FIND MORE
TIME

ALSO BY LAURA STACK

Leave the Office Earlier

FIND MORE TIME

HOW TO GET THINGS DONE AT HOME, ORGANIZE YOUR LIFE, AND FEEL GREAT ABOUT IT

LAURA STACK

BROADWAY BOOKS   NEW YORK

PUBLISHED BY BROADWAY BOOKS

BROADWAY BOOKS and its logo, a letter B bisected on the diagonal, are trademarks of Random House, Inc.

Visit our Web site at www.broadwaybooks.com

Book design and illustration by Lisa Sloane

Library of Congress Cataloging-in-Publication Data
Stack, Laura.
    Find more time : how to get things done at home, organize your life and feel great about it / Laura Stack.—1st ed.
        p.   cm.
    1. Home economics. 2. Housekeeping. I. Title.
    TX147.S77 2006
    640—dc22

                                                                        2005058110

ISBN-13: 978-0-7679-2202-9
ISBN-10: 0-7679-2202-6

PRINTED IN THE UNITED STATES OF AMERICA

10 9 8 7 6 5 4 3

For my Boopers

CONTENTS

ACKNOWLEDGMENTS

THANKS TO MY HUSBAND, John, my daughter, Meagan, and my sons, Johnny and James, for your constant love and support. Also to Eileen Stack, my wonderful mother-in-law, for giving your time to support my writing endeavors.

My appreciation goes to Tricia Medved, my talented editor from Broadway Books, for her continued enthusiasm for my projects.

I'm grateful for the guidance and friendship of my incomparable literary agent, Robert Shepard, who patiently listens to my wild ideas and manages to steer me in the right direction.

To my mentor and friend, Dianna Booher, CSP, CPAE, author of forty-two books, for kindly giving me countless hours of her time to school me in the publishing process.

My gratitude goes to Jenny Bardsley, my wonderful assistant, for keeping the office humming.

Thanks to my independent editor and proofreader, Barbara McNichol, for her eagle eyes and incredible writing skills.

In addition, my gratitude goes to the many thousands of seminar participants I've met over the years, for sharing your success stories with me and validating these concepts. I am humbled by the gift of your time and attention and privileged to be able to help you in some small way.

Particular thanks goes to my corporate clients, who recognize the significance of this material in improving retention rates at work and satisfaction in life. Thank you for your confidence and partnership.

Lastly, most of all, my eternal gratitude goes to my Lord, Jesus Christ, for continuing to shower His blessings upon my life. I pray this work is acceptable in His sight.

INTRODUCTION

YOU HAVE A SINK FULL OF DISHES to wash, three loads of laundry to do, seventeen bills to pay, you're not sure how many e-mails to answer, a big stack of novels on the nightstand you'd love to read, and zero—count them—*zero* minutes of free time.

"Where does the time go?" you lament. "I just need to find more time!"

Suddenly, a time fairy appears, waves her magic wand, and says, "Your wish is granted. You now have a thirty-hour day!" and then she disappears. At first, you're delighted. But strangely, within three weeks, your list has mysteriously expanded and now your thirty-hour day is just as full. And you *still* have a pile of projects to start, books to read, places to go, bills to pay, chores to complete, and things to do.

You begin to realize: *I will never get it all done.* This is the harsh reality of time. There will always be more things to do than time to do them. In fact, you don't *need* more hours in the day—you just need different habits. You *do* have the time; you're just not using it well.

The problem isn't time *shortage*; it's time *usage*.

My first book, *Leave the Office Earlier,* focuses on the workplace and teaches professionals how to leave the office on time, every time. But busy professionals said they want more. "Great! I've used your systems to get my work life in order," they told me. "Now what about my home life?"

So this book picks up where *Leave the Office Earlier* leaves off. Now that you're more productive during your workday, this complementary book teaches you how to get things done at home, rather than feeling that you never have enough time. You can create a fulfilling, productive life . . . or just wander through it aimlessly, never quite satisfied with what you accomplish.

I wrote *Find More Time* for busy men and women who work long and hard on the job (outside or inside the home) and also face kids, chores, and household projects. Using the ideas in this book, professionals will get more done than ever before. They'll learn ways to free up time for leisure, volunteer work, and plain old "quiet time." And they'll learn how to leave work behind at the end of the day.

College students will also be thrilled to have this book, as will moms and dads who work in the home full time. So will single working adults who want time for more leisure activities, CEOs who don't have time for grocery shopping, homebodies who like to garden, parents who can't seem to accomplish anything with the kids around, and parents whose children left long ago but who are busier than ever in "retirement." Readers will span generations and cover the gamut of life experience. Regardless of the differences in our ages and situations, the things we have to get done in our personal lives are fairly universal. We all have to eat, have clean clothes to wear, and live in sanitary environments. Handling those tasks efficiently will allow us time for more fulfilling things.

After reading and implementing the concepts in this book, you'll feel like you're controlling your life instead of your obligations controlling you. The ideas will help you create and sustain a productive home environment, so you'll have more time for enjoyment. *Find More Time* will also help you organize your space, time, and information to reduce your stress. You'll be able to focus your energies without letting things fall through the cracks.

You'll create a home environment that lets you avoid burnout and keeps you relaxed and having fun. When you're productive, your home and schedule reflects who you are, what you want, and where you're going. By getting things squared up around the house, you'll gain time to achieve those loftier dreams and relax into them.

Whether you need help with just a few things or feel like your life runs completely out of control, read this book and learn how to:

- Picture your ideal situation and determine where you want your life to go.
- Schedule family activities and community work.
- Complete those projects you've been thinking about.
- Organize your storage areas, kitchen, closets, and kids' rooms.
- Accomplish your housework and chores more quickly with shortcuts and timesaving techniques.
- Eliminate procrastination and multitasking.
- Manage paper, mail, personal e-mail, and phone calls.
- Find time to invest in your own self-care and leisure.

If you're thinking, "Ugh, I work hard all day! Why would I want to be productive at home?" I understand your anxiety completely. It's difficult to think about productivity at home, especially in today's "do more with less" world.

But understand this: Productivity isn't your enemy. Being productive is essential, since the reality is that all of us have so much to do—and that isn't changing.

Productivity is not about cramming more into your day. Rather, productivity helps you create more space and time, so you can get to the important things in life. Without it, you'll take on too many tasks; have too many late nights and too little sleep; increase your stress level; miss deadlines; and find yourself living in the same cluttered mess you started with.

If you embrace productivity, you can get clear about what you really value; realize your life goals; feel a sense of control; and change your life for the better. Productivity helps you reduce frustration by finding a purpose and direction in your life while adding structure to your day. It allows you to put your head on the pillow every evening with a sense of accomplishment.

Think about how a home in a high flood zone is constructed. It is most likely built on a platform supported by strong pillars or columns. If one or several pillars are weak or missing, the house's stability is threatened. But if the pillars are strong, they can save the home from damage when a hurricane or flood comes through.

In the same way, pillars also support your life—your personal "house." The strength of your supportive structures determines your ability to perform at your productive best. When one pillar is weak or nonexistent, you feel unstable and your life begins to tilt. If several of your life pillars need repair, you may feel like the walls are collapsing around you—or may even feel like you might crash.

But when the pillars are strong, you won't be bothered at all when the "floods" hit: activities to schedule, meals to cook, laundry to do, and projects to tackle that you hadn't even anticipated. It's vital to discover and strengthen the weak pillars in your life, so you can weather the challenges that come your way—or at least reduce their impact. With proper life support—with strong pillars—you can function optimally.

You're not a house, of course, but a person. So what are these pillars that hold you up? This book identifies eight pillars of personal productivity that support successful lives. Each pillar is a chapter and begins with the letter "P."

PILLAR 1: PLANS—helps you outline the desired direction for your life based on your ideal vision for yourself.

PILLAR 2: PRIORITIES—explores your life balance and determines where you want to spend your time in support of your plans.

PILLAR 3: PERSONALITY—encourages you to look at your behavior, habits, and choices—and then figure out which ones to adjust to support your desired direction in life.

PILLAR 4: PESTS—looks at the "termites" that eat away at your foundation: the time wasters and robbers that keep you from accomplishing what you set out to do. This could actually be thought of as "pest control," the problems you need to eliminate to keep this pillar strong.

PILLAR 5: POSSESSIONS—addresses items you've accumulated that might be weighing you down and putting pressure on the other pillars—everything from toys and clothing to tools and household items you simply don't need.

PILLAR 6: PAPER—suggests solutions to make your bill paying, filing, reading, and scheduling more manageable.

PILLAR 7: POST—refers to your job. This chapter shows you the most productive ways to accomplish your day-to-day tasks, chores, errands, and responsibilities.

PILLAR 8: PLAY—explores the importance of fun, leisure, wellness, and stress reduction. Helping you find time for the activities you enjoy is one of this book's main goals. Play is more than something "extra"—it's the final solid pillar upon which your life really rests.

The concept is simple. When all eight pillars of productivity support you equally, you're better able to accomplish your life goals.

Most people, though, have strengths in some areas but weaknesses in others; it's only natural. If you want to strengthen your Play pillar but your spouse isn't giving you time for yourself, it means your Plans pillar isn't strong enough to support your goals for your free time. If you want to accomplish a redecorating project but can't discipline yourself away from hours of television each night, it means that your Personality pillar is interfering with the stability of your Possessions pillar. Understanding where your "house" is off-balance gives you a systematic plan to conduct routine maintenance, a build-out, or even a complete "remodeling" of your life.

As in *Leave the Office Earlier*, each chapter in this book features a quiz that details the most important components in determining the strength of the pillar. The quizzes are organic; the learning is created from within them.

Realize *you do not have to read the chapters in order*. After all, you wouldn't choose to work on the same issues that others select. The comprehensive eighty-item quiz that follows guides you to "jump" right to the chapter and specific items that addresses your weakest pillar. The questions will be repeated within each section of the book. If a question isn't clear, you might want to browse that section for an explanation before answering. To customize your personal productivity program, I'd recommend taking the quiz first and starting with the chapter where your score is lowest.

Remember that the larger things you want to get out of life are interwoven through the hands-on, nitty-gritty details. The psychology of life balance (the *why*) is integrally tied to the details (the *how*)—just as the balanced strength of a house is determined by how the timber and nails went in to building it.

Use these eight Pillars of Productivity to build a stronger house and have more time for yourself—and you'll be able to find more time for what's important.

The Eight Pillars of Personal Productivity Assessment

PRODUCTIVITY QUIZ 1
PLANS

To what extent do I ...	1 = to no extent	2 = to a little extent	3 = to some extent	4 = to a considerable extent	5 = to a great extent
1. Have a personal mission statement for my life.	1	2	3	4	5
2. Maintain a list of my life's goals and dreams and make plans for their accomplishment.	1	2	3	4	5
3. Try to gain flexibility at work.	1	2	3	4	5
4. Keep effective to-do lists so things don't slip through the cracks.	1	2	3	4	5
5. Break larger projects into smaller ones.	1	2	3	4	5
6. Prepare for the next day the night before.	1	2	3	4	5
7. Plan for chaotic transition periods during the day.	1	2	3	4	5
8. Prevent crisis by preparing well in advance.	1	2	3	4	5
9. Embrace flexibility and weather change.	1	2	3	4	5
10. Continuously work to improve my efficiency and effectiveness.	1	2	3	4	5

TOTAL FOR QUESTIONS 1–10 _____

PRODUCTIVITY QUIZ 2
PRIORITIES

To what extent do I ...	1 = to no extent	2 = to a little extent	3 = to some extent	4 = to a considerable extent	5 = to a great extent
11. Spend enough time with the people who are dear to me.	1	2	3	4	5
12. Volunteer in ways that feed my spirit and make a lasting contribution.	1	2	3	4	5
13. Eliminate time-zapping addictions from my life.	1	2	3	4	5
14. Limit my children's activities to manageable levels.	1	2	3	4	5
15. Make my health a number-one priority.	1	2	3	4	5
16. Exercise consistently.	1	2	3	4	5
17. Enjoy the way I spend most of my day.	1	2	3	4	5
18. Practice healthy eating habits.	1	2	3	4	5
19. Get enough sleep.	1	2	3	4	5
20. Make time to feed my intellect and continue my learning.	1	2	3	4	5

TOTAL FOR QUESTIONS 11–20 _____

PRODUCTIVITY QUIZ 3
PERSONALITY

To what extent do I . . .	1 = to no extent	2 = to a little extent	3 = to some extent	4 = to a considerable extent	5 = to a great extent
21. Control perfectionism, realizing that some things are good enough.	1	2	3	4	5
22. Refuse requests when appropriate.	1	2	3	4	5
23. Ask for help when I need it.	1	2	3	4	5
24. Avoid procrastinating on what I know I should be doing.	1	2	3	4	5
25. Know and honor my energy levels throughout the day.	1	2	3	4	5
26. Communicate clearly to avoid confusion and rework.	1	2	3	4	5
27. Consistently meet and usually beat deadlines.	1	2	3	4	5
28. Focus on completing one task before getting distracted by another.	1	2	3	4	5
29. Maintain a positive attitude.	1	2	3	4	5
30. Stop trying to please all of the people all of the time.	1	2	3	4	5

TOTAL FOR QUESTIONS 21–30 _____

PRODUCTIVITY QUIZ 4
PESTS

To what extent do I . . .	1 = to no extent	2 = to a little extent	3 = to some extent	4 = to a considerable extent	5 = to a great extent
31. Confront problems head-on and make decisions quickly.	1	2	3	4	5
32. Complete tasks I start; don't let projects stall.	1	2	3	4	5
33. Keep interruptions from wasting my time.	1	2	3	4	5
34. Create shortcuts to get things done quickly.	1	2	3	4	5
35. Combine activities and routines.	1	2	3	4	5
36. Make good use of down time.	1	2	3	4	5
37. Turn off the technology when I'm with my loved ones.	1	2	3	4	5
38. Know and avoid my biggest time wasters and distractions.	1	2	3	4	5
39. Make productive use of driving or commuting time.	1	2	3	4	5
40. Eliminate aggravation and save time when traveling or flying.	1	2	3	4	5

TOTAL FOR QUESTIONS 31–40 _____

PRODUCTIVITY QUIZ 5
POSSESSIONS

To what extent do I . . .

		1 = to no extent	2 = to a little extent	3 = to some extent	4 = to a considerable extent	5 = to a great extent
41.	Have a systematic plan to get and stay organized.	1	2	3	4	5
42.	Eliminate clutter and resist adding more.	1	2	3	4	5
43.	Keep my briefcase, tote, or purse organized and clutter-free.	1	2	3	4	5
44.	Maintain clutter-free drawers and closets.	1	2	3	4	5
45.	Organize memorabilia such as photos and keepsakes.	1	2	3	4	5
46.	Keep kids' toys, clothes, and books organized.	1	2	3	4	5
47.	Set up and maintain my kitchen in an organized fashion.	1	2	3	4	5
48.	Keep my car organized and clean.	1	2	3	4	5
49.	Set up an effective office space in my home.	1	2	3	4	5
50.	Keep my house neat and tidy up daily.	1	2	3	4	5

TOTAL FOR QUESTIONS 41–50 _____

PRODUCTIVITY QUIZ 6
PAPER

To what extent do I . . .

		1 = to no extent	2 = to a little extent	3 = to some extent	4 = to a considerable extent	5 = to a great extent
51.	Consistently purge my files without fear.	1	2	3	4	5
52.	Create and maintain a filing system that allows me to find papers easily.	1	2	3	4	5
53.	Follow a daily processing system for staying on top of the mail and paperwork.	1	2	3	4	5
54.	Handle my bills in a timely fashion and keep up with bookkeeping.	1	2	3	4	5
55.	Know where to put every piece of paper I receive.	1	2	3	4	5
56.	Handle phone calls and voice mail productively.	1	2	3	4	5
57.	Use technology to reduce paper and complete tasks quickly.	1	2	3	4	5
58.	Keep insurance, medical documents, wills, and important papers up-to-date and easy to locate.	1	2	3	4	5
59.	Use a calendar system to track family members' schedules.	1	2	3	4	5
60.	Organize and keep up with my reading.	1	2	3	4	5

TOTAL FOR QUESTIONS 51–60 _____

PRODUCTIVITY QUIZ 7
POST

To what extent do I . . .	1 = to no extent	2 = to a little extent	3 = to some extent	4 = to a considerable extent	5 = to a great extent
61. Hire out tasks requiring a level of expertise I don't have.	1	2	3	4	5
62. Hire out simple chores to helpers.	1	2	3	4	5
63. Have goods delivered to avoid unnecessary time at the store.	1	2	3	4	5
64. Complete shopping efficiently.	1	2	3	4	5
65. Run errands efficiently.	1	2	3	4	5
66. Function effectively as the social, child, and family coordinator.	1	2	3	4	5
67. Do routine chores on a regular basis and keep my house clean.	1	2	3	4	5
68. Conduct preventive maintenance on my home.	1	2	3	4	5
69. Prepare meals quickly and systematically.	1	2	3	4	5
70. Expect family members to do their fair share of the housework.	1	2	3	4	5

TOTAL FOR QUESTIONS 61–70 _____

PRODUCTIVITY QUIZ 8
PLAY

To what extent do I . . .	1 = to no extent	2 = to a little extent	3 = to some extent	4 = to a considerable extent	5 = to a great extent
71. Close the mental office door and turn off work each day.	1	2	3	4	5
72. Leave work on time, so I can get home and enjoy my personal life.	1	2	3	4	5
73. Keep my stress levels low.	1	2	3	4	5
74. Rest, relax, and play daily.	1	2	3	4	5
75. Go on a long vacation each year.	1	2	3	4	5
76. Create fond memories and traditions with the people I love.	1	2	3	4	5
77. Have regular family time with loved ones.	1	2	3	4	5
78. Make time for a favorite hobby.	1	2	3	4	5
79. Force myself to slow down and stop rushing around.	1	2	3	4	5
80. Take care of myself on a regular basis.	1	2	3	4	5

TOTAL FOR QUESTIONS 71–80 _____

Scoring

Grand total of items 1–80:

337–400	Productivity Pro! Solid foundation!
273–336	Minor improvements considered necessary
209–272	Preventative maintenance needed
145–208	Major repairs required
80–144	Red flag! Structurally unsound!

Plot Your Scores

Now graph your totals for each pillar and color in to your score. You'll quickly see where your house is sagging and needs reinforcement!

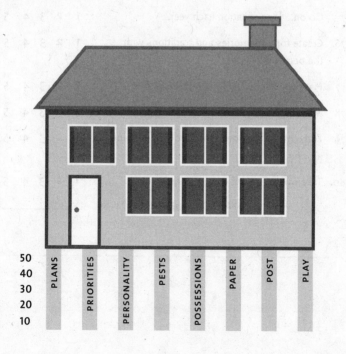

50
40
30
20
10

PLANS · PRIORITIES · PERSONALITY · PESTS · POSSESSIONS · PAPER · POST · PLAY

CHAPTER ONE

Mastering the First Pillar—

PLANS

WITHOUT A PLAN, life just sort of happens to you. But with a plan, you'll make sure your daily activities support what you want to create next week, next month, next year . . . until, at the end of your days, your activities will have contributed to creating and living a successful life. You don't want to accidentally create your life. Your plans should be purposeful, so your life moves in the direction you desire, based on your ideal vision for yourself.

My father is a veteran, a retired colonel in the U.S. Air Force. I'm proud of my Daddykins (my pet name for him) for all the years of service he gave to our country. Thanks to Dad's success, I'm a veteran, too. Only my war wasn't the Gulf War, Afghanistan, or Iraq—it was the turf war that comes from moving a lot as a kid.

Today, when people ask me about my childhood "home," I think about the pink bedroom in Colorado, the yellow kitchen in Ohio, the whitewashed porch in Texas. I've moved nearly thirty times in all and hated *every single* one of them. The fact is, moving is a traumatic experience—considered the third-highest stressor behind death and divorce.

So I survived by taking control of what I could. I became a master at packing and organizing. Before the movers had finished unloading the van, I had my room up and running. And I'd already moved my Barbie and Ken into *their* house. Every stuffed bear, bunny, and unicorn was neatly arranged in precise formation on my bed—exactly as they'd been in the house before—at attention for the Colonel's inspection. My friends used to laugh at my perfectly clean bedroom, my compulsive list making, and my overwhelming urge to organize.

But these experiences helped me with my life plan. The upheaval of my childhood taught me how to create order out of chaos, which laid the foundation for my work today. My background helped me build the systems I use today as The Productivity Pro®, teaching professionals how to spend their time moving closer to their goals in work and life.

You must also have a clear plan for your life's goals and dreams. When you clearly define your priorities and work productively toward them, you'll be able to accomplish your goals sooner. Planning reduces crisis and lowers your stress; buys you a night of rest, without you lying awake, thinking about tomorrow; gives you time to assess whether your schedule for tomorrow is realistic; and allows you to start each day feeling confident and ready. You have your marching orders. All you have to do is—march!

PLANS quiz item 1

---

1. _____ Have a personal mission statement for my life.

Who Am I? Where Am I?

Unless you're independently wealthy, you must work in some capacity. Some people don't get paid for their work in dollars but still contribute significant value to their families or communities. Some people work because of a calling to be a missionary or social worker and may not receive a lot of money for that work. Other people are paid very highly for their work outside of the home. But your work is just a part of your life. You need money to provide food, clothing, and security so you can do important things with your life. You work to live; you don't live to work. You are so much more than what you do for a living! Be careful not to get caught up in *what* you do, lest you define yourself by your job. To remind yourself of this truth, first create a personal mission statement that will help you evaluate how to spend your time.

A personal mission statement is an essential written document that helps you make decisions about the way you spend your time and evaluate your choices. It guides you in the right direction when you're faced with many choices. Defining your values helps you describe where you want your life to go based on your ideal vision for yourself and your definitions of success.

To write your mission statement, sit down in front of a computer or grab a journal and pen, and write down the most important values in your life: for example, health, happiness, justice, spirituality, family, truth, love, happiness, and so on. Then write a paragraph about each one to define what that value means and how you would determine if you successfully lived according to that value. Ask, "At the end of my time on this earth, how will I know if I've succeeded in life, not by anyone else's standards, but by my own desires and expectations?"

Here's my personal mission statement as an example:

> First, the most important thing to me is my relationship with Christ. My success is first measured by how I serve the Lord with my time, talents, and treasure. I make decisions based on what Jesus would want me to do, not what I feel like doing. Second, I am a faithful, encouraging, supportive wife. I will be a loving, caring, and nurturing mother, sometimes even sacrificing my own needs to ensure my children's are met. I work to live, not live to work. Lastly, I take care of myself physically, so I will have the energy and ability to work for the Lord and my family.

This is who I am. It's what I'm all about. My mission statement governs my life and my decisions around time. I keep copies of my mission statement where I'm sure to see them frequently. It constantly reminds me of what I want to create and helps me make difficult choices when life presents them.

For example, if I state that I will take care of myself physically, my actions aren't supporting my mission if I watch five straight hours of television while devouring an entire pizza by myself . . . even if it's a giant Chicago-style pepperoni pie and I'm watching the *Star Wars* series twice through. Although they're two fine activities, doing them doesn't support my mission. But perhaps your mission statement includes time to play and relax; for you, these activities might be okay occasionally.

If you choose work that doesn't fit with your values, for example, you doom yourself to approximately forty years of daily activities pursuing false values that actually compete with your happiness. To live a balanced life and experience inner harmony, your values must be the foundation for everything you do and everywhere you spend your time.

Now is the time. Get out a blank piece of paper or get on a computer and write a paragraph about each of your top three values.

PLANS quiz item 2

> 2. _____ Maintain a list of my life's goals and dreams, and make plans for their accomplishment.

Is "Lose Weight" a Good Goal?

Based on the mission statement you just wrote, ask, "What would have to change about the way I'm spending my time right now in order to obtain the vision I described for myself?" Your answers describe the gap that would need to close to take you from where you are now to where you want to be.

In December 1992, when I was twenty-three years old, I remember sitting down one evening and making a list of all my dreams. I brainstormed everything I wanted to do before I died. I listed forty-three lofty goals I wanted to achieve in the next twenty-five years. It included things such as, "Have speaking engagements in twenty-five states," "Ride in a helicopter," "Learn to water ski," "Visit Laura Ingalls Wilder's home in Missouri," "Travel to the Bahamas," and "Be a successful published author." As of 2005, I've completed thirty-three of them.

Other dreams, such as "Be married twenty-five years," "See a kangaroo in Australia," and "Publish an article in the *Wall Street Journal*," are yet to be realized. But goals are simply dreams with a deadline. I know I will accomplish them; the only question is when. Your goals are specific guideposts that keep you moving forward toward your ideal life. In the end, your goals will help you make sure your life has been worthwhile.

One thing I know for sure: You won't accomplish your goals and dreams if you don't plan for them. I suggest that you take each dream and phrase it in the form of an objective statement, using the following format:

I will (verb) (measurement) by (date) because (motivation). I will evaluate my progress by (date). I will reward myself through (_____).

For example, a poor objective would be "Get a new job." A better objective is "I will get a more challenging and satisfying job as an engineer in a different industry and realize an increase of $7,500 per year by June 2007. I will buy myself that new truck when I land this job!"

Create three goals that describe the changes that would have to take place to get you from where you are now to where you want to be.

PLANS quiz item 3

> 3. _____ Try to gain flexibility at work.

Which Half of the Job Do You Want?

An important component of planning is determining how the business of life and the game of work are going to fit together. Strive to create a lifestyle that is flexible, in which your personal life works with your job and your job works with your life. Wherever you work, whatever you do, find a way to make your job fit into the rest of your life.

As better technology explodes on the scene and people can work from anywhere, the blurring of your work life and home life is inevitable. Dual career couples, each feeling equally passionate about their jobs and families, want to participate more fully in each, regardless of gender. In more and more situations, sacrificing one for the other is no longer required. Managers have become increasingly aware of the need for flexibility, recognizing that a worker who leaves in the middle of the afternoon to visit an ailing parent will log into the intranet on the home computer later that night anyway.

Flexibility could come through telecommuting, an off-site work arrangement that permits employees to work in their homes for all or part of the workweek. Challenger, Gray and Christmas, a Chicago-based international outplacement firm, conducted a survey with two hundred HR professionals in different industries throughout the country. The survey noted that 43 percent of those polled believe workers will become increasingly mobile with far more telecommuting.

However, flexibility doesn't only mean telecommuting, which may not be as desirable to some people as other solutions. Indeed, the definition of "flexibility" is morphing. It might mean seasonal hours, such as different hours during the school year and summer. It might be rotating jobs part time so one or the other spouse is always home when a child arrives home from school. It might mean "desk share," allowing workers to share a job in the office and take turns working remotely, or "compressed workweek," in which you do a full-time job in fewer than five days and have a long weekend. Sometimes workers come in early and leave to beat horrendous traffic patterns. In summary, managers in a truly flexible workplace don't care when or where the work gets done as long as it gets done with great results. It hinges on giving workers more authority and responsibility.

How can you add flexibility to your life? Check with your human resources department to find out what alternative schedules are available. If your child gets out of school at four o'clock and no after-school program is available, ask about arriving at work extra early on some days and leaving early to pick up your kids and your neighbor's kids on other days. Perhaps your neighbor can work the opposite schedule. Or possibly you could do your job from home, which would allow you to take short breaks for drop-off and pick-up runs.

If you want flexible work hours but believe that your boss wouldn't dream of it, get brave! The trend to add flexibility is gathering steam. Even if an official policy isn't on your company's books, you may be able to create your own program. People often avoid pursuing a telecommuting arrangement for fear of their bosses' reactions. Usually, however, the concern of most supervisors comes down to this: "How can I manage an employee I can't see? How do I know if that employee is working or not?" This trend demands that managers learn to focus on results and achievements instead of attendance. An employee who is "present and accounted for" is not necessarily productive.

Is Your Job Right for Telecommuting?

Even if you think you have a "telecommuting personality," your job has to fit the situation. If you want to approach your employer to discuss a telecommuting arrangement, use this list to spur some introspection before proceeding. HR professionals actually use this list as a conversation document to assess the viability of this arrangement with interested employees. It notes the following characteristics of good "work at home" jobs:

- Jobs that require frequent use of the telephone
- Jobs that don't rely on person-to-person contact
- Jobs in which most of the work is done on computers
- Jobs that deal with a series of projects that have definite beginnings and endings
- Jobs that can be done in small, possibly confined areas
- Jobs that don't rely on constant feedback from coworkers
- Jobs requiring tasks that can be done by one employee or combined with the work of other employees at a later date

Once you make sure you're suited to working from home and have a job that supports it, be proactive in securing the necessary approvals to make it happen.

Whatever solution you choose, you must be proactive in gaining flexibility at work; it's rare that others will do it for you. Plan to actively pursue work that fits your life, rather than trying to squeegee your life into your job.

PLANS quiz item 4

4. _____ Keep effective to-do lists so things don't slip through the cracks.

I Know There Was Something I Was Supposed to Do Today!

One important planning consideration is what you're going to accomplish each day. In his role as the dean of creativity for the Walt Disney Companies, Mike Vance had a strategy he called Do-Doing-Done. The idea is to start a task in the Do column, move it to Doing quickly, and then move it to Done as quickly as possible.

That's a fine idea, but it doesn't really matter how you format your list. What *does* matter is that you *have* a list. In fact, you need several lists. Without them, your brain forgets many of the things you have to do as well as the cool ideas you come up with. Having lists will enable you to plan your day most effectively and will relieve that nagging sense of "what did I need to get done . . ." Chapter 6, Paper, also contains information on tools for planning.

I use several types of lists, outlined here:

1. **TASKS.** *Goal: Keep track of actions involving a single step.* You need at least two task lists, a master and a daily list:

- **MASTER TO-DO LIST(S).** This is a running list of everything I need to do that only has one step. Think of it as your memory list. I have one for work and one for personal. Every time I think of something I need to do, I write it on the master list. The only exception is if I plan to do something that very day, then I'll write it on the daily to-do list. Having a master list keeps your daily to-do list from having eighty-seven things to do on it. For example, my master list currently contains "Replace border in James's bedroom" and "Investigate LCD projector options."

- **DAILY TO-DO LIST.** Essentially my daily plan, this captures everything I truly intend to get done that day. It's *not* an ongoing list of everything I need to do, as in the master list. I integrate my personal and professional lives into a single list because the lines are blurred in my life. If I don't get something done, I go through the exercise of writing it again on the next day's to-do list, which actually motivates me to work productively so I don't have to carry it over. Besides, I hate not accomplishing what I'd planned! Each week, I'll review my master to-do lists and select tasks that are ready to be "time activated," or scheduled. I put a dot (●) next to each selected item on the master list so I know it's in progress. From there, I select a day to do each task and write the task on the corresponding daily to-do list.

2. **PROJECTS.** *Goal: Keep track of actions with multiple tasks or steps.* Each project plan lists the individual tasks required to complete the broader project. Each task has a corresponding entry on a monthly or daily to-do list so I can ensure the project will be completed in an efficient fashion and nothing gets forgotten. For example, "Redecorate living room" is one of my current projects for the house, as is "Develop media campaign for new book" for the business.

3. **COMMUNICATION.** *Goal: Keep track of items to discuss with someone else.* I keep a communication list (or log) on each person I communicate with frequently: operations manager, sales manager, mentor, assistant, spouse, children, and mother. Each time I think of something I need to chat about, I write the item on that person's list. I check in once a day with these individuals and cover all the items on my list, rather than interrupting them ten times through the day for one item each. Doing this helps me focus better, and they appreciate being able to work without my constantly reprioritizing their days (emergencies aside, of course).

4. **CATEGORY.** *Goal: List items pertaining to each category.*

   a) Books to read
   b) Groceries to buy (even though "go to grocery store" may be a task, this list contains the individual items I need to remember to buy)
   c) Shopping to do (a list of things I need to remember to get when I'm running errands)

d) Honey-do's for John

e) Gift ideas (one for each person)

f) Meagan's friends (I can never remember their names)

g) Johnny's friends

h) James's friends

i) Neighbors (who lives where, kids, pets, etc.)

j) Passwords (I know I'm not supposed to do this!)

k) Combination locks (so I can take the sticker off)

l) Babysitters (so many to keep track of)

m) Phone lists (company directory, trade association staff list, etc.)

n) Girl Scouts (who's in the troop, photocopy electronic list)

o) Soccer (who's on the team, photocopy electronic lists)

Any list your brain can imagine, you can and should track!

Where should you keep your Category lists? If you use a paper planner, you can file them behind the A–Z tabs. A–Z tabs are normally used for addresses and phone numbers (as mine are), but they also work as a paper filing system. I use lined pages the size of my planner and write the name of the list across the top—gifts, shopping, errands, projects—and file it behind the letter of the list. For example, I keep my master task list under *M*, my question list for my mentor Dianna Booher behind *B*, and the staff phone directory of the National Speakers Association behind *N*.

If you're an electronic person, you have several options. Some people prefer to use Outlook Tasks on their computers, using a category to sort the different lists. Others use the Notes feature and create a new note for each of the categories, adding items as they think of them. Some people prefer Excel spreadsheets or Word documents . . . it doesn't matter, as long as you *pick one method and stick with it*. You will confuse your brain if you handle information unpredictably.

I still love paper and use a traditional paper planner (I use Franklin Covey) for my calendar and lists. I also carry a multifeature cell phone/PDA, so I can access my e-mail and contact database. I know how to use the PDA features, but I still prefer to handwrite lists. Bottom line: There is no right/wrong to this approach *as long as you pick one method and use it consistently.*

PLANS quiz item 5

> 5. _____ Break larger projects into smaller ones.

What to Do First?

Let's say this is your to-do list for a Saturday:

- Water plants
- Pay the mortgage bill
- Buy new reading group book
- Return socks to Wal-Mart
- Put up new border in James's room

Which of the five things will you most likely have accomplished during the day? If you're like most people, you've completed everything but the last—the one you've had on your list for five months. Most people are inclined to knock off the little items first, rarely getting to the bottom of the list and getting the "big" things done. Why? "Put up new border in James's room" is too big. So is "Get photo albums arranged." So is "Get down balloon stuck in eighteen-foot-high ceiling fan." Each involves multiple steps. If you don't break them down, you will not be able to systematically tackle them. You must first break large tasks down into smaller ones and create a project plan.

If you want to put up a new border, you must:

- Shop for and buy new border
- Gather supplies for removing old border
- Move and cover furniture
- Remove old border
- Hang new border

If you want to get your photo albums arranged, you must:

- Determine if you're going to use books, boxes, or scrapbooks
- Purchase the necessary supplies
- Put stickers with months and years on the floor
- Identify and sort photos into piles or on the computer
- Print them, if not printed already
- Arrange in albums

If you want to get the balloon down, you must:

- Back the car out of the garage
- Move snow blower, bikes, and wagon out of the way of the ladder
- Get down the ladder
- Get someone to hold the door
- Bring the ladder inside
- Set up ladder and cut down balloon

Without clearly listing the pieces of the project (on paper or in your head), the task will simply swirl around in your head. With the project listed as a series of individual action steps, you will eventually be able to finish one big job. If necessary, schedule only *one piece* of the big project for the day, so you have time to fit it in with the mortgage bill you have to pay and still see progress.

If you never break larger projects down into manageable steps, you might not ever have time to complete them, because the rest of the small stuff will take all your time. When you approach your to-do list, make sure to include a small piece of a larger project, so you can see movement on your goals.

PLANS quiz item 6

6. _____ Prepare for the next day the night before.

I'm Not Ready for This Day to Be Here!

A productive day must start well each morning so the day will be organized and pleasant. The way you begin each new day will have a direct impact on how the whole day shapes up.

One way is to get a good head start on it. As the night draws nigh, you put your plans in place for the next day. When the sun comes up, simply execute your plan rather than create it from scratch.

BETTER YET, A WEEK AHEAD. You've probably all heard the advice to put out the clothes you'll wear the next day the night before—both for you and your children. Take that a step further. How about picking out clothes for the week and then tucking the outfits inside a colorful hanging sweater organizer labeled with the days of the week? This takes one step out of your family's morning routine. And it lets your kids get dressed themselves, without you having to worry they'll walk out the door looking like raga-muffins. We have a temperature sensor and transmitter outside; a quick glance at the receiver on the counter tells us if the boys need a light jacket or heavy coat, both of which can be found in their cubbies by the garage door. Having clothes in predictable places helps your children become more independent in dressing themselves.

GET THE KID'S DAY STARTED. Pack (or have your kids pack) a box lunch if they don't buy at school; make sure the clothes are se-lected down to the last hair bow and shoes; lay out breakfast dishes; fill up the backpacks (don't forget homework, permission slips, lunch money, show-and-tell, gym clothes, musical instru-ments, etc.).

SET THINGS UP IN ADVANCE. Dump out the days' vitamins from your vitamin sorter; load your briefcase; run the dishwasher; set the coffeepot with the timer for the next morning. Lastly, if you have the energy, do your own personal grooming routine (shav-ing legs, shaping eyebrows, taking care of skin, filing nails, etc.).

PREPARE MEALS THE DAY BEFORE. Before he goes to bed in the evening, John looks at his menu list, takes something out of the freezer for the next day, and puts it in the refrigerator. Set up your breakfast. Measure out the water for your oatmeal and have it waiting on the stove. Put all your fruit, milk, and yogurt into the blender pitcher and store it in the refrigerator overnight.

A little bit of work now setting up your evening systems will save you much time in the morning. Just like you, I'm often ex-hausted at the end of the day. You may have just enough energy to clean up dinner and crawl into bed. But by developing the habit of doing as much as you can at night, your days will run more smoothly and take less of a toll. So leave as little preparation as possible until the last minute. That way, when you come downstairs in the morning, you can quickly grab your cup of coffee and get breakfast moving. You'll thank yourself for all the planning you did the night before.

PLANS quiz item 7

> 7. _____ Plan for chaotic transition periods during the day.

Surviving the Witching Hour

Transitions are the most difficult times of the day: from nighttime to morning; from workday to evening; and from evening to bedtime. These transition periods are called "witching hours," and they are fraught with stress and chaos. Every person, every household, has at least one witching hour, sometimes more. Even though transition times are only a small portion of the day, they can pack enough punch to spill over into the rest of it. However, with proper planning, you can flow through these high-stress periods more easily.

FROM WORKDAY TO EVENING. We have affectionately dubbed ours "the five o'clock melt-down hour." We've been working hard all day. The kids have been stimulated at school. When we pick them up, they have a million things to talk about. Dinner needs to be made and the table set. The kids start to fight. Meagan talks to me a mile-a-minute, as ten-year-old girls do. I can *feel* my blood pressure rising. Before long, I'm short-tempered and hungry. My ears are ringing from the sudden rise in decibels. "Will you kids just be quiet?" I shout, which makes things worse. Sensing my stress, James starts teasing Johnny, and Johnny begins whining, to which John responds by sending everyone to his or her room. What a great way for the night to begin!

Rest assured that this is the normal scenario in households across America—yes, even in The Productivity Pro's house— trust me. But you can plan for this witching hour and do something about it once you know what the patterns are.

Because John is the chef in our family and is busy cooking dinner at our witching hour, it makes sense for me to pick up the boys from day care. With Meagan having returned on the school bus, it also makes sense for her to drive with me and download her day so she isn't competing for attention with the boys at home. Since they're hungry and cranky when they get home, it makes sense to pick them up at 5:00 instead of 4:45 so they can eat a snack with the class. Once we get home, Meagan sets the table and helps John while I take the boys to another part of the house, connect with them, and keep them occupied. Once John rings the dinner bell and we sit down to eat, our entire household mellows out.

FROM EVENING TO BEDTIME. Perhaps bedtime is your battle, trying to do baths, brush teeth, read books, and get everyone ready for the morning. When it comes to bedtime, a consistent routine is the best way for kids to transition from awake to asleep. Don't wait until they say they're sleepy—it may be too late! Start their bedtime routine at the same time each night, and use a checklist to remind and guide them through the process. Set aside at least thirty minutes every night so you don't have to rush. Even before your kids can read, you can use a checklist using pictures and stickers. Our kids each have two checklists of activities they must complete—one for the morning and one for the evening. We simply have to say, "Do your checklist," and most of the time (many times with encouragement and reminders like "where are you on your checklist?") things get done without repeating the message ten million times—and getting frustrated doing so.

You can even put timed deadlines on each activity so they know where they should be in the one hour of time designated to get out the door. At first, give rewards for making the deadlines. After a while, start to use penalties: for example, miss more than two deadlines and you lose your television time.

Here is a sample checklist to get you started that you can modify to meet your needs. This list was created when my daughter was in first grade (obviously, they change as the child gets older, although some older children still need reminders to flush!). If you'd like to download and modify electronic copies of these checklists, visit www.TheProductivityPro.com and look for Free Stuff under the Resources menu.

CHECKLIST FOR GETTING READY AT NIGHT

CHECK OR STICKER	ITEM
	Do forty minutes of reading
	Do homework
	Give notes to Mom from backpack
	Set and clear table
	Eat snack
	Brush teeth
	Check pet's water and food bowls

CHECK OR STICKER	ITEM
	Go potty
	Flush potty
	Take shower (every other day)
	Wash face
	Brush hair
	Get pajamas on
	Feed fish
	Make sack lunch, if needed
	Make sure room is clean
	Get bed ready
	Put on lotion
	Turn out light
	Pray
	Kiss parents goodnight

When your children get to bed easily, maybe, you won't feel too rattled to relax. You might even think about tackling the mountain of bills and filing you've been putting off.

FROM NIGHTTIME TO MORNING. Perhaps your witching hour is first thing in the morning, trying to get everyone out the door. Assuming I've set myself up for a great day (see quiz item 5), I want to get my morning off to a great start. If I have scheduled to be in my office all day, my morning goes something like this: get myself ready first so I'm not shouting directions and moderating disagreements from inside my bedroom; toss the comforter on the bed; focus on the kids, making sure Meagan is up and getting the boys dressed for school (John usually drives them to day care in plenty of time to participate in the school breakfast—healthy, faster, and cheaper); have my breakfast and coffee; take a few steps around the house and tidy up; toss in a load of laundry if something can't wait until the weekend; put my husband's stray papers into the newspaper bin (a subject of another conversation); unload the dishwasher. Then I'm ready to begin my day!

As for my children getting themselves ready, here is a sample checklist we created for Meagan that can be a model for you.

CHECK OR STICKER	ITEM
	Go potty
	Flush potty
	Eat breakfast
	Get dressed
	Put on shoes and socks (wear tennis shoes if it's PE day)
	Feed fish
	Make bed
	Clean up room
	Put away pajamas
	Turn out light
	Wash face
	Put on lotion
	Brush teeth
	Put snack and lunch in backpack

CHECK OR STICKER	ITEM (CONT.)
	Put in show and tell if it's related to learning
	Put library book in backpack if it's Monday
	Put daily folder in backpack
	Brush hair
	Fill pet's water bowl and food if empty
	Put on coat

Understanding your transition times, figuring out your patterns, what happens when and why, and then scheduling and planning for them will make a big difference in making your witching hour disappear.

PLANS quiz item 8

8. _____ Prevent crisis by preparing well in advance.

Urgent—Urgent—Emergency

No matter how well you plan, an unexpected emergency will occasionally sock you right in the kisser. School closes unexpectedly for a day. The cat runs away. The garage door won't open. The kids wake up with fevers. The car won't start. To cover these contingencies, make sure you have a backup strategy, a Plan B, and perhaps a Plan C and D, in place. At a minimum, make arrangements with a neighbor if you have an emergency day-care pickup need. Keep a helper's cell phone number with you at all times.

My mother-in-law steps in when we have a day-care emergency, and we know how blessed we are that she is available and willing.

However, there's a difference between a true emergency and a crisis that was created because you didn't do something in a timely manner.

Here are some examples:

- Wrap the present days *before* the birthday party (not in the car on the way).
- Refill your prescription several pills *before* you take the last pill (not when you're out, forcing you to wait at the pharmacy thirty minutes before work).
- Find your tax receipts a month *before* taxes are due (not when you're forced to file an extension).
- Buy greeting cards *before* your card box is empty (not when you have to go to the store to buy one single birthday card).
- Get your car checked out when you hear a noise *before* it breaks down (not when you're on the side of the road calling AAA).
- Restock toilet paper *before* you run out (and are forced to use tissue).
- Stock up on stamps *before* they're gone (and you have to stand in a one-hour line during lunch to mail a single bill).
- Take your printer in for maintenance *before* it breaks down (and you're forced to purchase another so you can get a mailing out while that one's in the shop).
- Get your tooth checked if it's hurting *before* it gets infected (and has to be pulled).

Participants in my time-management classes gave me all of these examples. I share them so you can understand you're not the only one! But you can change any patterns and take care of things before they become crises. Call it contingency planning, prevention, time padding, time shifting, pre-work, or frontloading—it saves you trouble later.

You will be amazed at the level of calm you experience when you do things before they are due or you need them. Over a period of weeks and months, if you spend ten minutes more a day (building to thirty and sixty minutes more every day) doing activities before they're required, soon you'll have shifted your time wisely. Yes, you're still doing the same activities, but you're no longer doing them under deadlines. The biggest bonus, however, will be the amazing sense of tranquility you feel by racketing down your "emergencies."

Here are a few universal time crunches that can be better managed:

PREPARE YOUR HOME FOR THE CHANGE IN SEASONS. If you've ever wanted to snuggle up with your sweetie in front of a blazing fire during a snowstorm, but lit the logs and had black smoke come billowing out into your living room, you know the importance of winterizing your home (Florida, Nevada, and Arizona residents, ignore this). A month or two before the first snow blows in your area, put the following items on your monthly to-do list and crack at them over several weekends: clean and store your warm-weather tools and equipment; cover your air conditioner; make a list of supplies and purchase items like shovels and salt; check and change your furnace filter; cover the outside of your windows with plastic sheeting; roll and store hoses; service your snow blower; seal drafts in windows; change the batteries in smoke detectors. Then when the snow flies, you'll be ready to relax in front of that fire. Have a glass of wine on me to congratulate yourself.

HO-HO-HARRUMPH. The best time of year to think about the holiday season is long before it starts! Will this year be a season of joy or a season of stress? Avoid waking up tired and blurry-eyed from wrapping fifty gifts until 2:00 a.m. the night before Christmas. Instead, set up a wrapping station in a utility room, corner, basement, or closet. Wrap gifts as you purchase them. Keep rolls of ribbon organized on a paper towel rack hanging on the wall, and put up pegs or hooks to hang tape and scissors. Put wrap on a card table or stand it up in a tall wastebasket. Purchase a gift-wrap organizer for flat sheets and nametags. Keep your wrapping station set up throughout the year, if possible.

REPLENISH HOLIDAY ITEMS RIGHT AFTER THE HOLIDAYS. John is a big shopper. Yes, he's a guy and actually *loves* to shop (strange, I know)! One of his favorite traditions is to hit the sales the day after Christmas. He especially loves going to Target, where he picks up decorations and wrapping paper at discounted prices. He also hits Ace Hardware or Home Depot to add yet one more lawn statue to his (already large) collection. We also purchase sale holiday gifts for the next year—the gifts that won't go bad—and it just takes some planning.

PLANS quiz item 9

9. _____ Embrace flexibility and weather change.

Watch Me Do a Backbend!

There is no going back to the good old days. Whatever we do, wherever we do it, everything—work styles, economic conditions, technology, corporate structures, global communications, and lifestyles—changes at a dizzying rate.

Here's evidence:

- In ten years, at least one-fourth of all current "knowledge" and accepted "practice" will be obsolete. The life span of new technologies is down to eighteen months—and decreasing.
- Within ten years, twenty times as many people will be working from home as today.
- Two-career families will multiply; currently 50 percent of all families have two paychecks, a number that will increase to 75 percent.
- If you are under twenty-five, you can expect to change careers every decade and change jobs every four years, partly because you choose to and partly because industries will disappear and be replaced by others we haven't heard of yet.

In this new and unpredictable world, everything is moving faster. What we need to know and how we need to act has changed and will continue to change. Dealing with this change requires a whole new way of thinking and a lot of flexibility, personally and professionally.

Organizations are learning that flexible policies provide a strategic advantage in retaining the best employees. To help people balance life and work, some organizations are instituting work/family policies, allowing time off to attend children's school activities, building on-site day-care centers, and even giving a half-day off on Fridays. Not surprising, many employees find these changes help them get as much done in half a day as they do during a regular workday. They prioritize work better, have more energy, and waste less time on these Fridays because a one o'clock departure is a firm deadline they *want* to keep.

KNOW IT WILL PASS. You, too, must plan to be flexible with all the changes you will face in life. Learning more about yourself will help you handle change better. Examine your behavior in times of change. When I had children, I would get frustrated because of the toys and clutter strewn about the house. I had to be flexible with the expectations I was placing on myself to have a constantly organized home. Books didn't have to be sorted in the bookcase by height and type; as long as they were stuffed in there and off the floor, I learned to be happy. My kids wouldn't be young forever. This too will pass! Now that they are older and can store books correctly, I wonder why I ever stressed out about it. Now if only they would do what I tell them to do the first time! Things change in good and bad ways, but one thing is for sure—things will change. You must be flexible as you move through life's phases and stages, because life won't always be the same. Something you're dealing with today won't be an issue later, so hang in there.

BE PROACTIVE. Why do we have to be overweight before we decide we need to exercise? Why do we have to have a heart attack before we realize we need to watch our diets? Why do we have to wait until we have a stroke before we reduce our stress? Why does our blood pressure have to go sky-high before we take care of ourselves? Why do we have to be on the verge of divorce before we tend to our relationships? Be flexible and willing to change aspects of your life that aren't working. Don't simply be content to coast and maintain the status quo. Change might be scary, but change is required for you to continue to grow and be happy.

CHECK OUT YOUR EMOTIONAL STATE. Upset emotions signal you when something is wrong and needs to change, they tell you when something is wrong. Self-awareness of emotions can work as an alarm that prompts you to make needed changes and take care of yourself.

Listen to yourself. How are you reacting? Are you jumping on people? Crying a lot? Withdrawing? If you look at your life and are happy with what you see and getting what you want, great. Keep doing it. But if you're not happy, be flexible about the way you're doing things and choose to change. If you don't make any changes, don't expect things to be different. Remember the old cliché: "insanity" is doing the same thing over and over again and expecting different results. And if you always do what you've always done, you'll always get what you've always got.

Some run their lives like watching a soap opera: you can turn it off for six months, turn it back on again, and see the same old thing. So check out your emotions, be flexible, and make necessary changes.

PLANS quiz item 10

10. _____ Continuously work to improve my efficiency and effectiveness.

Inch by Inch, Step by Step

I put this quiz item last to serve as a pep talk after a lot of seemingly time-consuming dictums. Don't throw your hands up in despair and think, "There's no way I can do all this!" You can! You might just be stuck in a rut. You get into a certain routine and have fixed habits that are hard to break. You know you're not performing up to your ability, but hey, you're getting by, so it's good enough. Break out of that fix you're in! Your beliefs are self-limiting. You can always do better than you are now.

For example, people once believed it was impossible to run a mile in less than four minutes. It was called the Four-Minute-Mile-Barrier. For many years, athletes tried to break this barrier, and no one could do it; in fact, there was a multitude of scientific evidence to support the fact that it couldn't be done. Then in 1964, Roger Bannister, a British medical student, broke the barrier. As you'd suspect, it was a huge deal and made headlines in the world of sports. Guess what happened after he did it? Yep—a lot of people started doing the very same thing—five or seven athletes that year. Why? Simple: He had shown them the possibility and encouraged them to break through their own limitations.

When you believe that something is impossible to do, you don't even try or you do it halfheartedly, so that when it doesn't work you say, "See, I told you I couldn't do it." "It's impossible! I knew it was!" This is the infamous self-fulfilling prophecy. If you think you can get better and be more productive, you can, and you will.

Always think, "What if?" Take stock. Think about your daily tasks and ask some important questions. "How can I do this better next time?" "How can I be more efficient?" "How can I get these results with less effort?" Occasionally, you must take the time to stop, step back, and ask yourself these questions. You can't just keep plowing ahead without occasionally regrouping and re-assessing what you're doing or have become blind to doing.

Here are a few concrete and immediate ways to begin making changes.

SITTING BOMBS. You've passed that magazine twenty times—you know, the one that has a great article for your mom—and keep telling yourself, "I need to send that article." Do it now. Decide that, whenever possible, you will dispatch routine tasks immediately. If it takes less than three minutes, do it right then.

APPOINTMENTS. Your friend repeatedly cancels lunch dates at the last minute. This drives you crazy, but you continue to put up with it. Next time, don't avoid dealing with the issue. If the person is important to you, explain how frustrated you are.

WAITING TIME. It makes you nuts to have to continually wait for your doctor, who is always late (we must go to the same doctor). Instead, you decide you will make good use of this time and now carry cards and magazines in your tote and catch up on your note writing and reading.

FORGETFULNESS. At the end of the day, you had to rush out the door and leave that project half done. You're always frustrated, because when you return the next day and look at the page, you can't for the life of you remember what you were thinking or doing. Before quitting for the day, jot a few notes on a sticky note about where you left off and what your next step is.

POST-VACATION SLAM. You return from vacation and are so overwhelmed by your overflowing paper and e-mail in-boxes, you're more stressed out than before you left. Decide instead to return a day earlier, so you can get unpacked, do the laundry, and sort your mail.

When something is bothering you, do a bit of introspection to see what's going on and how you might approach it more efficiently or effectively next time. If you're in a rut, and you've grown accustomed to low productivity, change may not be comfortable or easy. Take an honest look at your life, determine what's no longer working, and change it.

CHAPTER TWO

Mastering the Second Pillar—
PRIORITIES

DADDYKINS QUICKLY MOVED up the ranks in the Air Force, so with each new promotion, our family got a bigger house. More boxes to pack. More crates to label. More uncertainty in our lives.

My two brothers and I quickly learned the packing drill: Open the box, tape the bottom, layer with paper, heavy things first, seal, label, stack. Repeat and stack. Stack. Stack. Stack.

I think it's one of life's cruel ironies that, at the point in my life when I finally stopped moving, I ended up marrying a man with the last name of Stack. (I guess it could have been worse. For all I know, there's a guy out there named Bubblewrap.)

When I was growing up, our family lived a fast-track life, following my dad's fast-track life, so I lived a fast-track life: Owned my first lawn-mowing business at age twelve; skipped my senior year of high school and graduated at age sixteen; graduated college at nineteen; earned my MBA at twenty-one; and started a company at twenty-three. (See what you can do if you're organized? And have no life!) At the rate I was going, I should be retired and playing bridge in an assisted living facility by now.

But there was something definitely wrong with this picture—my priorities were out of line. Today, when people ask me, "What was your hurry?" I don't have a good answer. I lived my life like I was running a race. The problem was, I was racing . . . to nowhere.

I was perpetually on the move. Pushing to accomplish "it," without ever defining what "it" was. By the time I was twenty-four, I was married, working sixteen-hour days, traveling three weeks out of a month, and feeling burned out. My priorities pillar was teetering. Moving fast without clear priorities took a heavy toll on my career, on my family, and on my health. Without the *why* in my life, the *how* became harder and harder. I was moving up the career ladder, but I was paying an extremely high price.

In 1995 when I was twenty-six, my first child, a daughter, Meagan, was born. Being pregnant. Giving birth. Raising a child. None of this slowed *me* down. I could change a diaper with one hand and type a proposal with another. An *excellent* proposal, too. I was determined to succeed and moved any mountain in my way to do it.

The problem was, my life was insane. I wasn't working to live; I was living to work.

But then I got this wake-up call.

When I was on the road, I would telephone my nanny at the end of each day to check in.

"Angie, hi. How's Meagan?"

"Oh Laura. We had a wonderful morning. Meagan walked today."

I felt like I had been punched in the stomach.

"Meagan walked today."

And where was I? Sobbing in the lobby of a Holiday Inn in Mansfield, Ohio, 400 miles from home. *"What am I doing?"*

I had missed one of the most important moments in my daughter's young life. And for what? I was moving so quickly in my career that I hadn't stopped to weigh the costs. Missing these moments with our kids serves as a wake up for many men and women, highlighting the lack of a satisfying balance in life.

At that moment, I knew what I had to do to achieve my plans: I had to change my priorities. I stopped worrying about the quantity of work I was producing and focused instead on the quality of time I spent with Meagan. I was still committed to success—just a different kind of success.

I started to tune out all the background noise in my life and focus on what mattered most. And suddenly, the *how* really did become easier. I learned that productivity is not about speed. And achievement is not about money. Sadly, it wasn't until I was divorced and a single mom that I figured that out. I hope you figure it out faster than I did!

This chapter explores your priorities and helps you determine where you want to spend your time in support of your plans. What are you committed to changing in your life?

PRIORITIES quiz item 11

> 11. _____ Spend enough time with the people who are dear to me.

Allow Me to Introduce Myself

In April 2002, I had a speaking engagement in San Diego, California, just a few miles from where my paternal grandfather lived in the town of Santee. I decided to fly in a day early and spend time hanging out with Grandpa Herbie, who was then eighty-four years old. We played several games of pool in the recreation center in his apartment complex (in all of which he decidedly stomped me). We ate at a wonderful seafood restaurant while watching the sunset on the bay. We took a walk along the winding path by the water's edge, held hands, and laughed about bygone days. He told me many stories of his life as a young lumberjack in the big woods of Minnesota and his career as a letter carrier. He talked about my grandmother, who'd passed away, and my father as a little boy.

A week after I returned home, he called to tell me he had been diagnosed with lymphoma (cancer of the lymph nodes). On December 31, 2002, he passed away, less than a year after I had spent this memorable time with him. Because he seemed so perfectly robust and healthy when I was with him, his death was surreal. But I'm so grateful I had those moments to share with my Grandpa Herbie, not knowing that would be the last time. After he got sick, he didn't want me to see him. Instead, he begged me to remember him as he was in April. So I respected his wishes and didn't see him again until he was laid to rest.

The obvious takeaway message is to never take your time with your loved ones for granted, for they may not be here tomorrow. Treasure every minute. Make time when none exists. Put aside your work to look into the eyes of your child for ten minutes and really listen.

It's possible to fit your life into your time; you just need to know when and where the different elements can fall into place. Here are some suggestions.

COMMUNICATE YOUR PLANS. When you need to leave work to attend important family events, let your boss and coworkers know well in advance. If you frequently spend personal time on work activities, don't feel guilty about leaving work early once in a while to attend a personal function.

COMBINE ACTIVITIES. A woman in one of my seminars shared that she was continually upset at her husband during the summer because he would play golf with his buddies every Saturday. They didn't have any children and he wasn't shirking his home responsibilities; she just didn't want to be left alone on the weekends. I suggested that this was more her issue than his, and perhaps she needed to find something to do with her imposed alone time rather than complain at him for giving himself permission to have fun. Two weeks later, she e-mailed me and excitedly told me she had decided to take up golf lessons. Her husband was enthusiastic about the idea and offered to let her join his group as a foursome. She had increased her exercise and social time, and was spending time with her husband. Where can you use this concept of combining activities? Taking family walks? Meeting a friend at the gym? Learning a new sport?

MAKE GET-TOGETHERS A HABIT. Schedule time with friends and family into your calendar. We have four couple friends we like to keep up with. I know people who have so many "friends," they don't have time to enjoy outings with the ones they really like. *I suggest limiting the number of people you purposefully connect with so you can grow the depth of your friendships and family ties.* Once a month or every six weeks, we schedule a Saturday date with one of our couple friends (we are blessed to have my mother-in-law as our standing babysitter every Saturday night). When we're with these friends, we don't leave each other without putting the next play date on the calendar. It's the same with our families. My parents only live an hour away, but with all of our busy lives, we have to put a get-together date on the calendar in ink. Things occasionally come up and we have to change the date, but for the most part, if we plan for it, it happens.

PRIORITIES quiz item 12

12. _____ Volunteer in a way that feeds my spirit and makes a lasting contribution.

Am I Richly Rewarded?

I always make a special effort to greet and thank the volunteers I meet at the hospital; the greeters at the airport offering directions; and the ushers who help me find a seat at church. These people give cheerfully and unselfishly from their hearts. Remember, the minute you start to dread going to volunteer, it will show. You can give up the position. It's okay. For those of you who don't volunteer because you think you're too busy, it may be an important added piece of your life. Volunteering is fulfilling, but it has to exist within the context of your overall mission.

VOLUNTEERING SHOULD GIVE YOU ENERGY. Volunteering shouldn't feel like work; it can be hard but should be enjoyable and done willingly. At our church, my husband and I teach a weekly Christian Sunday school class for kindergarteners called Bible Blast. Our sons Johnny and James love having their mommy and daddy as their teachers, but admittedly, it's an often-arduous volunteer commitment. We teach at the 10:30 service, but we still want to attend church ourselves, which means being at church for the 8:45 service. Given that, every Sunday morning looks like this: get up early, rouse the kids and get every-one ready, eat, and head out for church. We're gone by 8:15 a.m. and don't return until noon. But even though it takes up our en-tire Sunday morning, we love doing it. We feel uplifted (albeit tired), not resentful, when we arrive home. We look forward to connecting with our kids each week and bringing them closer to God.

YOU CAN ALWAYS CHANGE YOUR MIND. Perhaps you continued to say yes to a volunteer position that you wished you'd said no to. It's never too late to change your mind. I remember when I was into my second year as a director on the board for my local Colorado chapter of the National Speakers Association. In the middle of the term, I had my third baby and just knew I couldn't contribute at the level that I desired and others expected. So when I went to the first board meeting after my baby was born, I announced that I was vacating my position. The president quickly appointed a replacement, and that was that.

Horrors, you may think. Doing something like that looks bad to your peers. It could sabotage your future assignments and ca-reer advancement. Nonsense. In fact, quite the opposite. My col-leagues respected that I was honest about my ability to give to this volunteer position. Two years later, I was elected to a three-year term as president-elect, president, and past-president. Then I was elected as a director to the national board for three years. Doing what you know is best for the volunteer position beats staying in office and giving it a halfhearted effort.

BE CREATIVE. At the beginning of each year, my children's teach-ers send home a "Volunteer Sign-up Sheet," which conveys the expectation that each family will help out. The entries include items such as "Make copies and put together Friday folders," "Be a reading buddy on Tuesdays and Thursdays," and "Plan and host special parties." These activities require a time commitment during the day, so they're clearly more appropriate for parents who don't have traditional office jobs. Unlike many of the parents, I don't have the time to support this type of volunteer work. I always feel torn: I want to support Meagan's school events but can't commit to something on a regular basis.

To deal with this, I called her teacher and suggested two new categories of volunteerism: roving field trip chaperone and special reward contributor. I would be able to check my calendar for availability on upcoming field trips, and I'd donate money, rather than time, to purchase special little gifts for exceptional performance. As a result, Meagan's teacher now informs me about upcoming events that require parental assistance (like going to the zoo), and I attempt to plan my calendar around the dates. Yes, I can make a day trip once in a while; I just can't commit to an activity on a regular basis each week. I also purchased prizes for her to give as rewards for task completion or outstanding behavior.

I've decided that giving treasures like this is just as valuable as giving time or talent. The key? To be creative in actively determining with others what a good contribution could look like.

PRIORITIES quiz item 13

13. _____ Eliminate time-zapping addictions from my life.

I'm Playing Video Games in My Dreams!

The U.S. Bureau of Labor Statistic's Time-Use study, released in September 2004, showed that watching television was the one activity that occupied the most leisure time, accounting for about half of leisure time on average for both men and women. The adult population in the United States averaged 2.57 hours of television *every day*, with men who watch television logging the highest number of hours: 3.43 hours a day.

Television is only one of many such addictions that sap our time. Add mindlessly surfing the Internet, talking excessively on the phone, Instant Messaging with your friends, and playing video games, and you've added countless hours of wasted time to your life each day.

Here are some suggestions to control these addictions.

LIMIT YOUR TELEVISION WATCHING. How many hours of TV do you watch each day? If it's a lot, I highly recommend breaking yourself of this habit. Many people feel guilty after overindulging in television time. Sensible limits will relieve this feeling, while freeing up time for more worthwhile pursuits. If you can't bear to part with your cable service, then break the surfing habit. Use your *TV Guide* to plan your programming each week and limit yourself to five hours. Turn on your TV when the show begins, don't change the channel, and turn it off at the end of the program. When we choose to watch a particular show, we use our TiVo service, so we can bypass the commercials. By taping your shows, you can also watch them at a more convenient time.

DESIGNATE A "NO TV" NIGHT. One night a week, declare television off-limits. Read, play outside, play board games or do crafts, or catch up on chores instead.

LOG YOUR SCREEN-WATCHING HOURS. Set a time limit for yourself and your children for television, video games, IM time, phone, and Web surfing. Any combination of the above is allowed, but not all. I'd start with a maximum of ninety minutes a day and reduce it from there. Require each person to annotate the log when spending budgeted time in one area. Keep the log (with a pen attached) near the activity area to make it easy for each person to complete. Review the logs often so you know what's going on.

ENCOURAGE EXERCISE. How about focusing your children's energies away from technology? For birthdays and holidays, buy your kids toys that will force them to use their bodies. Roller blades, scooters, bicycles, soccer bounce-back nets, and sports equipment are all excellent choices. Force yourself to suggest an outside activity that gets everyone off the couch. Children are much more likely to engage in an outside activity if you lead the charge. Go ahead! Climb on the swing, jump on the trampoline, or throw a ball to your spouse. You'll be amazed how quickly they follow you outside and engage in the fun.

PRIORITIES quiz item 14

14. _____ Limit my children's activities to manageable levels.

Hurry! We're Going to Be Late for Basket Weaving!

In this society, you've likely been brainwashed to believe that you aren't a good parent unless your child plays competitive soccer by the time she's ten, is active in the Girl Scouts, can play the piano masterfully, and swims beautifully . . . and, by the way, leases a horse. Hear a little sarcasm in my voice? For years, I bought into this notion as well and dutifully enrolled my little girl in ballet, piano, church programs, choirs, Girl Scouts, basketball, and more. I used the rationale that "she has to try everything so she can find out what she likes."

Many children are so overscheduled, their stress levels race sky high and the entire family comes apart at the seams. Many parents feel guilty because of the number of hours they spend at work. As a result, they overcompensate by signing their children up for myriad activities to show their commitment. When they aren't working in the evening and weekends, they shuttle their kids back and forth between activities, never realizing any quality time together. Your children don't *want* all that activity—they just want *you*.

Still, parents tell themselves that all these activities are good for their children. Yes, you may see long-term benefits—but at what cost? What cost to your children's stress levels? What cost to your relationship with them? What cost to the sanity of your family? What cost to your spouse—the person you never see anyway because soccer games are held on complete opposite ends of town? Can simply spending quality time together strengthen your relationship?

Having made big changes in my thinking in this area, I offer these suggestions that might work for you.

ONE ACTIVITY AT A TIME. Sometimes it's easy to make excuses for why your children are involved in so many "good" programs. For example, we have a Wednesday night program at our church that Meagan joined for a year. "My goodness," I thought. "We have to be able to make time for her to learn about the Lord." Forget that she was already participating in another program on Sundays that required her to study lessons during the week. Forget that she had Girl Scouts every other Monday, piano lessons on Wednesday after school, and soccer practice on Monday, Wednesday, and Thursday evenings, with games on Saturday morning. Aaaarrrggghhh! I soon realized that it was easy to justify the need to participate in yet one more thing because it was a church function. So we gave up going to this program and felt good about the additional family time we'd gained. The benefits of that time are arguably better than what she'd get from attending the church program. The key is to achieve a good balance.

ONE SEASON, ONE SPORT. Tell your child he or she must choose only one sport to focus on each season. For example, if playing on both volleyball and basketball teams occur in the same season, pick one over the other. If your child really enjoys soccer but also wants to ride horses, take a hiatus from riding during the spring soccer season. Then ride during the summer until soccer begins again in the fall. When it's too cold to play soccer or ride horses, take a few months of swimming lessons at an indoor pool.

FIND ACTIVITIES MORE THAN ONE CHILD LIKES. When John and I teach Sunday school, we tend to arrive at church feeling a bit frazzled and thrown-together after getting three kids fed, dressed, and out the door. But one of the other teachers always looked amazingly put together, despite the fact she has four young children at home. So I asked about her family management tips for being relaxed and happy. She told me one of her secrets was to find a single activity that all the children could participate in together, no matter what their ages. That way, she wouldn't be running around so much. She let her children decide what sport to be involved in, and they chose swimming. Practice times are the same for everyone and the meets happen at the same place. What a great idea!

15. _____ Make my health a number-one priority.

Healthy as a Horse

If you aren't in good health, you won't be able to do much. If you don't take care of yourself, your ability to take care of others will decline. And certainly if you don't feel well, you won't be able to be productive at home or work. You must take personal responsibility for this immensely important priority in your life.

BE A PHYSICALLY ACTIVE ROLE MODEL. Instead of watching television, plan family outings that include a physical activity such as biking, hiking, or strolling through the zoo. We have a beautiful open-space trail behind our home that winds around for miles. One of our favorite things to do after dinner is to take a family walk around the neighborhood. We don't necessarily walk for exercise, but rather for the social, family, and leisure roles it fills.

KEEP UP WITH DOCTOR, DENTIST, AND EYE CARE APPOINTMENTS. Don't ignore warning signals. Listen to your body when it tells you something is wrong and tend to it immediately. If something bothers you, take care of it!

When I married John, I was amazed at how many things were "broken" that he never took care of. Because he didn't come with a warranty, I couldn't return him, so I set out to fix all the things that bothered him. Lord knows the man wasn't going to do it himself! Over time, he had a bad vein stripped from his leg, a finger surgery to repair a joint jammed in high school, a nasal surgery to cure a mild deviated septum, a clearing up of skin-care issues, a crown repaired and moles removed, eyes surgically corrected with a laser, a flat-foot problem fixed with custom shoe inserts, and an elbow shot with cortisone to relieve pain. Added to that was "fixing" his propensity to get me pregnant. It's amazing that one person could have so many things go awry and not address them. After taking care of these issues he is a happier, more productive, healthier person than he was before.

SCHEDULE SCREENINGS FOR YOURSELF AND YOUR CHILDREN. Don't trust routine screenings at your child's school. Meagan had been getting her eyes checked by the school nurse in a regular screening at the beginning of each year. After every one, she came home with a note marked 20/20. However, I began to observe that she couldn't see signs in the distance—ones that I could see plainly and thought she should easily be able to read. Being concerned, I scheduled an appointment with my eye doctor to check her eyesight. Indeed, she was nearsighted and needed to wear prescription glasses to see far away. After getting glasses, she was amazed. Now movies, a flying soccer ball, and Christmas lights are all easier to see. She had no idea she couldn't see before! You are responsible for child's well-being, and routine exams help avert health-care crises.

DRINK ENOUGH WATER. You must drink sixty-four ounces of water each day for optimal health. Water can eliminate headaches, increase energy, and decrease blood pressure. It also makes you feel better overall and boosts your mental performance. In fact, mild dehydration can give you a headache and impair your ability to concentrate. If you work outside of the home, make sure you have a sixty-four-ounce container or enough water bottles to get you through the day. Try to finish your water allotment by 5:00 p.m. to avoid midnight trips to the bathroom.

STOP SMOKING. I know about this one from personal experience. Many people are surprised to find out I'm an ex-smoker. When I was in school, my friends and I considered smoking to be cool. I loved smoking, and I smoked from the time I was thirteen until I was twenty-two. Then I went cold turkey, which was probably one of the hardest things I've ever had to do (except have a baby). So I know telling you "just quit" isn't easy advice to follow.

In addition to all the things you hear about why smoking is bad (causes cancer, costs money, makes you smell, gives you bad breath, gets on fabrics), smoking lowers your productivity. Can you relate to this? When I wasn't having a cigarette, I was thinking about the next time I was going to have a cigarette. When it was getting close to time to have one, I couldn't concentrate well because I was getting antsy. When I needed another cigarette, I took a "smoke break," and lollygagged with my smoker buddies. Clearly, the nonsmokers didn't take nearly as many breaks as I did. Cumulatively, I wasted a lot of time during the day being a smoker. Looking back, I know quitting was absolutely one of the best things I ever did for myself.

I encourage you to get determined, get some help, improve your productivity, and live longer. Stop smoking!

PRIORITIES quiz item 16

16. _____ Exercise consistently.

You Can't Make a Difference if You Can't Make It Up the Stairs

If your doctor told you she had a new drug that would prolong your life, reduce your chance of death from all causes by 50 to 70 percent, enhance your quality of sleep, and improve your ability to manage stress, would you take it? Yes, it exists! It's called exercise. According to the Harvard School of Public Health, as few as fifteen minutes of exercise a day can greatly improve your health and quality of life.

The Facts

- 60 percent of Americans don't exercise regularly.
- Americans watch an average of fifty-seven days of television each year, not counting surfing the Internet and playing video games.
- Most U.S. jobs require countless hours in front of the computer and very little physical activity.

According to the Office of the Surgeon General, obesity has more than doubled since 1980. In addition, 26 percent of U.S. children watch four or more hours of television each day. Do you think there's a connection? Studies by the Department of Health and Human Services show that children who actively engage in physical and social activities have better social skills and family relationships, increased self-esteem, and healthier lifestyles than their sedentary peers. Dare I say this applies to adults as well?

JUST DO IT. Doing nothing could be hazardous to your health and can cause diseases like arthritis, depression, and sleep problems. In fact, according to a group of health experts, if all you do is sit around without getting much physical activity, your lifestyle could actually kill you by setting up a condition called sedentary death syndrome, or SeDS. "Physical inactivity, which can start during childhood, can lead to a wide range of diseases that, coupled with a poor diet, kill a quarter-million people each year," says Frank Booth, Ph.D., a physiology professor at the University of Missouri, Columbia, and founder of the group Researchers Against SeDS.

It's estimated that conditions like obesity, Type 2 diabetes, and heart disease are all increasing because of SeDS. Being sedentary, combined with poor eating habits, claims about the same number of lives annually as smoking tobacco. Overall, the SeDS group says that 60 percent of all Americans are at risk of dying sooner because of their own inactivity.

We know we should exercise. We beat ourselves up for not doing it. If you're like me, it's easy to see why. When it comes to exercise, I'm fundamentally lazy. I just can't seem to get off my fat bottom and take care of myself. I simply don't *like* it. But I know I have to do it or I can't indulge in the wonderful desserts I love, so I've figured out a few tricks.

DO ACTIVITIES THAT YOU LOVE. Personally, I enjoy walking. I like getting out into the fresh air and sunshine. I feel energized and invigorated when I've finished a long walk. Not long ago, I heard about a program called Colorado on the Move through one of my clients. So I registered The Productivity Pro® stepping team for this program and invited my newsletter subscribers to join me. An amazing twenty-two people signed up.

The key to succeeding in this program is developing a "step culture" in the environment in which you live. It requires using a pedometer to track the number of steps you walk in one week as your baseline (with no increase in activity that week). Then you set a goal of adding 2,000 steps a day over the next fourteen weeks.

When I took my baseline steps I was amazed at what a slug I was; I had actually thought I was fairly active! My goal was to add 8,000 steps a day, and along the way, I discovered some creative ways to add steps to my pedometer when my energy was running low. (You don't have to have a pedometer to implement these tips because every step counts toward good health and happiness. Remember, small changes make big differences!)

Try some of these ideas to get moving:

- Walk during your lunch break.
- Take the stairs instead of the elevator.
- Force yourself to park far away from the entrance of the mall or grocery store (instead of driving around in circles for five minutes trying to find the closest spot).
- Walk on your treadmill while watching television (my husband's favorite trick).
- Walk the longest way around the block to get the mail.
- Walk the dog instead of just letting it out in the yard.
- Meet your friends and walk together.
- Walk up and down a flight of stairs for ten minutes.
- When you need to use a copy machine or restroom, go to one on a different floor than yours.
- Take a couple of ten-minute breaks during the day to walk a few laps around your floor.
- Walk to a colleague's office rather than send an e-mail.
- Get up and walk over to the TV to change the channel instead of using a remote while sitting on the sofa.
- Walk around your office and use a speakerphone to conduct business.
- Walk to any destination that is less than one mile.
- Don't take the moving walkways at the airport. (This makes

my husband nuts when I do this. He always takes the walkway, but I always beat him to the end.)

- Take the kids out for a family walk after dinner, or if you live close enough, walk to and from dinner at a restaurant.
- Unload groceries from the car in several trips.
- Talk to your friends on a cordless phone and walk around the house.
- While your son or daughter plays soccer, walk around the perimeter of the field while you're waiting.

You don't have to run a marathon to get into better physical condition. Moderate exertion will almost certainly be enough to keep you from joining the two-thirds of the American population who are either overweight or obese. It's fairly easy to increase your activity once you make a conscious effort to get moving.

STICK WITH A FRIEND. When I had a workout buddy, I exercised more than any other time in my life. There's nothing like the pressure of a friend waiting for you at 7:00 a.m. at the gym and knowing she'd be upset if you didn't show. It's easy to put dates and times on the calendar in blocks when you're going to exercise, but it's much harder to actually do it when the time arrives (because most likely I won't feel like it). It helps to have peer pressure to make you follow through on your commitments.

GET A PERSONAL TRAINER. After my workout friend moved to Florida, I stopped going to the gym. No surprise there! It was such a pain to get up early, get dressed, drive somewhere in the cold air, work out with a bunch of strangers, come home, and get chilled on the way back. Then, strangely, I thought of my daughter's piano teacher. All the other piano teachers I talked to wanted me to drive Meagan there. Michelle, however, drove to our home and gave lessons on our own piano. The boys might still be in the middle of eating their dinners or I'd be doing dishes, but it didn't matter, because the lesson could carry on regardless.

The convenience of having someone come to the house dawned on me as a great benefit, so I decided to hire a personal trainer. Not the type who works at a gym and meets you there, but one who'd come to me. Enter David. He requires me to work out three times a week, and I'm likely to do it, for several reasons. One, I'm paying for it, and I hate wasting money. Two, we schedule a week in advance so I'm forced to schedule around his visits, rather than fall back on the excuse that "I'm too busy." Third, he just shows up at my home. Now I'm not exactly going to purposefully leave my house to avoid him. So I work out. And it's just what I need. He's fun, energetic, and motivational. He does the workout with me and encourages me the whole time. Even if you have to sacrifice in another area of your budget each month, I highly encourage cutting out something and getting a trainer.

DECIDE TO STOP MAKING EXCUSES. Before I joined the Lady Fitness in my area, I had a million reasons why I didn't have time to work out. Then I decided to practice what I preach and look for solutions to all of my usual excuses. "I have nothing to do with my boys when I'm working out, and I don't want to saddle John with watching them all the time" became "Lady Fitness has child care and a play place right in their facility. I'll just take them with me." "I have to drive Meagan to soccer practice right at the same time I'd want to take a class" became "Let's switch Meagan's activity of choice to horseback riding, so she can take lessons on the weekends rather than practicing during the week." "I'll get sick doing yoga too close to eating dinner" became "We'll pick up the kids and eat a half-hour earlier on class nights." And my favorite excuse of all—"I have to do the dishes after dinner" became "Oh, duh, I can soak everything and do them when I get back."

TRY SOMETHING DIFFERENT. If you're bored with your same old routine and dread your workouts, remember that variety is the spice of life! I got tired of walking on the treadmill and literally going nowhere. I also didn't particularly like the co-ed recreational center I could use in my town because it was crowded and difficult to get on a machine. The aerobics floor (made of hardwood) aggravated my back. Then I saw an ad for a ladies only gym five minutes from my home and went there for a visit. The environment was pleasant, it offered a wide variety of classes, and the floor was carpeted! So I joined and attended a yoga class the next day. I'd never tried yoga before but heard lots of great things about how relaxing it could be. Now I love attending my yoga class every Saturday morning.

What could you try that's new and different?

- Walking a new route in your neighborhood
- Biking
- Exercise classes
- Pilates
- Shooting hoops
- Toning with a video series
- Weight lifting
- Water activity

Here's the most important part: Stop feeling guilty when you take time for yourself to exercise. You *do* have time, and you must *make* time. You can't tell me that you don't even have ten minutes a day to do *something*. When you do, you'll be taking care of the most important person in the world! If you don't, you might not be around for long to enjoy being with the people you love.

PRIORITIES quiz item 17

17. _____ Enjoy the way I spend most of my day.

She Works Hard for the Money

Some of you work outside the home; some of you work just as hard within it. Regardless of where you spend the majority of your time, you should enjoy it.

How you spend your time should also fit within the overall context of your personal mission statement. If you said your career is one of your top priorities, I'd expect to see you devoting a great deal of time to your work endeavors. Many people spend lots more than the required hours at the office, but it's not something they value or sometimes even enjoy. If you spend time in ways that don't support what's important to you, life can seem empty and hollow.

Interestingly, some self-admitted workaholics have confessed to me they don't even like what they do. But they've attached their sense of self-worth to their ability to succeed in the workplace, so they keep giving more than they should to feed their addiction.

"The trouble with the rat race," Lily Tomlin once observed, "is that even if you win, you're still a rat." In your quest to get ahead, don't leave your values behind. You might be making a great living and failing to make a life. You owe it to yourself to do work that matters to you. It's easy to put in too many hours and take on too much stress to work at something that isn't personally fulfilling and exciting. Why not spend that time crafting a more fitting career?

Talking with thousands of people in hundreds of different jobs, I have observed that people who succeed in finding work they love are naturally more productive.

When I was in junior high and high school, one of my best friends, Suzanne Ellis, was an amazing dancer. No wonder: Her mother, Barbara Ellis, was a renowned dancer. She also owned the dance studio where we took lessons. Of course, Suzanne was a natural dancer. Her body moved in ways I could never get mine to do.

I wanted so much to be a dancer back then, and I tried so hard, I really did. But I was always jealous of Suzanne's superior talents in dance. She danced professionally after college and made a career out of it. I had to settle for being our high school mascot.

Looking back, I understand that I simply wasn't destined to dance a lot. But I can sure talk a lot! Daddykins has a Ph.D. in philosophy and taught ethics at the Air Force Academy. Mom was a psychologist and lectured frequently at conferences and church. I guess speaking is just in my blood and a natural part of my personality.

Once I discovered my calling to be a professional speaker, everything else fell into place, and life became *easy*. When you *love* what you do, you never have to worry about being productive. You'll find that you become naturally productive and work from the sheer joy of it. Is writing this book my work? Yes . . . but it sure doesn't feel like it. Is standing in front of an audience and sharing my truths in the hope of bettering their lives my work? Yes . . . but I feel blessed and privileged every minute I'm on the platform. I'm productive partially because I was conditioned to be this way from my parents and my background, but also because I simply love what I do, so I take time to master the skills.

If you love what you do and immerse yourself in it, even work can provide the kind of escape that psychologist Mihaly Csikszentmihalyi defined thirty years ago as the state of flow. When you experience flow, you lose track of time. You lose yourself in an activity and experience utter contentment. One of my girlfriends stays home with her two children and works harder than many people I know. Amazingly, she can immerse herself in laundry or mopping the floor, actually enjoy it, and feel like time is flying. Some people experience this during leisure activities like quilting. I've heard of others working through lunch without knowing it, as they dive into a work project that really moves them.

Here are some important questions to ask youself:

- If you didn't get paid for what you do and didn't need the money, would you continue working in that particular job, field, or industry? If money were no issue and all jobs paid the same, would you still be doing what you're doing? Don't sell out your soul for money.

- Does your work make you feel excited to get out of bed every morning and start your day? You shouldn't have to check your life at the door of your office and then pick it up on the way out. Life and work don't have to be separate.

- Does your work fit your lifestyle? For me, traveling every week and staying out for days at a time in sleek hotels was great when I didn't have kids. After my experience of missing Meagan's first steps, I quickly learned that living out of a suitcase would be both undesirable and impossible if I wanted my happiness. If your work severely clashes with your joy in life, you have nowhere else to go but the door.

- Is your work fulfilling? Have you actually reached the goals you set for yourself and outgrown your current job? If your job no longer jibes with who you are, it's time to start looking elsewhere.

BEING BORED IS WORSE THAN BEING TOO BUSY. Sirota Consulting, which specializes in gauging employee attitudes and morale, surveyed 800,000 people at sixty-one companies worldwide and found that those who say they have "too much work" scored an overall job-satisfaction rating of 57 on a scale of 100, while those who had "much too little work" scored lowest in all categories at 32. Those who work harder are more fulfilled than those who don't do enough, so don't make the mistake of staying in a job that underutilizes your skills in the long run.

DECISIONS AREN'T PERMANENT. If your work doesn't satisfy you, don't stop searching for the magic! If you left a traditional office environment to be home with your children, either because it was expected of you or you thought it was best, and you're miserable because you miss the pace or challenge, then consider other options! You're not constrained by an either-or decision: either make a living or make a life. You can do both! In fact, when you ignore your values and set goals and plan activities that won't meet your long-term needs, you won't feel fulfilled. Look for something that makes you put your feet on the floor every day and say, "Yes! I can't wait for this day to begin!" Perhaps you could lobby for a flexible schedule that allows you to occasionally use day care and work at home part-time. Don't feel limited by or tied to earlier choices. You can always change your mind.

Of course, many jobs combine truly satisfying work with a lot of grunt work, so strive for work that is more satisfying and less grunt. Work to see the value and necessity of the difficult parts of your job. When your day-to-day activities fall in line with your values, you'll discover your natural productivity. In fact, it will come bursting through without your even trying.

PRIORITIES quiz item 18

18. _____ Practice healthy eating habits.

Ice Cream Has Milk, So It Must Be Health Food

As a society, Americans are clearly in a state of nutritional crisis and in need of radical change. After thirty years of solid research aimed at lowering dietary fat, Americans have grown collectively fatter than ever.

When I'm traveling out of state for a speaking engagement, it's tempting to order a big, fattening dessert from room service. "After all, I am working hard so I deserve it," I might justify. But when I feel sluggish and bloated the next day, I realize that eating that dessert is never worth it. Saying "I'm out of my time zone; I'll have jet lag tomorrow" becomes my excuse to avoid working out in the hotel gym. The result: low energy during my speaking engagement. When at a friend's wedding, I think, "Well, she's only getting married once so I'll only be able to eat her wedding cake once" might be an excuse for a second serving—and a need for walking an extra twenty minutes on the treadmill. When I'm at my annual speaker's convention, it's tempting to eat the yummy dessert at my place every single meal. But why would I work so hard to get in shape before the convention, just to ruin it with a week's worth of desserts? Instead, I take a couple of bites of the dessert and push it away.

Statistics from the American Dietetic Association

- Poor eating habits can make you fuzzyheaded and less productive.
- People perform less efficiently on an empty stomach.
- Fatigue from low blood sugar levels leads to poor concentration.
- It's easier to catch viruses when your body is weak from a lack of nutrients.

So, realizing how easy it is to eat poorly and recognizing how important it is to eat healthily, you have to make eating a priority. Here are some items you should add to your regular shopping list.
Shopping list:

- Whole fruit, especially blueberries, strawberries, and apples
- Nuts, especially almonds
- Dried fruits, such as raisins, prunes, or apricots
- Protein bars or low-fat granola bars
- Ready-made protein drinks
- Snack cans of fruit
- Cereal with a high-fiber content
- Raw ready-to-go veggies like celery, carrots, broccoli, and cherry tomatoes

Having these items on hand makes it easier to reach for something healthy. Make sure you're stocked up at work as well, so you don't end up in front of the vending machine when you're hungry.

19. _____ Get enough sleep.

If You Don't Sleep Like a Baby, You Will Act Like One

Sleeping well is not a luxury . . . it's a necessity. Sacrificing sleep for any reason is actually counterproductive. A March 2001 National Sleep Foundation (NSF) poll of 1,000 adults found that one-third get fewer than seven hours per night and only one-third are getting the recommended eight hours a night. John Shepard, medical director of the Mayo Clinic Sleep Disorders Center, says that most adults need between seven and a half and eight and a half hours of sleep a night, teens need nine hours and fifteen minutes, and small children need more than that.

The NSF poll actually showed that 85 percent of people would sleep more if they were convinced it would contribute to a healthier lifestyle.

Statistics from National Sleep Foundation

- The foundation reported that drowsy workers cost U.S. employers an estimated $18 billion annually in lost productivity. Too little sleep also suppresses your immune function, which leads to increased infection and illnesses, creating more absenteeism. If you add errors, damage to property or equipment, and health consequences, the costs go even higher.

- Overall, the quality of work, the amount of work, and your concentration *each* decline by 30 percent when you're sleepy.

Sleepiness also impairs memory, reaction time, and alertness. Talk about a productivity loss!

- A lack of sleep affects your personal life, too. Among those having sleep problems, 77 percent also said they had less marital satisfaction. And 38 percent of married respondents said they have intimate relations with their spouses less than once a week because of fatigue and lack of time. Tired people are more moody, less patient with others, and less interactive in relationships.

- Inadequate sleep causes problems similar to drinking too much alcohol. Nodding off at work isn't just unproductive; it can be disastrous. The National Highway Traffic Safety Administration reports that sleepy drivers cause at least 200,000 crashes each year. The 1989 Exxon *Valdez* Alaskan oil spill was reportedly due at least in part to the severe fatigue of the tanker's sleep-deprived third mate. Worker fatigue was also a factor in the crash of the *Challenger* space shuttle and the nuclear accidents at Chernobyl and Three Mile Island. In rats, prolonged sleep deprivation resulted in death.

When I take an informal poll during a seminar and ask participants if they think daytime sleepiness is normal, about 75 percent say yes. Most people also believe that feeling sleepy in the afternoon is normal. However, sleep experts tell us that daytime sleepiness is *not* normal if you're getting the correct amount of sleep for your needs. When people start nodding off, they blame the heavy meal they just ate, the stuffy air in the room, or the boring movie they were watching. These things don't *cause* sleepiness; they just unmask it. Many people don't make the connection between the amount of sleep they get at night and how drowsy they feel during the day.

The Sleepiness Scale

Answer the following questions "yes" or "no":

1. Do you get sleepy while at your desk during the day?
2. Do you consistently get grumpy or feel low?
3. Do you need an alarm clock to wake you up in the morning?
4. Do you hit an afternoon slump after you eat lunch?
5. If you were a passenger in a car for an hour during the day, would you nod off if you didn't take a break?
6. Would you fall asleep if you sat quietly and read during the day?
7. Are you likely to doze off while watching TV during the day?
8. Do you get fewer than six hours of sleep at night?

Total number of "yes" answers: _____

Check your score to see how sleepy you are:

1–3.   Congratulations, you are getting enough sleep!

4–5   You are sleep deprived.

6 and up Seek the advice of a sleep specialist!

My husband John was thirty years old before we discovered he had a sleeping disorder. I used to think he was just exhausted from a long day of work at the U.S. Postal Service and just needed a nap. He was frequently cranky and moody. Then, when we had a baby, I'd get up at night to feed him, come back to bed, and find John not breathing. Well, he was sort of breathing, but he would go for long periods of time between breaths, and then gulp air quickly. I told him about my observations and started paying close attention to his sleep patterns in the middle of the night. Then I alerted our physician, who ordered a sleep study. A medical supply company brought an oxygen-level measuring device over for John to sleep with, and we discovered his oxygen levels were dipping well below normal. After a full-blown sleep study at the hospital, John was diagnosed with upper airway resistance syndrome. An ear/nose/throat doctor corrected John's deviated septum and enlarged glands, which improved his ability to breathe and sleep. Bottom line: Take your sleep problems seriously. You might not even realize you have them because you're, well, asleep.

Test your knowledge of good sleep habits. Answer the following questions "true" (T) or "false" (F):

1. You should sleep in on weekends to catch up on the sleep you missed during the week.
2. To sleep well at night, you should get as much bright light as possible during waking hours.
3. The best time to exercise is two hours before bedtime, so you will sleep soundly.
4. Avoiding coffee, tea, soft drinks, and nicotine after noon will help you sleep better.
5. An alcoholic drink or two before bedtime will help you sleep more soundly.
6. To get a good night's sleep, you should not nap at all during the day.
7. Experts recommend reading in your bed before sleeping, so you can drift off naturally.
8. You should not eat or watch TV in your bed.
9. The average adult requires seven hours of sleep a night.

10. You should not watch TV one hour before bedtime.
11. Reading, listening to music, taking a bath, and writing are all good activities to do prior to bedtime.
12. You should eat a snack prior to sleeping.
13. People sleep better in a slightly warm room, rather than a slightly cool one.
14. If you can't fall asleep, you should lie in bed until you drift off.
15. If you can't fall asleep, do not agonize about it.

Answers:

1. F
2. T
3. F
4. T
5. F
6. T
7. F
8. T
9. F
10. T
11. T
12. F
13. T
14. F
15. T

Here are some ideas to help you sleep better:

SLOW YOUR PACE. Avoid activities that stimulate you, such as fast video games, arguing with a spouse, or working out, at least an hour before bedtime, preferably more. With all its sounds, lights, and color, TV watching can be especially stimulating. Yes, you may get drowsy and doze off in front of the television, but you'll have to wake again to settle into a sleeping position, and then experience wakefulness during the night. Your body may be tired, but your brain is very active after watching television. Instead, select nonstimulating activities such as light reading, ironing, doing dishes, taking a bath, or writing letters for at least one hour before bedtime.

CLEAR YOUR MIND. Write down everything you're thinking about that must be done the next day. Lying in bed awake with all those reminders running through your head will prevent you from sleeping soundly. If you're stewing over an issue with someone, journal or write a draft e-mail but don't send it. (In fact, you're safest not to even put their e-mail address in the "to" field so your trigger-happy finger doesn't accidentally go off.) Waiting twenty-four hours after you've vented on paper will give you a better perspective, and you'll probably be glad you put time between your writing and sending that message. The bonus? You were able to get to sleep.

TRAIN YOUR BRAIN. I read an article about how some babies sleep better when exposed to the sound of a heartbeat or another white noise. I figured it couldn't hurt to try it on adults, too. So for Christmas last year, I bought John a sound machine. He played with the different noises and selected the ocean sound, with waves crashing on the shore. From December 25 until January 3, he played this sound while drifting off to sleep. On January 3, we went on vacation to Cancun, Mexico, with the family and were lucky enough to get an oceanside room. John didn't even need his sound machine! For someone who doesn't usually sleep well in hotels, I was so amazed how deeply and long he slept. He was always the last one to get up in the morning. I think that Cancun vacation may well be one of his favorites, simply because he got such great sleep!

FORM GOOD HABITS. Sleep experts tell us not to eat, read, or watch television in bed. Here's why. When you lie down to sleep at night, ideally your brain should associate your bed with sleep. If you crawl into bed and do other things, you'll only succeed in confusing yourself. If you like to read before bed, fine, but do it in a chair in another part of the house. Eat in the kitchen. Watch television in your family room. Then, when you go up to your bed to sleep, you will actually sleep. Make this a habit! If you wake up during the night and don't fall back to sleep in fifteen minutes, get up. Write down everything you're thinking about. Then try to sleep again fifteen minutes later. If you don't get up, over time your body will adjust to tossing and turning instead of sleeping.

RECORD YOUR "CAN'T MISS" LATE-NIGHT SHOWS. I often hear this excuse for staying up late: "I love the Jay Leno Show, and it's on late." That's no reason to not go to bed on time. Open your user's manual and finally figure out how to program your VCR to record your favorite shows. Then you can watch them on your own time, not when it's time to sleep.

PRIORITIES quiz item 20

20. _____ Make time to feed my intellect and continue my learning.

Learn from the School of Hard Knocks

All humans share the need to learn and grow. We're not just talking about education here, in terms of getting a degree to be more employable. If you want your brain to continue to serve you into your old age, you must keep it active. Be curious. Wonder. Stretch. Grow.

In this era of overwhelming stress, the world needs people who:

- Care deeply about what they do.
- Think independently.
- Are responsible for their own growth and development.
- Work tenaciously and proactively to improve their performance at work and home.

Employees are learning that it's their responsibility to remain employable by getting the new skills they need. Everyone is educated; some people simply lack a formal education but have learned from the school of hard knocks on the job and from their years living on this earth.

In March 2003, it was reported that Bill Gates was worth $52.8 billion. He'd been at Microsoft since 1975, the year he started the company with Paul Allen. With fifty-two weeks a year, five working days a week, and assuming no vacation, Gates had made $7,252,747 a day since Microsoft began. Not bad for a Harvard dropout! You can bet he never stops learning and growing. And he proves that you don't need to go to a university to achieve great things.

STIMULATE YOUR BRAIN. Even if you have no desire to attend school and earn a degree, you need to keep your brain active. I subscribe to a series of books from the Easton Press called the 100 Greatest Books Ever Written. The series includes titles such as *Moby-Dick*, *Wuthering Heights*, *War and Peace*, and so on. Pretty heavy reads. I order one book every other month because each one costs about fifty dollars—they are leather bound, with gold leafing, a satin bookmark, and beautiful artwork. I finish reading one book before ordering the next one. At this pace, I read six in a year, so it will take me almost seventeen years to complete the series. But that's okay! In fifteen years, I'll still be fifteen years older whether I read the books or not. In the meantime, I'll be able to discuss these great works intelligently and use excerpts as examples in my speeches. When I've completed reading them all, I plan to travel to the best places I read about.

ATTEND CONFERENCES. Like me, I'm sure you receive flyers on special one-day conferences being held for local associations, universities, and chambers of commerce. Every once in a while, don't throw the brochure away—*go!* You'll keep up with the thought leaders of the day, meet new people, and have interesting conversation material. I landed my first corporate client back in 1992 when I attended a conference held by Business and Professional Women. By chance, I sat next to the training director for Mobil Oil Company, and thus marked the genesis of a beautiful ongoing relationship.

CHECK OUT PUBLIC SEMINARS. Check out seminars offered by American Management Association (AMA), CareerTrack (www. careertrack.com), or Fred Pryor seminars (which owns Career-Track) when they come to your area. Explore new avenues of interest. Meet new people. It will be well worth your time and money.

SIGN UP FOR COMMUNITY COLLEGE OR CONTINUING EDUCATION COURSES. Our local community college sends out a catalog each quarter outlining the continuing education courses offered for no credit. If one looks interesting, sign up! Taking a course every Tuesday night for the next six weeks, for example, will add variety to your life and give your interest in learning a boost. Do it with your spouse or a friend and achieve more quality time with them to boot!

TAKE ADVANTAGE OF COMPANY EDUCATION PROGRAMS. Being in the training business myself, I'm often impressed by the wide variety of educational offerings available through many organizations. Several host learning luncheons each month, bringing in speakers to discuss everything from personal finances to yoga to time management. Some have an extensive catalog of open-enrollment training seminars offered on-site during work hours. A few even offer degree programs during the week, compliments of a university that offers special on-site classes. You get paid to learn and improve your skills.

CHAPTER THREE

Mastering the Third Pillar—

PERSONALITY

THIS CHAPTER ENCOURAGES you to look at your behavior, habits, and choices—and then figure out which ones to adjust in order to support your desired direction in life.

Being a mother of three and a career woman gives me lots of opportunities to ask for help. However, relying on other people can be hard. The hardest thing for me to do is let other people take care of my children. I tried to be a stay-at-home mother, I really did. But I almost had to enter the funny farm after nine months.

When Meagan entered kindergarten, her classes didn't start until 9:00 a.m. Since I often had to be at a client's offices at 7:30 a.m., Meagan attended before-school and after-school care (before John started working with me in the business). The plan was that these caregivers would drop her off at the front of the school where her teacher picked up the kindergarteners each morning, then pick her up at the front of the school, and drive her back to the child-care center for us to get her at the end of the day.

This sounded like a nice, tidy plan, but I thought I would be clever. I didn't have a presentation the first day we tried this, so I decided to spy on the caregivers' van. I sat in the parking lot in a back spot and cautiously followed behind the van so that they wouldn't see me. They got to school, and . . . wait . . . what are they doing? They pulled into the back of the school where all the big yellow buses were dropping off the older kids. Hey! That wasn't the plan! I watched in horror as Meagan walked quietly off the van and stood alone on the sidewalk. Then the van *drove away!*

You have never seen a mother park illegally so quickly and sprint across a school parking lot. As I approached Meagan, I saw the look of terror in my poor child's face—she had no idea where she was supposed to go! How dare they drive off and leave her standing there! I got to her in five seconds flat, ran up behind her, and said as nonchalantly as I could, "Surprise!" I won't soon forget the look of relief flooding her face as she saw me. She exclaimed, "Oh, Mommy!" while she flew into my arms. I played it like I meant to do that, like it was no big deal, because I didn't want to worry her.

In no time, Meagan was smiling and laughing while I tried to figure out how the heck to get to the front of the building. The doors were locked because students weren't allowed in until the bell rang, so we had to walk the entire perimeter of the school until we found her teacher. Meagan happily got into line and marched into school behind the teacher for her first day. All the mothers, including me, smiled and waved as they held back tears. The children acted much braver than we did.

My heart pounded as I imagined what could have happened if I hadn't been there. When I got home, I burst into tears. I felt so guilty. If I were a stay-at-home mom, none of this would have happened. I should be just like the other mothers who walk their kids to school.

I cleared up the error with the caregivers in a big hurry (believe me!) but I couldn't seem to shake the guilt I felt. I had lunch with a girlfriend/client that day and told her the entire sob story, breaking into tears at the thought of my little girl alone, confused, lost, not knowing where to go. I felt horrible and said, "I should have done this, I should have done that." Then my friend looked at me and said sternly, "Laura, nothing happened. You were *there*. You followed the van. You ensured that Meagan was safe. Now you have it fixed. You did your best. You arranged for her care. Mistakes happen. You can't feel so guilty or responsible and change your lifestyle completely because of one incident."

She was right. I was comparing myself to the stay-at-home mothers. Yes, I *was* there, I did fix it, and I did my best. I have to stop feeling guilty for relying on other people to help me.

Guilt—what a garbage emotion. Guilt keeps you from unlocking your true potential! Stop "shoulding" on yourself and let go of that guilt!

PERSONALITY quiz item 21

> 21. _____ Control perfectionism, realizing that some things are good enough.

Is Everything Worth Doing Right?

Perfectionists rarely experience satisfaction because they perceive their efforts as never good enough. A reader once told me, "I get hung up and obsess over small details instead of moving past them. I get an overwhelming feeling that if I don't get that one thing resolved, nothing else will come together." In her mind, she could have always done better. As a result, she hesitated to try new things because she didn't want to fail.

I know the feeling. I call myself a "recovering perfectionist." And it's taken me a long time to recover! One of my clients (who is also a friend), Lt. James Henning of the Denver Police Department, wrote me an e-mail saying, "Recovering Perfectionist? Like you were ever on the wagon! What do you do for therapy? Not squeegee your shower three days in a row? Leave the clip off the opened bag of potato chips? Let the TV remote fall between the sofa cushions? Send your socks through the wash solo? Go on vacation without your planner or, heaven forbid, hotel reservations? Wait a month to upgrade your Quicken software? File your taxes on April 14? Lose a receipt? Not send in the warranty card on the new DVD player? Let your spice jars go unalphabetized? Change your oil at 3,050 miles? Not RSVP? Not date your leftovers? Chew your pencil?"

His sense of humor illustrates an important concept: Not every task deserves your best effort. Another reader stated it beautifully, "I need help learning when to say 'enough.' Every 'A' doesn't have to have a 'plus' after it and every *wow* doesn't have to have an exclamation point after it. I don't want to say that I'm a perfectionist—I see it as striving for excellence and not wanting to settle for less. I think this can be detrimental to my time management and frustrating for my colleagues and family."

Here are some suggestions to curb perfectionism:

GET RID OF PICKY PARENTING STANDARDS. As long as you get the results you want, let people do things their way when it really doesn't matter or doesn't cause safety concerns. This lesson took me a couple of years to figure out.

Let me begin by saying *no one will ever be as good with your children as you are.* Parents are the best people to care for their little ones. But even parents who are compatible struggle with each other on the best way to do things. There is no right or wrong answer in parenting, just differences in style. Something may not be the way you would do it, but if it's not harming your child, allow it.

I used to think John played too roughly with our baby boys (I still do). Since my first baby was a girl, I was used to gentle, sweet play, lots of coos and cuddles. I cuddled, cooed, and used a gentle touch with my baby boys too. John, however, would pick them up and hold them high in the air, making loud noises and weird sounds. I would grit my teeth to keep myself from saying something when I thought he was playing "the wrong way." After all, this wasn't how *I* interacted with the boys. But you know what, darn if they didn't love it. Turns out he knew instinctively how to interact with boys—duh—and now they're teaching me.

I'd also get aggravated at the way John changed a diaper. It took him *forever,* and he didn't do it "right." Sure, I tried to coach him a few times, but then I forced myself to look the other way and leave him to his own devices. If I'd have complained, he would have quickly given me the dirty bottom to clean—and I would thus be enabling him to be labeled a "bad diaper changer" and never have to do it again. See how quickly you can pile things on your plate if you insist on picky-picky parenting standards?

ELIMINATE RIGID CLEANING STANDARDS. If you insist on always having things done your way, other people will be perfectly happy to let you do everything yourself. When Meagan was three years old, she was obsessed with spots on the kitchen floor. She would walk around with a wet dishcloth, hunting for spills. When she spied a culprit, she'd proudly exclaim, "There's one!" and run over to wipe up the mess. Now, it's not like she had a bucket of Lysol and a mop and cleaned the floor correctly. But, hey, wiping up spots made a difference! Instead of trying to teach her the "right" way to clean a floor, I decided that her efforts made our place look nicer and praised her for it. Best of all, she got to do something her way without being corrected for it.

If doing the laundry is normally your duty and your spouse pitches in to help, don't complain that it's folded "the wrong way." It might not be the way you would do it, but hey, it's done, so you can have more time to sleep. Pick your battles wisely.

LEAVE GOOD ENOUGH ALONE. You spent three weeks investigating a cell phone plan that combines long distance, e-mail, and Internet capabilities. You purchase the phone, get it all set up, receive the bill, and everything is going along swimmingly. Then you receive an advertisement in the mail about a new plan. Do you investigate? No! With all the time you've just spent, it's not worth more to save a few extra bucks. Don't just think about the hard costs of the phone, the plan, and the minutes. Think about how much time it will take to change once again, now that you've got everything working fine.

DON'T REINVENT THE WHEEL. The director of my boys' childcare center requires parents to complete a new contract, health record, immunization card, enrollment form, and emergency contact form each year. Completing these forms requires about forty-five minutes for each child. With two children in day care, these requirements become downright annoying, especially because none of my information has changed. If it had, of course, I'd need to suck it up and complete new forms. But in my case, I asked the director if I could see the forms I completed last year. She handed them to me, I crossed out the old date, and wrote in today's date and handed them back. She grouchily told me to complete them from scratch. I told her that was highly inefficient and wouldn't do it. Surprise—my kids are still enrolled in the school. Why reinvent the wheel?

PERSONALITY quiz item 22

22. _____ Refuse requests when appropriate.

I Dare You to Cross This Line

Do you know what always strikes fear in my heart? The snack sign-up sheet for my kids' parties. I don't particularly enjoy cooking (although I'm a perfectly good cook), but I'm jaded because I had a dreadful experience when Meagan was in preschool. Her teacher had asked me to bring brownies for their Halloween party, and I willingly said yes. So I went to a high-end bakery in town and bought some. When I proudly brought them to the teacher, she looked at me like I had horns. She actually asked me, "What's this?" She asked for brownies, yes, but she really wanted *homemade* brownies.

Well, that's completely different. If I had known she wanted homemade brownies, I could have politely explained that I'd be happy to pick up a dozen at the store, and if she didn't like that, she could find someone else to provide the brownies. Hooray! Less for me to do! (Here is a solution I've since discovered: If you take the bakery brownies off the plastic tray, put them on a doily on your own plate, sprinkle them with powdered sugar, and wrap everything with Saran Wrap, no one will ever know!)

Keep these things in mind when considering requests:

DETERMINE YOUR STANDARDS. Standards are rules to which you hold yourself accountable. They are choices you make about how you will behave and govern your life. "I will not use swear words" is a standard. One reader told me, "My manager says she doesn't expect me to work ten hours a day like I do, but yet she continues to give me more projects to do. I could work fewer hours, but then I wouldn't be meeting my own expectations for the quality of my work. Also, I don't believe that my superiors have a realistic expectation of how long it takes to do my work. My colleague who does the same job also averages ten-hour days. I think she believes we are inefficient, rather than competent professionals whose work requires that kind of time commitment." This makes me wonder if this person might need stronger standards around the number of hours he will work and how much work he takes on; in addition, his standards are too rigid and picky about completing a task when it's likely "good enough."

Having standards will later allow you to set boundaries. If you haven't decided on your own standards, it's harder to set boundaries, because you're forced to re-decide in every situation. Create your standards by thinking about what's important to you and writing a "rule" statement for each. For example, some of my family's standards are:

- Sunday morning church is mandatory unless you are ill.
- When we go to the grocery store, each of the kids may select one item under two dollars—don't ask for anything else.

- Children's books need to be put back on the shelves at the end of the day, but they don't have to be in order by size or alphabetized.
- John will absolutely not move the car until everyone's seat belts are buckled.
- No one touches the food on the table until grace has been said, even if we're in a restaurant.

Once you've put standards in place and have consistently communicated them to your children, family, and friends, it's much easier to set boundaries whenever people try to break them.

SET BOUNDARIES FOR OTHERS. Learning to refuse requests is critical if you want to increase your personal productivity. Many people end up chronically exhausted and dissatisfied because they take care of everybody else and not themselves. The solution? Setting boundaries. Having boundaries helps ensure that others don't intrude on your space, time, and energy. You're essentially creating lines that define what's acceptable and what's not. It forms the text of your personal rulebook. If your standard is "I don't work more than eight hours a day," your boundary would be to perhaps say to your boss, "I will be happy to complete that task tomorrow; right now I'm leaving, because I have a commitment I must adhere to."

PROVIDE ALTERNATIVES. Because you don't want to bust your boundaries, simply determine the need behind all requests and provide alternatives. For example, when the teacher asks for brownies, does she simply want something sweet? Will M&M's satisfy that need? Perhaps I could contribute by bringing something I can buy . . . plates? silverware? juice? napkins? I no longer approach the snack sign-up sheet with trepidation; instead, I ask the teacher what she *really* needs (yes, all my children's teachers have happened to be female) and find I can often suggest items she might not have even thought of.

SAY NO TO YOURSELF. When you find yourself sitting on the fence about whether to go to a meeting or social function (especially if you're not excited about attending), then don't go! No one has a gun to your head. That way, you'll have time to get to things you want to do or, just relax. If you're asked to chair the PTO, it's perfectly acceptable to say, "I'd be happy to contribute as a member of a committee, but I regret I can't take on the chair responsibility." If you planned to go grocery shopping, and you're dreading it because the sun is shining and you'd rather be in your garden, it's perfectly fine to change your mind and decide to do it tomorrow.

Place a note on your refrigerator to remind yourself to stop carrying the world on your shoulders:

> Dear [your name], You are not 100 percent totally responsible for everything, taking care of everything, or taking care of everybody. That's my job. Love, God.

PERSONALITY quiz item 23

23. _____ Ask for help when I need it.

What? I'm *Not* Superwoman?

Being known as The Productivity Pro® among my colleagues comes with a high level of expectation regarding the volume of work I can handle and the results I'm able to accomplish. I'll let you in on a little secret—I don't do it alone. You will be able to accomplish more than you'd ever hoped by surrounding yourself with a team of great contributors. Yes, be productive and work hard. But you'll produce more if you multiply your hands.

Discover how delegating can solve dozens of your productivity problems. By insisting on doing chores and hanging on to responsibilities that could easily be done by someone else, you sabotage your own time. Be willing to let go of your fear of losing control. Learn to ask others for help so you can gain more time for yourself.

These ideas will help you when you need to ask for help.

GO PUBLIC WITH REQUESTS FOR ASSISTANCE. One year, I was tasked with being the editorial advisory chair for my trade magazine, *Professional Speaker*. Each month, the mag features forty pages of fabulous articles and columns. The chair before me had painstakingly arranged for five to seven people each month to write a feature, plus she assigned different people to write the five to ten regular columns. I had volunteered part-time for this person, so I could learn the job I'd be doing. Knowing I didn't have the same amount of time she did, I decided I'd need ten column coordinators. Each coordinator would find someone to write a column (or write it themselves) for each issue. I also needed three issue coordinators who, every three months, would assign authors to write the feature articles.

So how did I recruit people to participate on a project of this scope? Specifically, I made my path public, directly solicited people, and told the world what I was up to. I also communicated these four things:

- I am a nice person and will be easy to work with,
- I need and want your help, and you are the perfect person for the role,

- Participating will be fun and rewarding, and
- You can be a part of a great team!

Commonly, people get nervous about going public, but truly productive people use the energy and gravity created to pull people into their causes. People also have an immediate attraction to focused, highly directed leaders because they convey that they have a definite direction and are going places. In fact, many people look for an opportunity to get behind something fun and rewarding; they willingly and enthusiastically contribute to the project when asked with respect.

TO GET REPEAT ASSISTANCE, SHOW GRATITUDE. Once your project's goal is achieved, *make sure you thank and reward your team*. For those who helped me with the magazine, I dipped into my own pocket to buy gifts for each team member at the end of the magazine year.

UNDERSTAND THAT PEOPLE WANT TO HELP. How many times have you attended a party where you rarely saw the hosts? They hid away in the kitchen, cooking, cleaning, and preparing. They left their guests to socialize with one another. But there's a better way—accept help! Here's how:

- If guests offer to bring something to the party, let them! Ask them to bring "their specialty," and you'll be thrilled with the sumptuous surprise goodies that appear.

- When your guests offer to help cook and clean up at the end of the party, don't play the martyr. You'll end up alone in the kitchen wishing you were part of the talk and laughter. Accept any offers gladly. Make the kitchen a welcoming place to gather and talk while dishes are being washed and put away.

- Or simply leave doing the dishes until later. Keep the kitchen door shut until everyone leaves. *Enjoy* yourself!

GET YOUR KIDS TO HELP YOU BY HELPING THEMSELVES. My boys Johnny and James are five and four years old, respectively. I have always encouraged them to be self-sufficient and "help daddy" or "help mommy" get them dressed, wash them, put their dirty clothes in the hamper, and so on. Now that they're able to put on their pajamas at night and brush their own teeth, I can get other things done while they're busy, and then we can all spend more rest or play time together.

DON'T TIE YOUR ASSISTANT'S HANDS. If you're lucky enough to have a personal assistant, admin, or secretary, allow that person to do all he or she is capable of—and more. When Jenny first started working with me, I used to open all my own mail. Then, when I went on a vacation with the family and left Jenny to hold down the fort in our home office, I gave her the mail key and asked her to grab the mail each day. "Shall I go through it for you?" she asked. "Oh, no," I replied. "You wouldn't know what to do with it." "Why don't I watch you do it for a few days, take notes, and I'll create a 'mail sorting' procedure to make sure you're comfortable." I soon discovered that she wouldn't have known what to do with it *only* because I hadn't shown her. Jenny is perfectly capable of opening the mail, sorting it according to my 6-D System (Discard, Delegate, Do, Date, Drawer, and Deter—see quiz item 53 in Chapter 6), and handling most responses independently. I realized that much of the mail I don't need to see, anyway.

> 24. _____ Avoid procrastinating on what I know I should be doing.

Can We Talk About This Tomorrow?

My mother has six brothers and no sisters. (Yikes! I thought I had it rough with only two brothers!) Among my favorite memories are my mom's family reunions. As a young girl, I'd sit in the living room of my grandparents' home while four of my uncles played the guitar, one played the piano, and one led the singing. They sang old Cajun favorites, patriotic songs, spiritual songs, and plain silly songs for us kids. One of my favorites was the "Arkansas Traveller and Rackinsac Waltz," a traditional American reel written in 1847 by W. C. Peters:

> *Oh, once upon a time in Arkansas,*
> *An old man sat in his little cabin door*
> *And fiddled at a tune that he liked to hear,*
> *A jolly old tune that he played by ear.*
> *It was raining hard, but the fiddler didn't care,*
> *He sawed away at the popular air,*
> *Tho' his roof it leaked like a waterfall,*
> *That didn't seem to bother the man at all.*

> *A traveler was riding by that day,*
> *And stopped to hear him a-practicing away;*
> *The cabin was a-flow and his feet were wet,*
> *But still the old man didn't seem to fret.*
> *So the stranger said "Now the way it seems to me,*

You'd better mend your roof," said he.
But the old man said as he played away,
"I couldn't mend it now, it's a rainy day."

The traveler replied, "That's all quite true,
But this, I think, is the thing for you to do;
Get busy on a day that is fair and bright,
Then patch the old roof till it's good and tight."
But the old man kept on a-playing at his reel,
And tapped the ground with his leathery heel.
"Get along," said he, "for you give me a pain;
My cabin never leaks when it doesn't rain."

I remember laughing so hard when they slowly sang the last line, the punch line "My cabin never leaks when it doesn't rain." How true! Doesn't this sum up the concept of procrastination well? We don't fix things when the sun is shining, and then we are caught unprepared when the rain comes. Yes, by putting off tasks that aren't urgent, we are creating self-inflicted pain when the crisis looms.

Isn't it easy to put off the things that you know you should be doing? As a client wrote, "When I was in college with a heavy homework load, my house was never cleaner. For some reason, I was obsessed with making sure everything in my surroundings was just right. Even cleaning the toilet bowl sounded like a better idea than writing papers, and I was always under the gun. Today, I still meet deadlines, but it usually means staying up all night or taking work home with me."

Her procrastination is quite understandable; it's human nature to avoid pain. After all, when you put off a task, it rewards you twice: First when you get to do something else that is more fun, and second when you don't have to do the undesirable chore. But when the task comes back to haunt you, it only pun-ishes you once. So it's easy to see why procrastination wins out! Unfortunately, in the end, the cost of putting things off out-weighs the reward.

Here's how you can deal with procrastination tendencies.

ANALYZE THE REASON FOR YOUR PROCRASTINATION. If you're rewriting an item on your to-do list for the third day in a row—*stop!* Before you transfer that task, ask yourself why you haven't completed it. Perhaps other tasks with higher priorities have justi-fiably pushed it away. If the task seems unimportant, quickly do an analysis to determine if you can justify your procrastination. Draw two columns and list your reasons for procrastinating on one col-umn and your reasons for getting started on the other. If your rea-sons to start are longer and more convincing than your reasons for waiting, perhaps you'll be persuaded to get going. On the other hand, the reasons for procrastinating may outweigh the reasons to start. This objective analysis may prove the task is indeed trivial and worthy of procrastination. If so, completely remove it from your daily to-do list and add it to your master to-do list. Review your master to-do list each month to see which items have changed pri-ority. If you don't have to stare at the listed item every day, you'll stop feeling guilty and stressing out over not getting it done.

ELIMINATE THE "LATER" FACTOR. "I'll do that later" is a phrase that makes me crazy. (Second in line is "I need to.") In redecorat-ing James's bedroom, we decided to sell much of his Beatrix Pot-ter Peter Rabbit collection on eBay. One piece that went with the set was a coatrack that was anchored to the wall. When John couldn't pull it down with his bare hands, he calmly said, "I'll get a screwdriver and get this off later." I quickly said, "No way!" He immediately went downstairs, got the screwdriver, and took the piece off the wall so we could photograph it with the rest of the set. Had I not insisted on doing it right then and there, it could still be hanging on the wall mixed in with James's new dinosaur motif. It would have delayed the whole selling process, too. The moral? Just do it!

VISUALIZE YOUR LIFE WITHOUT PROCRASTINATION. Act as if you're a go-getter. No excuses. Ignore that little voice in your head that says, "That sounds boring" or "I'm not in the mood." Don't wait—the mood may never come! Tell yourself you only have to work on a yucky task for a few minutes. Sometimes you just need to get momentum; that's when five minutes turns into fifteen. When you experience immediate success, you'll have the motivation to keep going. And once you see and feel the benefits, you'll want to achieve more.

STOP STRIVING FOR PERFECTION. Strangely enough, perfectionism and procrastination are related. Perfection can be an excuse to procrastinate because it is, by definition, unattainable. Perhaps you're looking with dread at your huge pile of items to file. You know your system needs to be completely reorganized, purged, and revamped, but that doesn't mean you can't use what you have and get started. No, you don't have to put everything in color-coded, neatly typed folders right now. Heck, even hand-write your labels to get by for a while. A simple system that you understand and use is more important than waiting until you have the perfect one. Focus on progress, not perfection.

PERSONALITY quiz item 25

25. _____ Know and honor my energy levels throughout the day.

I'll Just Rest My Head Here for a Second and *ZZZZ* . . .

You can know all the productivity tips in the world, but nothing will work if you don't have the energy to give 100 percent. Personal energy is a measure of how strong, invigorated, or up to a task you may feel at any moment. Nobody has an unlimited supply of personal energy. If you feel down, your zest ebbs, and you tend to produce mediocre work. In periods of low energy, your productivity sinks because you feel like you're slogging through a field of waist-high mud.

MATCH THE TASK TO THE ENERGY. Know your own rhythms and plan your work around them. If you tend to have a lot of energy first thing in the morning, do your most challenging work then. High energy gives you the ability to concentrate well, make critical decisions, perform complex analysis, or do any task requiring creativity or problem solving. When your energy is low, however, these tasks become more difficult, take longer, and often have poor results.

If you're like me, afternoons are hard, and sometimes you get in a plain bad mood. I know this about myself, so I prepare for and honor it. Some of the things we do for ourselves to counter low energy may not be healthy. Some bad habits like smoking and overeating are actually attempts to moderate low energy or a bad mood. If you didn't get much sleep last night, for example, you might reach for a third cup of coffee, and the extra caffeine will actually give you the jitters later in the day. Instead, choose a healthy way of dealing with low-energy periods, one that might actually bring you back to a state of alert productivity. When you feel like you simply cannot start a new task, take a break:

- Go for a brisk walk.
- Listen to upbeat music.

- Call a friend.
- Take a hot bath.
- Stand up, stretch, and move your body.

INCREASE YOUR METABOLIC RATE. Different people have different energy levels. Some people have the energy to work all day then run around and clean the house in the evening. Others drag themselves onto the sofa and watch television all night. While it's true that some people have higher natural energy levels, those with lower energy can use personal energy management techniques to make up the difference. The good news is you can impact your energy level and mood. You don't have to suffer from low energy!

One way to improve your energy level is to keep it from crashing in the first place. Just like the Energizer Bunny, you want to keep going and going and going all day long. To achieve that goal, you have to supercharge your metabolism and keep it high. Your body runs on blood sugar, and it needs a steady supply. If you typically have a muffin or doughnut in the morning or skip breakfast entirely, then grab fast food at lunch, you will be ravenous by 4:00 p.m. and munching on whatever snacks are sitting around the house. Instead, start out with a healthy breakfast and eat every three to four hours throughout the day, making sure to include protein and complex carbohydrates for prolonged periods of energy.

KEEP YOUR BLOOD SUGAR STEADY. The right amount energizes you, while too much or too little makes your energy plummet. If you go a long period of time without eating, your body starts to shut down to conserve energy, your blood sugar drops, and your metabolism goes in the basement. If you eat refined carbohydrates when hungry—white flour, sugar, processed junk—you will get a brief surge of insulin, prompting an even bigger drop in blood sugar, leaving you edgy, irritable, and hungry, which increases your appetite and drives you to eat the whole bag of cookies instead of just one. It's a vicious cycle that can really disrupt your entire day and negatively affect your health over the long term.

Instead, focus on eating a diet that includes whole grains, such as brown rice, oats, and whole wheat bread; colorful fruits and vegetables like berries, melons, leafy greens, and red peppers; proteins such as chicken, fish, cottage cheese, eggs, or tofu; and heart-healthy fats, such as nuts, olive oil, and avocado. And don't forget to drink six to eight glasses of water each day as well!

USE ENERGY BOOSTERS. If you haven't taken great care of your metabolism during the day, emergency measures may be required to counter low energy. Once you become aware of the time of day when you tend to experience low-energy or bad moods, make a conscious choice to change it. Instead of walking to the vending machine for a candy bar, try one of these healthy energy boosters as an alternative:

- Drink green tea. Green tea edges out coffee as an energy-boosting beverage. It has enough caffeine to pep you up but not enough to give you the jitters. Plus, the theophylline it contains may aid in regulating your blood sugar by dilating bronchial passages and thus improving the flow of oxygen in your body.

- Take your vitamins. Use vitamins C and E (two good antioxidants), plus Folic acid, B-complex (known to boost energy in women), and a good multi vitamin with 1000–1500 mg calcium, and vitamin D and magnesium for absorption. I like Emergen-C drink mix when I need a big shot of energy before an important presentation.

- Down a protein shake. These are definitely helpful if you can't get a meal on the run and need to supplement rather than miss a meal completely; and they are much better for you than a sugary soft drink or afternoon cup of coffee. EAS makes a delicious ready-made chocolate protein shake in a box that doesn't require refrigeration.

- Take a whiff of peppermint. Inhaling this essential oil through the day or eating peppermint candy can clear your thinking and boost productivity. Other revitalizing oils include lemon, eucalyptus, juniper, orange, and spearmint. Keep a bottle on your counter, uncap, and sniff as needed. To sustain energy after work, place a few drops on the vents and turn on the fan.

- Rub your ears. Your ears are particularly dense with pressure points; stimulating them can increase blood circulation and energy. Using your fingers, vigorously rub your ears all over for about one minute. When your ears start to feel hot, you should feel more alert.

- Splash on cold water. Your face, neck, and throat are quite sensitive. Wetting those areas with cold water provides a jolt that temporarily diverts blood to your brain, simulating the fight or flight reaction. Also gargle with something ice-cold.

Truly, the difference between an energetic and an unenergetic person is often that the former pays attention to his or her fuel gauge and takes action before it reads empty. Energy management allows you to detect and control any factors that might deplete your energy. Here's to eliminating outages!

> 26. _____ Communicate clearly to avoid confusion and rework.

What? You Can't Read My Mind?

Good interpersonal communication will help you reduce unnecessary problems and wasted time. Countless books have been written on the subject of how to communicate effectively, but my focus relates to helping you achieve the most efficient and productive results through communication.

Keep these principles in mind when communicating with others:

SHARE INFORMATION SOONER RATHER THAN LATER. I have discovered I'm a better social coordinator than my husband. So I end up scheduling our play dates with friends. I occasionally forget to share with John that we have plans. He'll come into the room whistling cheerfully and say, "Hey, why don't we go see *Star Wars* tomorrow night?" I'll say, "We can't because we have plans with so-and-so." He'll say, "Really? And when were you planning to share that information with me?" Oops. I know I don't like having plans sprung on me, and he doesn't either. It requires a different mindset to know you're expected to socialize tomorrow night rather than space out in front of a movie stuffing your face with popcorn.

STATE YOUR EXPECTATIONS. My administrative assistant, Jenny, has a genuine heart for service. Sometimes when I'm in a crunch, I ask her to do things for me I wouldn't normally expect from office personnel. Once, a news crew in our local market called and said they wanted to film me in my office in one hour. Our housekeeper was due to clean the next day, so the house needed attention. Jenny took it upon herself to vacuum, pick up stray items, and tidy up the kitchen while I prepared for this visit. What a giving person! But even when she goes over and above her duties, I'm often at fault in assuming she knows what I need her to do. For example, I had four presents for James's birthday party in a pile and asked her to wrap them for me. Jenny soon presented me with a single, big, wrapped box. I looked at her, confused, and asked, "Are the presents individually wrapped inside this box?" She said, "No, you asked me to wrap these up." She assumed I meant together, and I assumed she knew that I wanted him to open his presents individually. It was my fault because I hadn't stated my expectations clearly the first time.

BE SURE YOU ARE CLEAR ABOUT WHAT IS EXPECTED OF YOU. On the other hand, it helps to ask questions. If you're not sure what somebody means, speak up and find out! What is the due date? Do you have a certain level you want me to do this? What do you mean by "clean"?

BE SPECIFIC. When I'm tidying up the kitchen, I like everything off my counters that doesn't go there. Just one of my quirks, I guess. So I'll tell Meagan, "Please get this hairbrush off my counter," which she does. Ten minutes later, I'll pass the stairs and see the brush lying there. "What's this brush doing on the stairs?" I'll ask her. "Mom, you told me to get it off the counter." I have to hide a smile. "True enough, I did say that. I should have said to put it back where it belongs." "Ohhhh, now you tell me!" Meagan replies.

This principle doesn't just apply to children. For example, John will ask me, "Are the kids in the car?" and I think he's asking if they're ready to go. I'll shout, "Yes! They're ready to go!" Then I hear him getting his keys from the drawer and going out the garage door; I hear the door shut and open again. Then he yells up the stairs, "I thought you said they were in the car! They are in the van!" Things just run more smoothly when you're specific.

THINK BEFORE YOU REACT. More than once, I've received an e-mail from someone flaming me for something I've written. Yes, when one puts opinions on paper that comes with the territory. Not everyone agrees with me, and that's okay. But it still hurts my feelings when someone is rude to me—a complete stranger—for no reason or writes a cynical e-mail. I'm not afraid to speak my mind, but I have to remind myself to temper it with a dash of diplomacy. So I hit reply and remove the name from the to field, just in case my trigger-happy finger gets the best of me. Then I write a scathing reply, saying exactly what I want so my emotions come out. But then I hit save and keep it in the drafts folder. I wait several hours, usually a day. Then I go back to the message and revise the reply, taking out the nasties. I'm always grateful I gave myself time to simmer down, rather than saying exactly what came out of my mouth and wasting time repairing the damage.

PERSONALITY quiz item 27

27. _____ Consistently meet and usually beat deadlines.

If I'm Early, I'm Not Eating a Worm!

You may not like hearing this, but it must be said. Deadlines are for people who would otherwise be late if they weren't set. Deadlines eliminate some of the joy of accomplishment because you work toward the deadline and not the result. Some people would never do things if there weren't a deadline. If there is no deadline, you must artificially set one in your mind and work not just to meet it, but beat it.

When I was in college, our professors would inevitably assign term papers worth one-third of our grades. We'd know about the assignment the first day of the class (in September or January) and it wasn't due until the end of the class (in December or May). I was always hacking at it throughout the semester so I didn't have to worry about a lot of assignments coming due at once. And I always turned it in before the deadline. Then I watched incredulously as my classmates pulled all-nighters and worked furiously to complete the assignment the week before the due date. They produced their papers with a higher stress level and lower quality than they needed to. I don't tell you this to brag, but I graduated magna cum laude *not* because I'm smarter than anybody else, but because I generally produce better work by doing it *early*.

Let's say that you hired me to speak at a conference you were planning. You slotted me to be the opening speaker, starting at 9:00 a.m. What if, at 9:05, I came rushing in, exclaiming that I was trapped in a major traffic jam. Would you empathize? *No!* You could not care less about my reason for showing up late. You'd only care about your conference at that moment.

People expect you to honor their time and the commitments you make, just as you expect the same from them. Even if I gave an incredible speech and everyone loved me, would you ever hire me again? No! In fact, you would remember how embarrassed you felt because I was late. You'd probably even tell other people about my tardiness and recommend they didn't hire me either!

| *Late* says, "I can't make deadlines." | *Early* says, "I don't need deadlines." |

Late says, "I'm out of control."   *Early* says, "I'm in control."

Late says, "I can't look beyond   *Early* says, "I look ahead."
the moment."

So instead of thinking, "I begin speaking at 9:00 a.m.," shift your thoughts to something like, "I should plan on arriving at 8:00 a.m. to set up and get prepared." Then you'd have to figure out how long it takes to get there, leaving a buffer in case of heavy traffic. Working backward from the time you had to appear, you'd determine what time you'd need to drop the kids off at day care, what time to get them up, and what time you'd have to wake up to make all that happen. Besides, it never ever hurts to show up early. I always have lots of things to do once I arrive: I set up, pay bills, peruse magazines, read reports, write thank you letters—you get the picture.

Think *early*:

- If you invite friends over for a Saturday night two weeks from now, do you wait until that Saturday afternoon to think about what you're going to serve them? Do you scurry around, trying to clean up the house, thirty minutes before they arrive? Do you feel tired and sweaty when they arrive, instead of refreshed, ready to enjoy their company?

- If you have a trip coming up, do you pack the night before? Why not set the suitcase out and drop things in it during the *week* before you leave? If you have to run to the store for something you're out of, no problem. You won't be in a last-minute rush and picking out clothes at midnight and starting your trip tired, grumpy, and discouraged.

- When did you think about getting your family holiday cards? If you start in early November and get photos taken and reprinted throughout the month, buying your cards, creating your list, writing your newsletter, and stamping envelopes, by the time mid-December rolls along, they will be ready to drop in the mail. Does that make it easier to enjoy the holidays? You bet.

People ask me, "Well, what's wrong with just being on time?" Well, you can't really be on time. You're either going to be a few seconds early or a few seconds late. But, regardless, it's boring. It's average. Who wants to be average? It's not nearly as good as being early.

EVENT	LATE PEOPLE	ON-TIME PEOPLE	EARLY PEOPLE
Parking	Walk a mile, pay a lot	Fight another on-time person for the last, far spot	Get your choice of close spots
Leak in the roof	$50,000 rotting foundation	$10,000 roof repair	$100 quick fix
Flying	Sweat and run, high stress	Make the flight	Get ten little things done on the way and while waiting, low stress
Buying items on sale	Get the leftovers	Get goods already picked over by the early birds	Get best choice of everything

I hope you can see the benefits of not only meeting but exceeding deadlines. It might take a bit to catch up on any backlog, but once you're on top of things, stay one step ahead using a frontlog: Keep a list of things to do ahead of time. When you work ahead of yourself, you will experience a new peace of mind, knowing you're in control. If you are early (no extra cost, no strain, no explanations), you don't have to worry about deadlines. Make working ahead your style, convert "later" to "now," and you'll be much more productive in the future.

PERSONALITY quiz item 28

> 28. _____ Focus on completing one task before getting distracted by another.

Multitasking Mania

Do you get distracted easily and tend to blow like the wind in many different directions? Do you continually talk to yourself about all the things you need to do ("I don't know . . . do I talk to myself?")? Does it take you three hours to pay bills instead of half an hour? If so, then you'll probably benefit from less multitasking.

My mother could talk on the phone, prepare dinner, and tighten my ponytails all in the same moment. So what's changed? Partially, technology. Partially, the number of things we have to do. When we use machines that are capable of infinite multitasking, we're deluded into thinking we're infinitely capable, too. Then our brains become overloaded and run out of RAM, we crash, and we can't get anything done.

Here's a sample scenario: "I'm going to go to the grocery store. Wait, I should make a list. Put my keys down. Go through pantry. Yikes, this place is a mess. Throw out some stale chips, combine snacks, and put Oreos in a Ziploc bag. Whew, I'm hot.

Take off coat. Okay, milk, bread, and eggs . . . oh darn, my pencil broke. Go to the study to sharpen. Oops, this letter needed to go out today. I should stop by the mailbox on my way to the grocery store. Sit at computer to get address of client. Notice that I have seven unread e-mail messages. I wonder what's in here? Here's one from my sister with a link to a site. Click. Click. Click. Cool. Wait, the address. Write letter. Back to the kitchen. What was I doing? Shoot! Pencil. Back to study. I should just keep pens in the kitchen. Sort pencil holder to find some spare pens. Back to the kitchen. Put pens in drawer. Clean out old coupons. Yikes, finish list. I'd better go to the bathroom first. Bathroom. Coat. You know . . . if I ran the dishwasher, the dishes will be clean when I get back. Dishes. Notice grime in cracks of tile, gross. Spray with cleaner. Scrub. Scrub. Okay, I'm ready to go. Hey, where are my keys? Phone rings . . . I wonder who it is? Oh it's Mom . . . I'd better make sure everything's okay. Yack yack. Hang up. Darn, it's too late to go to the store now. I'll do it first thing tomorrow . . ."

This person flitted around from place to place and never made it to the grocery store or mailed the letter, the two most important things at that time. The dishes are clean, the grime is gone, and Mom is happy, but those things weren't the true priorities of the moment. However, this multitasker has the sensation of having worked hard from being so busy. But multitaskers don't stay focused and concentrate on what must get done. They experience a "flurry of activity" from doing a lot but actually accomplish little.

Instead, learn to focus *when* your full concentration is required. What are the benefits of extreme focus? Here are a few.

- Output is increased. You simply get more done when you're 100 percent attuned to your task. You'll get more letters written and more projects completed. When you multitask, you feel more frazzled and accomplish less. Complete engagement makes for peak performance.

- You perform optimally and do your best work. If you are giving your total attention to something, its quality will be better. Isaac Newton said, "If I have ever made any valuable discoveries, it has been owing more to patient attention than to any other talent."

- The time invested in projects is decreased. If you don't feel like doing something in the first place (like paying bills), wouldn't you rather have it over in half an hour instead of stretching it out over three?

- Less rework. Your focus reduces the time it would have taken you to correct the mistakes and omissions that are a by-product of inattention.

- Peace of mind is enhanced. There is an old legend about a man who travels the world searching for the meaning of life. One day he climbs a high mountain to a monastery to get the advice of a monk who is reputed to be the wisest man on earth. When asked for the secret to happiness, the monk replies simply, "*Do* whatever you're doing."

It's not a big deal to do two mindless tasks at once, such as making a phone call while tossing in a load of laundry or pouring a cup of coffee while listening to a voice mail message. It's quite another to try to write an important letter while checking e-mail, surfing the Web, and talking on the phone simultaneously.

When you try to do too many things at once, you make more mistakes, increase your stress, and actually reduce the amount of work you complete. But you just may be too distracted to notice.

The National Institute of Neurological Disorders and Stroke

reports, "The more things you have to keep in mind and switch between, the more it costs performance." You never, ever get a chance to pat yourself on the back for actually finishing something, because, in overload situations, the brain gets flooded with the chemicals norepinephrine and dopamine. They kick the brain into its more primitive, habitual mode, which makes us forget what we planned to do. According to research published in *The Journal of Experimental Psychology*, it takes your brain four times longer to recognize and process each thing you're working on when you switch back and forth among tasks.

Here's a sample scenario of a focused person: "Okay, in the next half hour, I've got to book this airfare, review this report, and load this software on the computer. Let's see . . . start the install. Let that run. A new e-mail; let it go. Call the airline. Hold. Put on headphones so I can write. Start reading report. Hello? Put sticky note where I left off. Make reservations. Remember that I need to call to confirm my meeting for tomorrow. Write it down and go back to task. Glance at computer and click okay. Finish install and registration. Continue reading report. Coworker walks in with interruption. Listen briefly. Low priority. Schedule phone appointment for tomorrow at 3:20. Back to report, write comments. Check. Now, I'm going to handle e-mail . . . and . . . what was it? Good thing I wrote that reminder down."

What's the difference between this and the previous scenario?

- It's written. Jotting notes to yourself pulls what you need to do out of working memory and relieves you of the burden of remembering it.
- It's purposeful. This person is still aware of the e-mail coming in, but decides to ignore it.
- It's chosen. You can proactively choose when multitasking is and isn't appropriate. For our family, dinnertime is sacred.

We don't watch television, look at mail, read the newspaper, or answer the phone. But scanning the paper over breakfast alone may be a good use of your time.

- It's based on priority. Identify and focus on completing your most important tasks first and concentrate until you're done. You may need to get a kitchen timer and set it for one hour to remind yourself when it's okay to check your e-mail.

- It takes advantage of technology. Turn off the function that allows you to show up on "buddy lists." Use caller ID. Send your calls to voice mail. Turn off the noises, pop-ups, and notifications on your e-mail. Take advantage of technology—don't let it take advantage of you.

PERSONALITY quiz item 29

29. _____ Maintain a positive attitude.

Yes, It *Is* Your Fault

Have you ever known people who accept no responsibility for their own stress levels? Some try to place responsibility on others and say, "I did not choose to be a person whose parents are divorced" or "My boss stresses me out" or "My significant other did this to me." These people are perpetual victims of what others do. Some people can get cut off in traffic on their way to work and seethe about it for the rest of the day. The other person involved doesn't even know about it and enjoys a perfectly good day. Do you see how even strangers can exert control over some people?

Try these suggestions for staying positive:

AVOID FOCUSING ON THE BAD. Negativity is a cultural manifestation of messages we're fed every day, mostly by the media. If we look for the bad, that's what we see. We're especially fascinated by atrocities. We've become convinced the world is a fearful, stressful place. Because we aren't fed by good news every day, when we hear it, the positive effects are brief. So we become *conditioned* to create drama in our lives. We actively seek evidence against reality, to confirm our thoughts that we can do nothing. We spend our energy in worrying, speculating, and creating worst-case scenarios, or reliving and wallowing in every bad experience, retelling the story of the rude, slow person at the grocery store, presumably to entertain our listeners while we vent.

CHANGE YOUR PERCEPTION. I'd like to challenge you to step back and ask yourself if you're playing to a self-induced drama. Life isn't as turbulent as you make it out to be. What might happen if you refocus your attention to positive, proactive experiences and open your thoughts to opportunities instead of problems? You are where your attention is. What you believe to be true is what your attention focuses on, thereby negating anything to the contrary.

For example, if you believe you have so much work to do that you have to work nights and weekends, you focus on the two hours you worked Thursday evening, forgetting you went camping on the weekend and attended a movie on Wednesday. If working late is a habit, you might tend to slack off your pace. You know there's no rush, you're not as focused, and you don't push yourself or prioritize your work as well. You waste time on things that don't need to be done or you socialize in the hall. We often convince ourselves that we *need* to work all those hours, then fall into a rut.

IDENTIFY "STINKING THINKING." If you generally view the world negatively, those beliefs typically show up in the way you behave. You can create stress with this "stinking thinking." If you want to change your attitude, first identify your negative thought patterns.

Here are some of the common patterns of stinking thinking:

1. **OBSESSING.** "Meagan did the dishes tonight. I should take all the dishes back out of the cabinet and wash them again. What if there is a glob of mashed potato that didn't come off? There could be germs on everything." Not letting go of certain thoughts takes your focus off positive things.

2. **CONTROLLING.** A coworker chews his gum loudly and it annoys you. Is it acceptable to request he doesn't chew so loudly? Yes. Can you *make* him stop? No. If you continually try to get him to stop, you cross the line from being assertive to being controlling. In fact, he is now in control of you if you choose to let him keep irritating you. Get earplugs!

3. **FEARING.** You've just arrived at work and see a note from your boss says, "Come see me ASAP." You immediately assume you did something wrong and start to worry about getting fired. Instead, think to yourself, "She is probably going to praise me for the excellent work on that presentation yesterday."

4. **VICTIM.** "Poor me. I just can't take this. I'm so stressed out, I think I'll just crumple up in a heap and cry today. There's nothing else I can do." This renders you helpless and increases your stress level. Think instead, "Wow, I have a lot

on my plate today. If I just focus on accomplishing one thing at a time, I will feel some momentum."

5. **HYSTERICAL.** "My daughter didn't come home on the bus! Oh my gosh, she was probably kidnapped and is going to die!" If you panic, you can't approach the situation calmly or react quickly and appropriately. Think instead, "Perhaps the bus driver was running late; I'll call just to make sure all is well."

6. **AWFULIZING.** "He didn't put his shoes in the mud room like I asked him to. That is the most disobedient child I have ever seen." This is making mountains out of molehills. When something negative happens, ask, "How bad is this, really? Is it worth getting upset over?"

7. **OVERANALYZING.** "She hasn't returned my call. I wonder what she's trying to tell me?" Don't try to analyze others and their intentions. After you finish a presentation, don't sit down and immediately start guessing what others' reactions mean or what they're thinking.

8. **DEMANDINGNESS.** "I have to finish this right now." Use of the words "should," "ought," "must," "have to," "got to," and "need to" can trigger you to feel upset and overreact in a negative manner. *Must* you go to work tomorrow? Absolutely not. You don't *have* to do much of anything except breathe, eat, and sleep. You may choose to go to work to avoid the negative consequences of not going in, but it's still your choice. Therefore, the must isn't really mandatory.

9. **EXAGGERATING.** "I can't stand it!" You're living proof that you *can* stand everything that has happened to you so far. In

fact, you'll always be able to stand things, except for whatever eventually kills you!

10. **CONDEMNING.** "What a jerk, driving that way." Directing negative thinking toward yourself, others, or the world can put you in a sour mood. Think of positive things and keep your mood optimistic.

Look for the good in every experience you have. The laws of nature tell us that every negative has a positive. Think of a time when a change occurred that really pushed you to the limit. What did you gain from it? How did that event positively affect your life? In life, I like to think that every negative experience comes with a good side to it, if you look for it.

PERSONALITY quiz item 30

30. _____ Stop trying to please all of the people all of the time.

I Just Can't Stand It If You Don't Like Me

I have a friend (who will remain nameless) who lives to please other people. She is overweight, depressed, and not doing well in business because she spends so much time trying to make others happy. It's as if she feels controlled by her need to please them. Sadly, people know this about her and take advantage of it. She's both addicted to their approval and feeling out of control because of the workload their demands have created. In short, being a people-pleaser isn't something to be proud of . . . it's a debilitating pattern that can create stress and ruin the productive pursuit of your own worthwhile goals.

Do these statements sound true for you?

- I am so exhausted after taking care of others that I have no energy for myself.
- I believe people wouldn't care much about me if I stopped doing all the things I'm currently doing for them.
- I believe that my value depends on my contributions to others, the team, and society.
- I have to do things for people to be worthy of their love.
- I expect to give far more in relationships than I will ever get back.
- I feel like I need to prove myself to others.

If you related to these statements, you too need to get out of the people-pleasing business. If you don't, your habits will take a toll on your health, your relationships, and your personal goals.

You may feel so stuck in your habits that it's hard to see a way out. Here are a few ideas to get you started.

STOP BEING THERE FOR EVERYONE AT EVERY MOMENT. You have to be okay with the fact that things aren't always going to be perfect in the lives of the people you love. You can't always fix things for them, nor should you try. Don't exaggerate your responsibilities and make unrealistic demands on yourself by taking on more than your share. You are not in charge of making sure everything goes well in every life that yours touches. Especially don't do what people should be fixing for themselves.

STAY OUT OF LOOPS. Ask if you need to be involved in a certain meeting, discussion, project, call, argument, decision, and so on. Understand that other people may try to drag you into webs you have no business being tangled in. Not wanting to be rude, you comply. But it's not helpful to you or others when you stick your nose in where it doesn't belong. For example, one of John's roles in our company as the COO is hiring. I'm happy to discuss a candidate's skills and qualifications with him and interview the candidate, but when it comes right down to it, it's his decision. Similarly, when issues that aren't yours enter your life, duck and say, "Keep me posted on what you do," or "I'll be curious to know how you handle this," or "I'm not in that loop." You might upset some people when you don't do their work for them or get involved in their dramas, but by saying no, you'll nurture problem-solving contributors who are better able to think on their own.

YOU CAN'T CHANGE GRUMPY PEOPLE. When you stop trying to change others, you become less affected by their moods. Perhaps you're in a book club, and you always secretly hope that one certain individual won't be there because she's negative and speaks critically about everything, no matter how minor. Learn to not take her comments personally and realize that very little of what she says actually affects you. You must learn to let others' comments run off you like water off a duck's back. Once you realize that others' behavior has nothing to do with you, you can tolerate negativity more easily. Hopefully, the negative person will respond to your increased patience with a more positive attitude.

GET RID OF THE NEGATIVE. Get rid of things that evoke negative emotions. If you absolutely hate that gift your mother-in-law gave you, don't display it prominently in your home just to make her happy. You will be irritated every time you look at it. It's your home, and you are not responsible for making sure others are happy with it. My home isn't decorated as elaborately as my friends' homes, but I want it to be child-proofed and comfortable, without worrying about my fragile knickknacks falling off a table and breaking. I don't decorate for others; I decorate for myself. Do things that make you happy. If you feel you absolutely have to keep that gift you hate, put it downstairs in a box where you don't have to look at it, then take it out and display it with a smile when your mother-in-law visits. Then put it back downstairs.

CHAPTER FOUR

Mastering the Fourth Pillar—

PESTS

A RECENT SURVEY of Fortune 1000 companies found that to-day's CEOs are so controlled by daily events and other people that they average less than sixty productive minutes a day. That's scary when you consider how much they're paid. Instead of CEO, they should be called the CIO—Constantly Interrupted Officer.

Yet other equally successful executives run huge organizations in fewer than thirty-five hours a week. They aren't working longer than you are and probably aren't smarter.

They succeed because they have eliminated all the pests in their lives—the "termites" that eat away at their foundations. Pests are the time wasters and robbers that keep you from being able to accomplish your goals. They are obstacles in your path.

My handheld phone/PDA allows me to access e-mail from anywhere; it is a time-saver during the workday and while traveling, but it is a pest when I'm fiddling with it while I'm supposed to be enjoying my son's T-ball game. Sleeping in on the weekend may be a necessary luxury if you've had a hectic week with little sleep, but it becomes a pest when being too lazy on a Saturday morning keeps you from accomplishing the tasks you set out to do.

It's amazing how good we are at eliminating time wasters when forced to. Are you ever shocked how productive you can be when you're trying to get things done before vacation? Let's say your boss called you in and said you were the perfect person for an extra job that would take twenty hours of your time this week. You couldn't slack off your demanding schedule at home, you had to complete your regular work, and you still had commitments in your community. But because you were excited about the opportunity for potential exposure from the assignment, you accepted. At the end of the week, you successfully completed the extra work and got everything else accomplished as well. Gads! How did you do it? You simply eliminated all the wasted time. You aren't even tired! On the contrary, you're invigorated by what you were able to accomplish. Getting rid of the pests that eat away at your foundation will keep it strong, so you have time to accomplish your plans and maintain your priorities.

PESTS quiz item 31

31. _____ Confront problems head-on and make decisions quickly.

I Just Can't Make Up My Mind!

Indecisiveness is a big time waster and a major pest in your quest to be productive. The ability to make quick decisions is the hallmark of a good leader and efficient person. Postponing decisions will only add to your problems, clutter your mind with things to think about, and turn into a snowball of consequences that can slow you down. Decide to decide sooner rather than later. Confront issues and problems head-on. If you avoid them, they'll multiply—and you'll have to deal with them anyway.

Many people suffer from "analysis paralysis" and prolong decisions unnecessarily. Granted, it's important to spend a significant amount of time making high-impact decisions, like an expensive purchase or a job change. But many routine decisions—such as where to go for dinner, what outfit to wear, what movie to rent—don't require a lot of time. Quickly weigh the pros and cons, and then make the choice that, in your estimation, results in the best outcome. Make the best decision you can at the time with the information you have. Which decision will result in the greatest possible benefits with the fewest negative consequences? If the long-term consequences are minimal or nonexistent, make the decision and move on.

Follow these suggestions for confronting your decisions and problems.

DEAL WITH RELATIONSHIP PROBLEMS. These problems are always simpler to handle when an issue first crops up. Decide to deal with problem people right away. If your best friend is taking advantage of you or is being inconsiderate, talk to him or her right away. If you don't, the behavior becomes a habit, and it will be much harder to deal with as time goes on. If a coworker constantly comes into your office to gossip and chat about things that don't matter to you, take a deep breath and discuss the challenge you're having with the behavior. Remember, silence implies permission. Delayed actions only prolong the agony and complicate matters. Move quickly!

BAN THE JUNK. Stop any unnecessary flow of paper coming across your desk or into your home. It's up to you to take action on eliminating the junk. How many e-mailed jokes, virus warnings, and newsletters do you receive? Halt anything that only creates excess amounts of paper or files to delete. How many newspapers and publications are you receiving and how many do you actually read? Do you need the daily newspaper or can you get by with just the weekend package? What about the junk mail and paper that comes into your house? Go to www.the-dma.org to get off many mailing lists completely.

REDUCE YOUR OPTIONS. Sometimes you can't make efficient decisions because you're bogged down by too many choices. There's no point trying to become more efficient doing things that shouldn't be done in the first place! Say "no" to some things in your life if you want to be able to say "yes" to others. Sure, you'll complete fewer things, but you'll feel much better about the activities you focus on. Getting rid of the past makes room for the new. Changing bad decisions makes room for better ones. The key is to get past your self-talk.

SITUATION	SELF-TALK	DECISION
There are 500 books on your shelf you haven't read.	I know there's good information in there I'm missing.	If you only read ten, you may as well only have ten, so get rid of the excess.
You get TV Guide each week and toss it.	This magazine subscription was really cheap, so I couldn't pass it up.	Why spend any amount of money on something you don't use? Cancel the subscription.
You're constantly cleaning your house.	People will judge me on my house.	Who cares? If that's all they care about, you don't need those kind of friends.
Your church is giving a free concert.	Wow, it's free, I should go.	You don't even care about the group that's performing. Skip it.
A friend invites you to attend a networking event.	Well, I don't have any other pressing obligations.	Unless you know the event will produce results, stay home and work on a project or relax.
You see something at a store you might be able to use some day.	Oooh, it's on sale; I should get it while it's cheap.	Don't buy something you don't have time to use. You can always get more stuff but not more time.

> 32. _____ Complete tasks I start; don't let projects stall.

When *Is* Later, Anyway?

When my youngest son, James, was soon to be born, we decided to remove the built-in desk in his room to give us more options for laying out the furniture. To install the desk, the previous owners removed a piece of the floorboard so the desk would lie flush against the wall. Removing it exposed the patch of missing floorboard. This was, of course, unacceptable to a mother with her third baby on the way. So my faithful husband went to Home Depot and bought the matching section of floorboard. Upon returning home, we discovered that the ends didn't match up, so John would need to cut the board. I bought him a big new circular saw that would do the job nicely, but it never got used. James is now four years old and that stupid piece of floorboard is still sitting uncut in the garage . . . and whenever I enter James's bedroom, I look with annoyance at that bare patch. However, this is John's half-done project, not mine. The big question is, does it bother him? Apparently not. So it's my choice to either ignore it or get someone in who will finish the task.

Here are some tips for eliminating the half-done projects from your life:

KEEP TRACK OF YOUR PROJECTS. I keep a running "Honey-do" list (as in "Honey, please do this," and "Honey, please do that"). I file it behind the *H* in the A-Z tabs of my planner. When John has some free time, he knows exactly where to look to remind him of what needs to be done around the house.

ALWAYS ASK, "WHAT'S NEXT?" I know I can't be the only one with such half-done projects all over the house. Why is it that things stall partway through completion? Because at some point, you stopped asking the question, "What's next?" What is the single next step you would have to take to see forward progress on the task? For John, it would be measuring the angle of the existing floorboard in the bedroom. If a belt is laying in the kitchen and needs to go upstairs in your room, you might just look at it and think to yourself, "I don't want to run all the way upstairs to put that belt away," so you leave it there. Instead, take the single next step and put it on the stairs. Every time you go upstairs, grab something to take with you.

SEEK TO RESOLVE INCOMPLETE PROJECTS. Take unpacking from trips as an example. Unpack the suitcases, put the dirty clothes in the hamper, and refill toiletries while you remember what's gone. I was in one woman's home office and noticed seven conference bags stacked against the wall. I discovered they were filled with her seminar notes, brochures, and vendor samples. She never spent time after the conference reviewing and activating her plans, so now she's afraid to even look in there, for fear of how much time it will take. In a case like this, when so much time has gone by, you may as well throw them all away. If you have a pile of magazines you haven't looked through in months, set a timer for five minutes, force yourself to scan the table of contents for each one, and toss or review it before the timer goes off.

BREAK DOWN PROJECTS INTO PIECES. Don't bite off more than you can chew. If you define your Saturday project as "clean out the garage," you're sure to fail. It's too much and takes too long. You will run out of steam before you're finished, give up, and leave it half organized, which is almost more frustrating than unorganized. Breaking down a project into smaller chunks of time is often called the salami technique—slicing up a big task into digestible slices. Schedule a one-hour "declutter assault" and define a specific goal to achieve in that time: "Label the drawers," "Tidy up the floor," "Organize the gorilla rack on the left wall," etc. Get an egg timer, set it for one hour, and then go at it! Dividing a task into small sections like this will allow you to see progress toward your goals and feel inspired rather than discouraged.

PESTS quiz item 33

33. _____ Keep interruptions from wasting my time.

Will You People Leave Me Alone?

I know you've had, as I've had, days when you felt busy all day but accomplished nothing significant. You started the day with the best of intentions and plans, but you wound up dealing with interruptions all day and had nothing to show for your efforts at the end.

This probably sounds odd, but my family and friends are my biggest culprits. Let me explain: I work at home. I work from eight to five. But my friends often think that because I'm "at home," I am able to chat with them. No matter how hard I try, certain family members and friends don't take my work seriously because I work in a home office, rather than a traditional office building.

If you stay at home, you probably experience the same thing: Your brother might drop in unannounced for coffee because "you're always home." An old friend might want to sleep on your couch for a week. A friend might be disappointed when you can't meet him for lunch. Perhaps a neighbor wants you to drop something off with the mailman when he arrives because "you're home." Or your sister calls to chat—for an hour! Just because you don't work outside the home doesn't mean you don't have work to do during the day!

Experiment with these suggestions:

IF YOU WORK AT HOME, EXPLAIN WHAT YOU DO AND ASK FOR SUPPORT. People may not realize that you work hard because they don't know what you really do. Sit down with your friends and family, and explain to them how hectic your days are. This blow-by-blow account will help them realize that you run a legitimate business. Then set guidelines with them about when it's okay to call and when they're interrupting you.

TAME THE TELEPHONE. People dropping in are my biggest interruption. Maybe yours is the phone. We have our home phone number set up to not accept unidentified callers and solicitors. Callers whose phone numbers come up "unknown" get a recording and have to punch their phone number in before getting connected. The recording also states we do not accept solicitations. Caller ID quickly shows us who's calling and lets us decide whether now is a good time to answer. If not, the call goes to voice mail. We *rarely* get these types of calls. When we do, I politely explain I don't do business over the phone, send me something in the mail, ask them to take me off the list, and hang up. Don't worry about being rude; they get used to being hung up on all the time. You don't have to cuss and slam the phone down, just state your limits and end the call. Remember, just because someone calls you doesn't mean you have to answer, and just because someone leaves a message doesn't mean you have to call back.

GO INTO HIDING. When people find out I'm an author, I often get a comment to the effect of "I'd love to write a book on _____.

I have all these wonderful ideas in my head!" When asked, "So how much do you have written?" they usually reply, "Nothing! I just can't seem to find the space and time." I always explain to them, "And you never will, if you try writing at home." Whether you are writing a book or just trying to get something done, sometimes you need to retreat to your "third place." Those who know me well know about my infamous three-day writing retreats. My favorite spot is currently Staybridge Suites by Holiday Inn in Lonetree, Colorado. It's inexpensive, comfortable, and has everything I need for a three-day stay, including a full kitchen. I don't even leave the hotel.

Perhaps you aren't a writer, so you don't need the absolute solitude of a hotel. My friend and speaking colleague, Mark Sanborn, often frequents Starbucks (mostly because he's addicted to their coffee) when he needs to plan. He sits there with a pad of paper and no technology and lets his thoughts pour out. If you absolutely have to get away for a solid hour without being interrupted, find an empty conference room, borrow a vacationing colleague's office, or go to the library.

To hide at home, explain your need for privacy to your family and sequester yourself in your bedroom or home office, with a "do not disturb" sign on the door. Or set a timer for a half-hour and tell your children not to bother you until it goes off. If all else fails, send your kids and spouse out of the house for several hours.

PESTS quiz item 34

34. _____ Create shortcuts to get things done quickly.

Over and Over and Over and . . .

Contrary to popular belief, you don't need more hours in the day—but you'd have more time if you got things done more quickly. Like you, I'm faced with too many things to do and not enough time to do them. So I've tried a lot of ways to streamline and simplify my life. Some of these shortcuts haven't worked, like trying to put on mascara on the way to church on Sunday morning while my husband (it seems) hits every pothole in the road. But many work well.

Here are some of my favorite tried-and-true shortcuts to help shave time off tasks without skimping on quality results.

BUY JAVA PODS. It's no secret that I love coffee. But I hate preparing the coffee. Grinding it. Measuring it. Pouring water. Cleaning the pot. What a pain! And buying coffee at Starbucks every day gets expensive, money I'd rather be spending on other services. I recently discovered, quite by accident, the Melitta One:One. I was surfing the Internet for a Christmas present for my husband and ended up buying this for myself instead. This nifty little appliance uses "pods"—premeasured, preground, clean. The water reserve holds enough for my entire morning coffee dose. Then I just toss the entire pod, and it's ready for the next day. Or you could use premeasured, self-contained packets of coffee in your drip coffeemaker.

KEEP AN ONGOING SHOPPING LIST. I get a supply of shopping list pads with a magnet on the top and bottom, so I can attach it to the refrigerator and it doesn't move around. Every time I think of something I need and it's not already on my master chart, it goes on the list. My family members also know: "If it's not on the list, it doesn't exist"—a nice little rhyming phrase even a ten-year-old can remember. Whoever uses the last of anything is responsible for checking the list and writing it down.

TIME STAMP YOUR PHOTOS. If your camera has a built-in time stamp feature, use it! Then you won't forget the date of the occasion when you go to organize them. If you don't have this feature, make sure your photo envelope or computer file has the date written somewhere on it. On the top of the envelope, I jot down the subjects, occasion, or activities, which is much easier than trying to remember the details later. If I have a minute in the store, I take it one step further and open the envelope and immediately toss any unflattering, unclear, or boring pictures.

CUT DOWN ON CLEANING. You're in the shower anyway, right? You'd have to get in the shower and run the water to clean it anyway, right? So keep cleaner within easy reach and spray the shower and glass while you're getting out of it! This saves you time when it's time to clean the bathroom. Wipe the bathroom sink after each use. If you're inclined to make the bed, pull up the quilt before you get out of it. Use throw rugs with rubber backs in heavy traffic areas. Change filters on the heating/cooling system frequently to cut down on the amount of house dust.

DON'T READ THE DAILY NEWSPAPER. I use www.slate.com to get a daily news update in my e-mail each day. I also like to do a quick scan of www.CNN.com, I read the *Wall Street Journal*'s What's News section, and glance at www.AssignmentEditor.com, which allows you to access any newspaper in the country. For news, I watch the thirty-minute roundup on Fox News. This takes less time from your day than reading the daily paper and keeps you in tune with world events. Or you could download a newsreader at www.-yahoo.com and get your news sent automatically to your computer desktop each day.

TAKE SHORTCUTS IN THE KITCHEN. If you're cooking a nice dinner, it doesn't take much extra work to make extra. Double (or triple) the ingredients and cook a large batch. Freeze some for a future dinner or freeze one portion in individual freezer bags if you're single or only cooking for two. While you're preparing your family's plates, put a portion into a plastic container with a lid so you can take it to work tomorrow. Then, when it's time for lunch, you simply pop it in the microwave and enjoy a hot, nourishing lunch, requiring no additional time on your part. And it saves time driving to fast-food restaurants, not to mention extra pounds! (You can save the extra pounds for eating cookies.) The next time you bake, put a cookie sheet covered with dough balls in the freezer. The next day, transfer them to a freezer bag. When the kids come home from school or your spouse is craving them, you can pop a few into the oven and have fresh, hot cookies anytime! Or you could buy chicken and beef in bulk, marinate it, grill, slice, and freeze it in individual portions. When you get home from work, you can quickly whip up stir-fry, enchiladas, or pasta with vegetables. It might even be wise to invest in a deep freezer so you can buy more when you shop and keep more ready meals on hand.

SHARE CHAUFFEUR DUTIES. When my daughter played in soccer tournaments, we spent hours driving to practices, games, tournaments, and camps. Families all arrived at once in our separate minivans and SUVs, a single girl would climb out, we'd watch the game, and then all drive home, caravan style. Wait a minute . . . what's wrong with this picture? I asked one family to split driving duties. We would pick up and drive to practice, and they would pick up from practice and drive home. That shortcut helped tremendously. We alternated for the games. If it wasn't one parent's turn to drive, but she wanted to see the game anyway, she could relax in the back while the other parent played chauffeur. Our system saved time and gas money—and was a lot more fun.

Don't feel guilty about taking shortcuts! Yes, go ahead and buy prewashed and precut vegetables. Do you think you'll be more likely to eat a salad when you can toss clean, cut lettuce, carrots, slivered almonds, cheese crumbles, and dried cranberries in a bowl and throw in oil and vinegar? Give yourself permission to spend a couple of extra dollars, save a lot of time, and eat healthier.

PESTS quiz item 35

> 35. _____ Combine activities and routines.

Hey, Mom! Watch How Many Balls I Can Juggle!

What's the difference between combining and multitasking? Combining involves the word "while"—you do X *while* doing Y. It's not multitasking, which is switching back and forth quickly from one task to the other. Combining actually means you are doing two activities at the same time.

Try these ideas for combining activities.

GET WORK DONE WHILE DOING OTHER TASKS. Dovetail supervising children's baths or homework, with other activities such as cleaning cabinets, checking supplies, mending, list making, ironing, washing dishes, or doing personal grooming. Or fold laundry while catching up with personal calls by using a headset.

FEED YOUR MIND WHILE FEEDING YOUR FAMILY. If you're the primary cook in your family, listen to tapes in your kitchen while preparing food or cleaning up. Keep a radio/tape player in the bathroom to listen to tapes or listen to the morning news while you're getting ready in the morning. Showering, shaving, fixing hair . . . these are necessary activities, but they aren't exactly life changing. Have something educational or entertaining to do simultaneously. Also purchase a portable tape player or CD player to use with earphones when you're in an airplane, at the supermarket, waiting in line, or just puttering in the garden. While you're cleaning the house, listen to a book on tape.

GET EXERCISE WHILE SPENDING TIME WITH LOVED ONES. In the warmer months, we love to go on "family walks." We're blessed to have a trail through the open space of our subdivision. We stroll unhurriedly, picking dandelions, running through the grass, counting bunny rabbit sightings, and looking at weird bugs. We all love the togetherness and are getting exercise to boot. When my daughter bought a trampoline with her own money, I got on with her to try it out. What a workout! Now I jump regularly with her to play and exercise. But there's nothing like a little peer pressure to get you to exercise. My husband joined a gym with his friend Jeff Vigil. When the alarm clock goes off at 5:30 a.m., he dutifully rolls out of bed. Not because he wants to, but because he knows Jeff is waiting for him. Having a workout partner gets him motivated and out of the house. I have girlfriends who meet each other in the morning for walks. The walk becomes a fun chat when they can catch up on each other's lives and enjoy spending time together. I know a man who took horseback riding lessons so he could share his wife's love of horses. The trick is to focus on activities that will give you great exercise and great fun at the same time.

COMBINE HOLIDAY SHOPPING WITH REGULAR SHOPPING. When you're out shopping for an item and you see something nice for the holidays, purchase it, and put it aside. Hide gifts in a special trunk, closet, or box. As December approaches, make your gift list. For items you still need to buy, go online and purchase what you can. Then plan remaining shopping trips, noting which items you can get at which store. Try to know exactly what you're buying before you go. Don't wander up and down the aisles hoping something will jump out at you. Getting started early and buying gifts with your regular shopping will help you avoid the last-minute crush.

BATCH TASKS WHEN YOU CAN. Small administrative tasks, such as entering receipts into your accounting software, making photocopies, writing notes, and paying bills, can seem like a waste of time when done one at a time. They are! It takes you a great deal of time to think about doing the task, switch your focus, find the needed supplies or equipment, do the task, and put it all back again (you do, don't you?). So instead, practice saving up these items. Put all your copies in a "to be copied" project file; your filing in a "to be filed" bin; your receipts and business cards into a "computer" project file. Pick a regular day and time to handle all these tasks at once.

PESTS quiz item 36

---

36. _____ Make good use of down time.

Hurry Up and Wait!

The only thing worse than wasting time is having someone else waste it for you! For example, is there *anyone* who enjoys waiting in the doctor's office? Once I thought I would be clever, and I made an appointment with my doctor for 8:30 a.m. I was *first*. No waiting. On the morning of my appointment, traffic was unusually light, and I made it to the doctor's office a half-hour before my appointment.

Being so early, I was a bit sluggish and craving that cup of Joe I'd skipped at home so I'd be on time. I looked over in the corner and saw a coffeepot that just needed a quick scrubbing and it would be ready to go. To my joy, the receptionist came over and got it. She went to the sink, filled it with water, and poured it into the machine . . . *without* cleaning it out first. Gross! Now I'm thinking, "Has she *ever* cleaned that coffeepot?"

I didn't know if there were any bacteria strong enough to survive that pot, but I wasn't taking any chances. So I jumped in my car and headed to the Starbucks on the corner, only to discover that every other caffeine-deprived person in Colorado had the same idea. Now I wanted that cup of coffee, but I really wanted to be *first* and there was no way I was going to miss my appointment. So I dragged myself back to the doctors' office to wait.

At 8:27, the receptionist called my name. Yes! My plan was working! I was ready to waltz right in. But instead of waltzing me in, she let me know she'd just received a call from the doctor, who, it turned out, had an emergency surgery that morning and was going to be late. "How late?" I asked. "I don't know," she said, "Maybe a half-hour." I thought, "What kind of emergency surgery only takes a half hour?" Then a lightbulb went on in my head! I told the receptionist, "I'll be right back!" I grabbed my stuff and drove over to the Starbucks. I was going to get my cup of coffee!

When I arrived, the line had diminished somewhat. I could actually see the counter from the end of it. As I inhaled the aromas, I looked around, and there—seven people ahead of me in line—was my *doctor*! My first thought was, "What kind of surgery could she be performing at Starbucks?"

As my mind tried to make sense of this, I watched her get her coffee and walk out the door, back to her office! I thought, "Oh no! She's going to beat me back to the office!" So I fly out the door, once again sans coffee, drove like a crazy woman, and beat her back by three minutes. It's 8:47, and the nurse called me in and told me to undress and wait in one of those little rooms. Now I'm waiting with no magazine, no coffee, and a gown two sizes too small. But hey! At least I'm *first*. At 8:57, the doctor comes strolling in, a half-hour late, and smiling because she's had her coffee. Being first doesn't always work, so be prepared.

TWO TYPES OF DOWN TIME. I distinguish between two types of down time—waiting time and during time. Waiting time means you're stuck somewhere—it doesn't really make sense to leave and come back—but you have a short amount of time available to you. You're not really doing anything. Sitting in the doctor's office is a good example. You don't want to attempt to leave the doctor's office and do something because you might lose your spot. During time happens when you're in the midst of another activity, essentially doing two things at once.

WAITING TIME. Since my doctor's office experience above, I've learned to plan for her to be late. In fact, I've been known to express disappointment if I am unable to complete the work I brought to do while waiting.

Learn to use your waiting time effectively. Complete a little task while you are:

- Sitting in a doctor's office
- Idling in your car while soccer practice wraps up

- Holding on the phone
- Watching your computer boot up
- Downloading a file
- Waiting at the bank drive-up window

You could:

- Call a friend you've been meaning to connect with
- Dash off a thank-you note
- Pay your bills
- Listen to movie show times
- Make dinner reservations
- Schedule your next date or spa appointment
- Review your calendar
- Tidy up the car

All of this means, however, that you'll have to be prepared. Keep stamped note cards in your tote. Have phone numbers programmed in your cell phone or your contact list updated on your PDA.

DURING TIME. You can generally do other things while in during time and shift your attention from one thing to the next. For example, you're watching television. A commercial comes on. You're now in during time. You can run to the dryer and grab a load of laundry to fold in front of the next viewing segment. You're walking on the treadmill (good for you). Ho-hum. You could listen to an audio seminar downloaded into your iPod and make good use of this during time. You're cooking dinner. Can't exactly get wrapped up in another activity for fear of the food burning. But you can listen to audiotapes while stirring or read your kids' school papers at the counter and pack lunches for the next day. You can use your cell phone wisely to get things done while you're driving home from work or walking from the office to the car or train: catching up with friends, making appointments, or checking in at home. During time can be a great way to get things done if it's not frittered away.

PESTS quiz item 37

> 37. _____ Turn off the technology when with my loved ones.

Honey, Call Me on the Cell If You Want to Talk

A 2001 survey sponsored by PriceWaterhouseCoopers and conducted by Harris Interactive shows that the increased use of technology such as cell phones, beepers, e-mail, and computers has had a tremendous impact on the feelings of overwork in America. The *four* out of *ten* employees who use technology *often* or *very often* for their jobs during typical nonwork hours more frequently feel overworked. About one-fifth of employees in the study said they *often* or *very often* have to be accessible to their employers during typical nonwork hours and nonwork days, while 30 percent said they *never* have to be accessible. Which group is more stressed? Employees who are more accessible to their employers during nonwork hours feel more overworked.

Consequences of Being Available 24/7

- Loss of time for loved ones, reflection, relaxation, and spiritual growth
- No "unavailable" time: intrusive

- Can violate desire for privacy
- Pleasurable activities (lunch with friends, a walk) quickly lose their pleasure when you're "on call"
- Feel like you have no control over your time

KEEP YOUR CELL NUMBER PRIVATE. Only five people have my cell phone number: my husband, mother, day care, best friend, and assistant. If you give it to everyone, you will never have private time. Unless your job requires it, give the number to as few people as possible, so you can turn it off and protect your privacy when you choose.

TURN OFF THE COMPUTER AND TELEVISION. How much time do you spend surfing the Web each day? Playing video games? Watching television? The Bureau of Labor Statistics' Time-Use Survey from September 14, 2004, states that on an average day in 2003, men spent about 2.7 hours watching television each day and women watched 2.4 hours each day. Holy cow! If you're among that group and you reduced your television time by only five hours a week, you'd gain almost eleven days a year. What could you do with eleven days a year? Spend more time with someone you love? Take a vacation? Think carefully the next time you reach for the remote.

BE FULLY PRESENT. Some people don't feel productive when they're not doing four things at once (such as driving, talking on the phone, drinking coffee, and putting on makeup). If this describes you, shift your focus. Avoid the tendency to multitask at home. Be especially attentive with children for their well-being. On weekends, turn off the technology completely. Resist the urge to sneak back into your office to check e-mail "just one more time" while your family hangs out elsewhere in the house.

DRAW THE LINE SOMEWHERE. If you stay connected to your e-mail and cell phone all weekend, you will go to bed physically and mentally exhausted on Sunday night. Instead of starting the week recharged, alert, and efficient, you will be sluggish on Monday morning. Slow down and rest. Reinvest in yourself.

PESTS quiz item 38

> 38. _____ Know and avoid my biggest time wasters and distractions.

Oops . . . Have I Really Been Playing Minesweeper for an Hour?

I couldn't teach a time-management seminar without talking about time wasters. Distractions are a big reason we don't make good on best-laid plans. I think of them like gnats—pesky little insects that like to fly around and annoy you—but you can kill them with a simple swat. The "swat" you need is a personal rule. Time wasters creep up on you and become part of your normal, everyday life without your noticing. You can stop them and prevent them from occurring again by becoming aware and setting certain rules. Everyone's rules are different, but you've got to determine what they are and commit them to writing.

Let's identify some of the time-wasting activities and distractions you find hard to resist when you should be working on other projects and priorities. Check the ones that apply to you, then add your own on the bottom:

_____ Television

_____ Hanging out around the refrigerator

_____ Lolling through the daily newspaper

_____ Checking e-mail as it comes in

_____ Surfing the Net

_____ Staying in bed too long

_____ Playing with your pet or a neighbor's (!) pet

_____ Taking personal phone calls

_____ Running for coffee

_____ Taking naps

_____ Dealing with home deliveries

_____ Doing home chores while you should be working

_____ Running errands one at a time

_____ Reading junk mail

_____ Socializing

_____ Letting guests overstay their welcome

_____ Working in your home office when you should be with your family

_____ Scheduling too many personal appointments during work hours

_____ Shopping

_____

_____

After you've identified your personal time-wasting activities and distractions, create a rule statement for each one. For example:

1. I get myself ready and get the kids to daycare in a manner that allows me to be at work by 8:00 a.m.

2. When work is over at five, I close the door. I will only go

back into the office for important personal things in the evening.

3. I am allowed to schedule doctor's appointments during the day, but nail and hair appointments must be scheduled on weekends.

4. I won't nap during the day.

5. I won't procrastinate by doing things around the house (except at lunch), like laundry, cleaning, and personal e-mail.

6. I will treat myself to lunch with a girlfriend once a week.

7. When I'm traveling for business, I will be productive and catch up on paperwork and reading.

Different people's situations are different; therefore, their rules are different. You might not stay at home or work from home, but you certainly have your own distractions to consider. You might be single with no kids, so you might have the flexibility to work later at night if you have the energy. Create rules that work for you and stick to them!

PESTS quiz item 39

> 39. _____ Make productive use of driving or commuting time.

Drive, Eat, Talk, Shave . . .

Travel time can seem like wasted time! I like being a passenger in a car much better than being the driver because I can observe the scenery, read a magazine, and catch up on phone calls. As the driver, you can't do anything (safely) that requires your hands or eyes. You're strapped into your car seat without much to look at except the bumper in front of you. So there's nothing you can do, right? Wrong!

Try these activities during long commute times.

USE THE PHONE. I'm one of those people who get aggravated while people are chatting away on their cell phones while driving . . . generally because they're not, well, driving. Many people have no idea how slowly they're going while they're on the phone. Plus, talking on the phone has proven to be unsafe and many states have passed ordinances against it. Often, you'll see someone pulled over to the side of the road to make a call.

That being said, you *can* get a hands-free phone installed, which uses a mounted phone and speakers. Many cell phones use Bluetooth technology, which allows you to wear a wireless earpiece and talk hands-free. By using these safe options, you can still use your phone to call clients or catch up with friends and family while still keeping your hands on the wheel and eyes on the road.

CLEAR YOUR BRAIN. Basically, use your morning commute as a warmup to your day. On the way to work, do whatever helps you focus and arrive at your desk raring to go. For mass transit travelers, that may mean reading the daily paper with a cup of coffee. Drivers may like to listen to news radio.

BOND WITH YOUR FAMILY. While driving together to away games or a relative's house, you can sing songs, quiz your child on his spelling words, play "I spy" or another travel game, or listen to stories. When your eyes are on the road, your child may feel more comfortable than usual bringing up a touchy subject, so be available to just listen as well.

SHIFT YOUR SCHEDULE. If you frequently get stuck in traffic, consider changing your schedule slightly to hit the road before or after the rush, and use the time on either side to organize your day.

USE A VOICE RECORDER. I knew a professional speaker who wrote an entire book by talking while driving. She clipped a microphone onto her shirt and talked into a recording device (there are many available). Then she simply had those tapes transcribed, hired an editor to clean it up, and printed it at www.instantpub lisher.com. She has published a book at the rate of about one a year using this method. Other people get voice recorders (Radio Shack sells a good one) with several minutes of tape and dictate their letters while on the go. If you're blessed enough to have an assistant, he or she can type your letters from the recording. Some cell phones also have recorders built into them, so you can make your to-do list or remind yourself of things as you think of them. Do *not*, under any circumstances, attempt to write while driving unless you're completely stopped.

LISTEN TO BOOKS ON TAPE. My favorite place to eat breakfast is a restaurant called Cracker Barrel . . . hash brown casserole, grits, and honey ham, baked apples . . . oh, sorry! The closest one to me is an hour's drive away, so I don't get to frequent it often enough because of Denver traffic. But if you're lucky enough to have one in your hometown or pass a sign for one along the road, stop. You'll notice that Cracker Barrel restaurants are always built right off an interstate exit. One of the founders' core strategies was to make them easy on, easy off from the interstate. You could get to the next one on a tank of gas, refuel, grab a bite, buy what you need (and what you don't need) in their little store, and get back on the road. Cracker Barrel has also come up with a clever books-on-tape program for frequent travelers. The next time you visit this restaurant, look for the spinning rack of tapes. You can purchase one audio book and, for a nominal fee, trade it in for another, anytime, at any other Cracker Barrel. Or, get tapes and CDs from your local library before you go on a trip. You'll notice that your perception of drive time is greatly reduced when you're listening to an audio book. Your brain gets engaged in the story, and time flies by. I have a friend who was planning a trip to France, so she listened to French language tapes while in the car. Within three months, she learned enough French to get around nicely.

CARPOOL WITH YOUR SPOUSE. If you work in roughly the same area, hitch a ride with your sweetie! You can use the extra time each day to talk. While one person drives, the other can take care of miscellaneous family business on the phone. By the time you reach your door, the calls will be done and you can enjoy more quality time together at home.

TAKE THE TRAIN INSTEAD. If you're lucky enough to have a great public transportation system, use it! Of course, many professionals are forced into taking commuter trains because of traffic or distance or speed. But many people have told me they live for their train time because they can complete light paperwork, catch up on reading, pay bills, or just nap. By the time they arrive home, they feel rested and can settle into the second shift.

PESTS quiz item 40

40. _____ Eliminate aggravation and save time when traveling or flying.

Fly Me to the Moon

Travel is a job hazard for many professionals. Some enjoy it; some hate it. I have a love-hate relationship with travel. I don't like the crowds, the lines, and the schlepping of baggage. I'll frequently pull a muscle trying to get my bag into an overhead bin. But I do love having the space and time to catch up on my reading, do some writing, and have some peace and quiet (with three kids, that's hard to come by).

Over the years, I've learned some tricks that have helped me travel more easily. Here they are.

GET AN AIRPORT DRIVER. "What? How spoiled is she?" you may think. Hang on and let me explain. If a friend or your spouse can drive you to the airport, that's great. But now that person also has to pick you up, and if children are involved, it adds an entirely different level of complication. One evening, my husband went to his Wednesday night men's group as usual. He came home and told me about a new guy who joined, Russ Johnson, who owned a sedan service. "Really?" I said. "Is that like a taxi?" "Sort of," John said, "but more like a limousine that doesn't cost as much." How much? To the airport, $120 round-trip. Now that seems like a lot of money, but let's talk this through. One-way costs $60. In the space of one hour, I could complete a task that is valued at far more than that—not to mention the $7.50 in tolls, the gas and mileage, and the parking costs at $18 a day. I wouldn't have to drag my pathetic self and baggage a mile (or so it seems) to the terminal because the driver would drop me at the door. When I return it's often late at night. I've had some scary incidents in dark garages that have convinced me of the value of protecting my personal safety. I decided that I can never overestimate the value of a driver standing there waiting for me at eleven o'clock at night. All in all, I think $120 is worth it.

PLAN YOUR WARDROBE IN ADVANCE. You should never have to rush around before going to the airport and worry about missing your flight. When you do, that simply means you didn't plan well. You should be ready to go to the airport before you turn in the night before your trip, no matter how late you get to bed. If you wait until the day of the trip, something always comes up or you forget something, and you'll find yourself panicking, throwing things into your bag, and still forgetting a key item. My girlfriend and fellow speaker, Rebecca Morgan, actually hangs her complete outfits together—suit, shoes, blouse, jewelry, hosiery, undergarments, and so on—and takes digital photos of the entire ensemble. Now she doesn't forget what she packed to go with what. I suggest not packing pieces of an outfit until you have the entire thing laid out. That way, you won't end up accidentally having to wear tennis shoes with your suit.

STICK TO ONE WARDROBE COLOR. Personally, I try to stick with black when I travel, so I don't have to worry about what goes with what, and I only have to bring one pair of shoes. Black also doesn't show the coffee I just spilled down my front. Try to find garments that are washable and dryable, and don't wrinkle at all, even when in a ball in your suitcase. Look for options that fit your style and budget but require little maintenance on the go.

IF YOU TRAVEL OFTEN, KEEP A TRAVEL BAG ALWAYS PACKED. You can partially solve any packing dilemma by always having a suitcase packed with travel essentials and ready to go. I use a folding toiletries organizer that's packed with small sizes of my cosmetics and lotions. It opens and hangs from a towel bar where I can access everything conveniently. It then folds back in one piece and into the suitcase. When I have a presentation in another state, I simply grab my carry-on suitcase, toss in the toiletries bag, a black outfit, and my pillow.

DON'T CHECK ANY BAGS. If you can figure out a system that allows you to travel compactly enough with one carry-on suitcase and one briefcase, you are golden! That way, if you want to stand by for an earlier flight, you're not handicapped because you didn't check bags. You can also leave one airline and go to another terminal for an alternate flight if your plane has a mechanical problem. No checked baggage equals free and flexible. I like Tumi and TravelPro suitcases, and my favorite briefcase is a Swiss Army rolling briefcase. It has four roomy sections in it, and amazingly, has ample space for my laptop, LCD projector, amplifier/speaker system, plus my files and planner. It still counts as a briefcase, and I can strap it on my suitcase and roll both at the same time. I stuff my purse into the front of my suitcase, so I never have to check bags! What a time-saver!

USE BAGGAGE-SHIPPING SERVICES. Family vacations are difficult even for normally savvy travelers . . . check bags . . . wait for bags . . . check bags . . . wait for bags. It's much easier to use a baggage-shipping service like www.luggagefree.com, www.baggageshipping.com, or www.uship.com. Your packed bags are picked up at your home and flown to your destination. No more schlepping baggage! The savings in time, hassle, and stress—especially when you're steering children—is definitely worth the money. Factor this service into your vacation budget!

ARRIVE EARLY. I have a friend who works right up until the last minute he possibly can leave and still expect to catch his flight—if there's no traffic, he doesn't need to check bags, there's no line at the security counter, and so on. It's no wonder he's always the one desperately running through the terminal and bursting onto the plane, the last one there—and sometimes he's the one watching his plane as it pulls away without him. That's no way to live! I know the airlines tell you to arrive sixty minutes ahead of your flight if you don't have baggage to check, but I'd rather give myself more cushion than that. I plan to arrive ninety minutes early with only a carry-on, and two hours early if I have bags to check. I have already checked the flight on the Internet at home and printed my boarding pass. My bags were already packed the day before. I do some work or read on the way to the airport, arrive feeling calm, wave to my driver, and walk to the security line. Give yourself plenty of cushion, so you won't be stressed out even if there is a line. And there's no running required.

USE CHECKLISTS. The way to *not* forget a key item is to use checklists—written checklists, not just lists in your mind. Because your brain is fallible, it will fail at some point, so don't rely on it. Here are some lists to get you started. Before you embark on your travel—whether it's a family vacation, a business trip, or a trip to the grocery store with your child—make sure you've run through your list. You can photocopy these lists or download a copy at www.TheProductivityPro.com under Free Stuff under the Resources menu.

1. DIAPER BAG

_____ Spare change of clothes

_____ Diapers and supplies

_____ Changing pad

_____ Wipes and napkins

_____ Drinks and snacks

_____ Utensils

_____ Tissues

_____ Lotion

_____ Sunscreen

_____ Pacifiers

_____ Antiseptic hand wash

_____ Toys

_____ Infant pain reliever/fever reducer

2. CARRY-ON SUITCASE

_____ Robe and slippers

_____ Undergarments

_____ Tennis shoes

_____ Swimsuit

_____ Jewelry

_____ Pillow

_____ Medicines

_____ Umbrella

_____ Travel alarm clock

_____ Hair dryer

_____ Shaver

_____ Facial products

_____ Socks and/or hosiery

_____ Workout clothing

_____ Business shoes

_____ Shoe buffer

_____ Sewing kit

_____ Pajamas

_____ Earplugs

_____ Clothing: suits, outfits

_____ Candle, small family photo

_____ Brush and comb

_____ Makeup

_____ Camera

_____ Shower cap

_____ Toiletries: shampoo, lotion, hair products, toothpaste, toothbrush, deodorant, Q-Tips, dental floss, ChapStick

3. BRIEFCASE AND/OR PURSE

_____ Laptop and cord

_____ Water and power bars

_____ Projector and cords

_____ Reading material

_____ Extra batteries	_____ Noise-canceling headset
_____ Planner or PDA	_____ Cell phone and charger
_____ Order forms	_____ Magazines
_____ Reading material	_____ Eye- and sunglasses
_____ Tickets	_____ Identification
_____ Wallet	_____ Paperwork

USE YOUR TRAVEL TIME PRODUCTIVELY. If you were fortunate enough to have ever met the late Art Berg, you would have been blessed. This pioneer of using technology in a way that helps people simplify their lives was the founder of the Internet calendaring system I use: www.espeakers.com. Art always told me, "Never waste your time on the plane. The more you get done while you're traveling, the more time you'll have available to be with your family when you return." I took his sage advice to heart and now *plan* on being able to knock out a bunch of work while I'm away from home. I don't just sleep, rent the movies, or listen to music on the plane—I work. I read business journals, trade magazines, write thank-you letters, complete routine paperwork, review large reports and board materials, or do project and advance planning. If I feel good about what I've accomplished, I have Oprah's current *O* magazine handy for pleasure reading. I take my office into the air and to the hotel. In the hotel, I don't watch television! If you're a television person at home, discipline yourself to say, "This is my time. Uninterrupted time. There's no one else to take care of but myself. I'm going to use it to get ahead."

USE THE LATEST TOOLS AND TECHNOLOGY. To be really productive, you have to be connected so you can stay in touch with your home and office. Without a good cell phone plan, for example, you'll hesitate to make long-distance calls. If you keep your Outlook calendar at work but don't have a printed copy or a PDA with you, it's more difficult to plan. If you don't have wireless Internet and a hot-spot subscription, you can't easily connect. It's worth paying the ten dollars (or whatever the hotel charges) to get wireless access in your room. If you keep up with phone calls, e-mail, and clients while traveling, you won't have a pile of correspondence waiting for you when you return.

CHAPTER FIVE

Mastering the Fifth Pillar—

POSSESSIONS

I CREDIT MY FATHER for instilling the value of hard work in me. He's living proof that you can do anything you put your mind to.

Secretly, though, Dad is a pack rat—an unfortunate trait in a man who spent his *entire* career on the move. With each relocation, he'd ship out an ever-growing battalion of boxes: precisely labeled, in exact formation, and still taped shut from the last move. And the one before that. And the one before that. We can go back as far as you want with this.

"Daddykins, are you sure you want to move these boxes? They've been sitting in the garage since our last move."

"Don't touch those boxes, Laura. They're full of tools I'll need at the new house."

Of course, he hadn't needed them at any of the previous seven houses . . . but maybe this next one was more of a fixer-upper. I'm thinking, "When we get to the new city, I'm going to take all these boxes to Home Depot. I bet most of the tools still have the price tags on them. I can get refunds on everything, Dad will never notice, and I'll have enough money to buy a car."

Of course, Dad would have noticed. Any good pack rat would. Pack rats may not use what they're storing, but they know if it's not there. He saved baby food jars from when we were infants and meticulously labeled each jar with the type of bolt, nail, screw . . . or three-inch piece of string labeled "string too short to use." He kept the baby food jars in drawers in a huge wooden workbench. He never used some of the items he kept, but, hey, at least he had them if he needed them.

In college, the timer on my microwave broke. My dad repaired it with a bathroom timer he had been holding on to for fifteen years. He said, "See! I knew that would come in handy someday!" I always wonder how much time, energy, and stress it took for my father to organize and reorganize things he could have bought for $3.89 at Wal-Mart when he actually needed them. He always argued, "Hey I might be a pack rat, but at least I can *find* what I want when I want it." The last straw was finding a drawer of combination locks, none of which he knew the combinations for!

This chapter addresses items you've accumulated—everything from toys and clothing to tools and other stuff that although you use regularly still counts as clutter. As in my father's case, these might be weighing you down and putting pressure on the other pillars.

41. _____ Have a systematic plan to get and stay organized.

Step by Step, Bit by Bit

The key to getting organized is focus. Most of us flit from one thing to the next and wind up with half-organized spaces. It generally works like this: You're cleaning the hall closet, you get thirsty, go to the kitchen for a drink, see that the kitchen is a mess, and begin to clean it. Stop! What's happened to your closet project? Focus on getting one thing completed before moving to the next area. Act like a postage stamp—*stick to one thing until you get there.*

Little by little, you will get there! Draw up a planning sheet with two columns—one marked "Weekend" and the other marked "Project." Post it in a prominent place in your home (refrigerator, bulletin board, or calendar) so everyone can see the goals. Select a different project for each weekend. If you plan ahead and prepare for each weekend in advance, you'll jump in and make the best use of your time when Saturday arrives.

Here's a sample six-week approach to begin conquering clutter in your home.

WEEKEND 1, CLOSETS. Clean and organize all the closets in your house. I teach my seminar participants that it's clutter if (1) someone else can use the item more than you can, and (2) it doesn't make you happy. Thus, the clothes we're holding on to until we lose some weight become clutter. You certainly aren't wearing clothes that don't fit, and your self-esteem takes a nosedive each time you look at them. Take a deep breath and give those clothes to charity—with no regrets. Rearrange the remaining clothes in sections—dresses, pants, suits, and so on. Then go through the closet in the front hall. If you never wear a coat, get rid of it so you can easily retrieve coats you do wear. Toss mittens and gloves that have no mate. Give away hats, extra sweaters, and outdoor gear your family doesn't wear. Lastly, sort through your linen closet, converting tattered sheets to rags and giving away table-cloths and towels you never use. This process could take a very long time the first time through, so you may need more than one weekend, but afterward, regular maintenance won't be so daunting.

WEEKEND 2, PAPER. Gather, organize, and toss paper that has ac-cumulated all over your house. Bundle up the daily newspapers that you've strewn all over the garage and take them to the recy-cling center. Go through your warranties and throw away the ex-pired policies. Sort your catalogs and toss those that you never order from. Review your magazine subscriptions and cancel those you never read. Take time to call companies that routinely send you junk mail and get off their mailing lists. Read any low-priority mail that you've been accumulating until you had some time to go through it. Select a few truly original pieces of your kids' artwork and throw the rest away (when they can't see you do it). Go through your coupon organizer and toss expired coupons. Spend time filing the pile of paper that's been growing unchecked. Then go through each of your files and purge paper you no longer need. Pull out and save records and receipts you need to save for tax purposes; put them in a storage box marked with the year. That way, you'll be ahead of the game *next* January!

WEEKEND 3, READING. To tackle your reading pile, how about considering a revolutionary step—throw the entire pile away and begin again? Or, if that's too drastic, throw away all but the current issues of *Newsweek* or *USA Today*. The rest is old news. Don't read magazines cover to cover; that's simply overwhelming. Go through the table of contents, allow yourself a maximum of three articles per issue, rip them out, and throw the rest of the magazine away. When you're through weeding through your stack, the actual task of reading your gleanings will be much less formidable. Spend the rest of the weekend catching up on important reading. You could try the timer technique for each article. Get an egg timer and set it for fifteen minutes for each item. When it goes off, toss the article. This tip comes from Nobel laureate Herbert Simon, speaking in *People* magazine: "Reading daily newspapers is one of the least cost-efficient things you can do . . . read the *World Almanac* once a year. What's happening you'll hear by lunch anyway."

WEEKEND 4, CORRESPONDENCE. To whom do you owe letters? Use letters, stationery, cards, e-mail, or the phone to return messages to friends and family you've been neglecting. Make a master list of the birthdays and anniversaries for all your friends and family you plan to buy for next year. Then take a trip to your local card shop and buy *all* (yes, all) of the cards at once. I go as far as addressing them ahead of time. Mark the important date lightly in pencil in the upper right-hand corner so the stamp will cover it when you mail it. File the cards in your tickler file (quiz item 52 in chapter 6). Stock up on all your stationery, envelopes, postcards, and stamps at once. Put them in a little basket in your nightstand or next to your easy chair so you can dash off a letter when you have a free minute. Put return address labels and stamps on blank white envelopes or keep address labels, stamps, and envelopes in a folder with your address book. Then if you're reading an article you think your mom would enjoy, you can simply rip it out and get it going out the door to her. Or if you have to mail bills that don't come with a preaddressed envelope, you have envelopes ready to stuff and mail. For holiday cards, tear off the return address label of each card you receive. Tape them to a piece of paper and add the addresses to your mailing list for the following year. Sort through the holiday cards you've been keeping for years and keep only the very sentimental. Pull photos from photo cards to keep and toss the card.

WEEKEND 5, STORAGE. This is generally clutter's last stand and could include your basement, garage, attic, or shed. The biggest problem with most storage spaces is that people stack items on top of and in front of one another, making everything hard to access. Solve these problems by creating a box storage system. Purchase industrial gray metal shelving from any home supply store. Get boxes that are all the same size and shape. Use strong, sturdy boxes of corrugated cardboard (moving cartons work best). Repack items you must store in a new box, clearly label the contents on the side, and store alphabetically (Camping, Christmas, Cooking) on the shelves. With this system, you can quickly spot and retrieve a box from the bottom of the pile. What items qualify for storage? Seasonal materials, hand-me-down clothes a child can soon wear, maternity clothes, baby gear, and infrequently used items such as camping or skiing equipment. If you bought a cappuccino machine to have for your grandfather's visits twice a year, you don't need to keep it on the kitchen counter between visits. Think about how much memorabilia you *really* need to keep, perhaps one box or trunk for each person in your family. Toss, give away to charity, or have a garage sale to get rid of items you don't use, need, or want.

WEEKEND 6, FIX IT. Dedicate a weekend to taking care of loose ends and getting everything repaired that needs it. Gather all the items in your house that need fixing. Make a master list of all the places you need to go or repairmen you need to bring to the house. Change the oil in your car, take your dog to the vet for a shot, and catch up on your mending. Fix the handle that fell off the dresser and put the pedal back on your bike. Bring that tie tack with the broken pin to the jewelers, the coat with the torn inside pockets to the seamstress, the skirt that needs to be altered to the tailor, and the DVD player that isn't working to the repair shop. Buy a new battery for your watch, a new blade for the lawnmower, and a new hose to replace the leaky one. Call the repairman to tune up the dryer and fix the icemaker. Try to get as many of these things done over the weekend as you can and put the rest on a list to handle during the week or the following weekend.

You see, you don't have to wait for spring to get organized! Use your time effectively and plan for success. If you're tired, take a break, and start up again in another month. But if you get some momentum going—keep going! Weekend 7 could be cabinets, weekend 8 drawers, weekend 9 photographs, weekend 10 housework . . . You get the idea.

Repeat the system each year, and subsequent years will take less than a day and be a little easier. Once you get clutter under control in each of these areas, use the following tricks and philosophies to keep on top of it so it doesn't back up again. You may have to work hard a few weekends in a row to clear the current backlog, but those smart choices will result in more time for you in the months and even years to come.

POSSESSIONS quiz item 42

42. _____ Eliminate clutter and resist adding more.

You Might Be a Clutterer If . . .

The way you label a moving box is every bit as crucial as how you pack it. My father was very specific: We had to write, in marker— a big black permanent one, of course—what was inside the box, whether the contents were fragile, which room the box should go in, and which way was up. I sometimes added drawings of ponies as well, but these weren't technically part of my father's system.

He was right. Moving professionals tell you that a properly labeled box has a better chance of arriving undamaged, ending up in the right room, and getting unpacked at the right time.

We build piles of possessions and stacks of stuff. It's hard to pack—let alone label your boxes—when you can't sort the treasures from the trash.

As you might guess, I dislike clutter. Even worse, I don't like the excess that usually surrounds it. When you can't keep track of your possessions, you tend to buy more. Before you know it, your house looks like a Wal-Mart. You end up with three of everything because you can't locate the first two you bought.

If you have bundles of newspapers from the Eisenhower administration, you just might be a clutterer. If you're thinking about adding on to your three-car garage—and you only own one car—you just might be a clutterer. If you have keys to things you no longer own, you just might be a clutterer. The more you own, the more time you're obligated to spend cleaning, maintaining, and moving your stuff.

If you are serious about de-cluttering your life, take it in small steps. Don't plan to organize the garage in one day. First you have to take stock of what you have. Select one small project each weekend that can be de-cluttered in about an hour. Don't select "the bedroom," because that's too big. Choose perhaps "these two dresser drawers" instead.

Get five boxes labeled *give away, toss, store, put away,* and *goes here.*

One at a time, take an item from the designated area and put it into the appropriate box.

If you have a hard time tossing anything, just take a deep breath and toss something that feels negative—like clothes that don't fit you, lipstick that looks awful on you, a tool you never use, or an heirloom that's really an eyesore. Then give yourself a reward. Repeat the process. I promise—it will get easier.

Adopt these ideas:

DON'T KEEP UNHAPPY REMINDERS. A lot of people have a hard time parting with things. Do you still have all your old love letters and corsages? Throw away anything that conjures up a negative image—reminders of things gone wrong, of unrealized dreams. For example, let's say your dear great-grandfather brought you a vase when he visited Russia last summer, and it's a valuable item to you emotionally. Then, let's say you were robbed and the burglar used it to knock you unconscious. Now every time you look at it or hold it, it upsets you. This no longer has a positive emotional value to you, and you should give it away.

If you can't bring yourself to give or throw away certain items (games you never play with, camping equipment you never use, or clothes that no longer fit), store them for a "trial period." Label and date the box and tuck it away for a year. If you haven't needed the items after a year, don't open the box at all—simply give or throw it away immediately. Or, if you can't do it, get a ruthless friend who is willing to do it for you.

STOP BEING AN INFORMATION HOG. You really do want to read all those magazines, I know. You want to be informed! There's probably really good information you'll miss in that newspaper if you throw it away! Who cares? The *potential* benefit of that information doesn't matter a bit if there's no *actual* benefit. You'll have to live with the reality that there might be something good you will miss. I believe people with above-average interests have above-average frustration in this area, and it's really hard to toss potentially good reading material. But having it lying in wait for you to get to it is a mental burden. Practice letting it go!

LESS IS MORE. Here's a challenge. Go through your recipes, books, tools, self-improvement tapes, Internet bookmarks, sporting equipment, and so on, and get rid of 25 percent of them. You'll have fewer things, but you'll actually use a higher percentage of things you own. Remember, you can't do or read it all. If you try, you'll enjoy each item less and tend to feel anxious about something you should be doing or reading.

SURROUND YOURSELF WITH THINGS YOU LIKE. If you get gifts you dislike and don't want to throw them away because others will wonder where they are, create a "gifts" box. Put the items in that box, take it out when they visit, then pack it up again. Or, better yet, if you get a gift that you hate, say thank you, and remember—it's the thought that counts. Keep the thought and get rid of the gift. Thoughts don't take up space. In fact, think of someone who could really use it and give it away!

DON'T BUY THINGS JUST BECAUSE THEY'RE ON SALE. Similarly, never buy at yard sales just because you're getting a bargain. You're only getting someone else's junk! What if you buy something and never have time to use it? My husband bought this nifty steamer to clean the carpet in his car but has yet to use it. My daughter bought a cotton candy machine only because it was on sale, not because she wanted it, and it's never been out of the box. Of course, if you're shopping for that specific item for a birthday or holiday, getting it on sale is best. You can save money, reclaim your storage space, and purchase items on purpose when needed now or wanted for a future gift.

LABEL AND LIMIT. If you're unsure about how to go about decluttering your closet, use this simple labeling system. Put a tag on each article of clothing you own and date the tag one year from today. When you wear the article of clothing, remove the tag. In a year it will be easy to see which items you didn't wear. Pack up those items and move them out. This simple labeling system makes life easier. You will know what you actually wear, spend less time planning what to wear, and won't buy more than you need.

PRACTICE THE "ONE-IN, ONE-OUT" PRINCIPLE. This one is really simple. If you get a new sweater, give away one you never wear. In a similar way, encourage your children to go through their toys and give away those they've outgrown. That way, you make room for the new toys and they learn to give to children who are less fortunate.

BE SENSITIVE ABOUT CLUTTER WHEN GIVING GIFTS. Most people don't have the cash or the time to purchase gifts for everyone on their list. See if you can break tradition and reduce the clutter for everyone by drawing names at holiday time or just sending cards. Tell the people you're not buying for that you've pared down your gift list out of necessity and ask them not to buy for you as well. If you want to purchase gifts for them, flowers and blooming plants make welcome gifts—especially for people who don't want more clutter in their lives. Flowers are like visiting relatives—they come in, they are enjoyed for a short time, and they leave.

43. _____ Keep my briefcase, tote, or purse organized and clutter-free.

I'm a Walking Junk Drawer

I used to carry around a behemoth briefcase, packed with my planner, folders, and projects "just in case" I had time to work on them. After discovering I rarely had time to get them out and suffering chronic neck pain from a huge weight on my shoulder, I pared down. Now I carry a very small all-in-one wallet/purse and a smaller leather briefcase with my planner. I've also recently switched planner sizes from the Franklin Covey Classic to the Compact version. I've determined that if I'm productive during the day at work, there's no reason to attempt to take work home. My mantra is now "light and portable."

ALWAYS PUT IT BACK. If you put your keys and cell phone back in your purse each time you use them, you'll never have to launch a fifteen-minute search in the morning when you're racing out the door. Then always put your purse and briefcase in the same place so you don't wonder where you left them. Never say, "I'll just put this here for a minute" or "I'll only do this once." That's a bad habit waiting to be formed.

LOADING YOUR BRIEFCASE. Here are some ideas.

- Start with something lightweight and durable. I like Swiss Army and Kenneth Cole totes. Look for something with several built-in compartments and zippered pockets.
- Once a week, dump out the contents of your briefcase.

- Get rid of old pens, dry cleaning slips, extra change, and receipts you no longer need.
- Put library books in your car to be returned on your way somewhere.
- Remove and file project folders you no longer need and 100-page reports you won't have time to get to.
- Put items you use every day back in your briefcase—your PDA, phone, planner, and iPod—in their own slots/pockets.
- Organizing accessories are not just for women! Add a sunglass case, a zippered case for important documents like airplane or train tickets, and a mesh bag for small, easy-to-lose items like Post-It flags or pens.

JUST FOR WOMEN. If you must haul a mini-medicine cabinet, convenience store, and portable office with you, then at least do it smartly. Here are some additional tips for organizing a purse.

- Unload your purse each day. If you stuck a toy or snack for your kid in your purse or a magazine clipping someone handed you, be sure to take it out.
- Pare down multiple items. Do you really need to carry around six different colors of lipstick?
- Go through your purse and throw away grocery lists and receipts, old film and dry cleaning tickets, receipts for purchases you made six months ago, photos of people you don't know, and so on. Put toiletries and emergency items (like first-aid wipes and Band-Aids) into small mesh bags.
- It's inefficient to keep transferring items from a larger to a smaller purse when you don't want to carry the bigger purse around. If you're going to the zoo and might need those Kleenex, safety pins, and antiseptic gels, carry them separately in a fanny pack or backpack.

- If you work, it's always a good idea to keep your briefcase and purse separate, but have enough room in the briefcase to hold a (very small) purse. When you are carrying both of them or traveling, you can consolidate into one bag. However, when you want to go on a shopping trip, you don't want to take your entire briefcase with you.

POSSESSIONS quiz item 44

44. _____ Maintain clutter-free drawers and closets.

If It's Hidden, Am I Still a Slob?

June 2 each year (which happens to be my birthday) is recognized by Chase's Calendar of Events as National Leave the Office Earlier Day. I created this holiday to spark awareness of the need for productivity at work. In 2005, a television film crew came to my home office to interview me. As soon as I took that phone call, I told John that Fox News would arrive in one hour to film me for a segment that evening. "One hour?" he said. "You've got to be kidding!"

I heard the sound of rustling, dragging, and occasional dropping as John rushed to make his office presentable—just in case the camera guys wandered into it. After the interview with me, sure enough, the television team turned their attention to John. "What's it like living with her?" they wanted to know. "Are you organized like this, too?" John should have just fessed up right then and there, but he said something like, "I'm not too bad." So they wanted him to prove it!

When I walked into his office, I was rather surprised—it

looked great. The film crew was impressed. But I couldn't resist for long. I casually sauntered over to his desk and opened a drawer to reveal to the cameras the piles of paper he had simply stuffed in there. After interviewing me for one hour, I figured there was no way they'd include that ten-second bit filmed in John's office, but I was wrong. Apparently they found it funny enough that they aired it—and John has yet to live that one down with his friends.

Drawer Tips

USE TRAYS OR OTHER DIVIDERS. Having dividers allows you to find what you need when you need it and not purchase supplies just because you didn't know you already had more than enough. When purchasing supplies, look at your needs before going shopping, not once you've arrived at the store. Think of them as accessory items and products to support whatever you need *once you've determined what you need*. If you haven't yet decided, you'll simply add to the clutter with unnecessary products that caught your eye. Keep the clutter contained by using the best containers for your needs.

USE THE BABY FOOD AND KEEP THE JAR. You can take my father's idea and use baby food jars for thumbtacks, paper clips, and rubber bands—items that you really *do* use that can quickly spread out of control in your drawers.

KEEP EXTRA SUPPLIES AWAY FROM YOUR DESK. Keep a supply cabinet separate from the supplies you really use. You don't need ten boxes of staples, three rolls of tape, and twenty Post-It note pads in your desk drawer. Better yet, keep a supply caddie organizer on top of your desk for the items you need everyday and store the rest elsewhere.

PERMIT YOURSELF TO HAVE ONE JUNK DRAWER. Yes, you are allowed to have one junk drawer! I give you permission. If you have things you have no idea what to do with (film, spare keys, batteries, and other miscellaneous items), designate a drawer. But don't keep useless items that should be tossed such as dead batteries, dried-up pens, and leftover condiment packets from past lunches.

Closet Tips

Let's face it. You're not going to suddenly fit into those size-6 dresses you've kept since high school. And even if you can, they won't be fashionable. While they may have looked great on you, that ankle-zip, acid-wash pair of jeans from the eighties will *not* make a sudden stylish comeback. You need a closet overhaul! Here are some ideas to get you started.

BE CHARITABLE WITH ITEMS YOU GIVE AWAY. Go through your closet with the goal of trying to give away rather than throw away. Adopt the point of view that what clutters up your life may be useful in someone else's life. Give away shoes that hurt your feet. Weed out items you haven't worn in a year, that are saggy or too tight on you, or aren't comfortable. If you (or any member of your family) have outgrown clothes, find a better home for them than yours—it is called *Goodwill*. Only give away clothes that are in good condition, not those that are soiled, damaged, or worn out.

HOLD A TRASH BAG CEREMONY TWICE A YEAR. Throw away anything that has a negative image in your mind, of things gone wrong, of unrealized dreams. So if the color looks terrible on you—*out!* If you feel uncomfortable when you wear it—*out!* You'd be embarrassed wearing it if you ran into an old girlfriend—*out!* Fill that trash bag at least twice a year.

KEEP THE CURRENT SEASON'S CLOTHES IN YOUR CLOSET. Store out-of-season clothes in suitcases, in under-bed storage units, on closet shelves, in old trunks, or in large plastic trashcans with lids—anywhere but in your closet. Extra clothes make it hard to organize and find the clothes you need to get to quickly every day. I find time on Memorial Day weekend to switch to spring/summer clothes and Labor Day weekend to switch back to fall/winter.

DESIGNATE BINS AND BAGS. If you have a walk-in closet, you probably have room to keep three separate laundry bins for whites, darks, and colors. Sort your dirty clothes as you get undressed to make your washing chore easier. Keep a dry cleaning bag, a give-away bag, and a mending bag in your closet as well. When you notice a button is missing or a seam is coming apart, don't wear the item—put it right in the mending bag.

INVEST IN YOUR CLOTHES. Fellow speakers sometimes chide me about my insistence on wearing only St. John knits (an upscale line of women's clothing that travel well and don't require ironing) when I keynote a conference. However, I speak to one hundred different audiences in any given year, so I rarely see the same people over and over again. I prefer to buy only a few expensive suits each year rather than a lot of clothes at bargain prices. As a bonus, having extra space in my closet keeps my clothes from getting jammed together. Women need to learn from men, who don't seem to mind wearing the same clothes more frequently. Buying extra accessories such as belts and scarves can change the look of the outfit without adding extra pieces.

THINK "DEPARTMENT STORE" ORGANIZATION. Think about the signs that hang from the ceiling in a Target store; they indicate where you can find different types of items. In a similar way, hang your clothes by category and color. Use every inch of wall space for shelving or pegboards for costume jewelry. My husband even went so far as purchasing a label maker and creating labels for each type of item in his closet (heavy sweaters, light long-sleeve sweaters, short-sleeve sweaters, etc.), and stuck a label on the shelf beneath each pile to mark the contents. He added shelves to the wall above the hanging bar to store out-of-season sweaters. While business and dress clothes require hanging to stay wrinkle-free, sweaters, T-shirts, and workout clothes don't need hanging. If your closet is stuffed to the gills, try to move some items to drawers and shelves.

POSSESSIONS quiz item 45

> 45. _____ Organize memorabilia such as photos and keepsakes.

You Kept the Cork from the Wine Bottle?

Before taking the time to organize memorabilia, determine if it's something you should be keeping in the first place.

I can't tell you how often seminar participants have approached me to talk about a parent who's recently passed on and the difficult time they're having sorting through that parent's possessions. Instead of expressing joy at the treasures discovered, they express amazement at all the junk the parent kept: old bills, receipts from twenty-five years before, and photos of people they don't know. Most disturbing are the items the parent kept from childhood—not the childhood of the parent, but that of the child—such as identification tags from the hospital, a moldy pacifier, the first tooth. "I have no idea why my mom/dad kept this for me all these years. I don't want it and want to throw it away, but I feel bad since mom/dad kept it." Don't make the same mistake wasting time as your parents did.

Generally, people keep items that have sentimental value for *them* as reminders of people or good times. Their children rarely feel the same way about those items. Resist the urge to say, "I'm holding on to this for my kids, because they'll need it when they're older." Keep in mind that they may feel distressed about what to do with all the "junk" saved on their behalf. Before keeping a sentimental item, ask grown children if they want it saved for them. When children are young, limit the amount of things you allow yourself to keep to a large plastic container. Then gift it to a child at a certain age, say sixteen, so you don't have to tote it around all your life, just to have your child discard it when you die.

Check out these ways to keep things organized:

ORGANIZE PHOTOS INTO BOXES. Lisa Hill is a friend who's an amazing scrapbooker. Our daughters go to school together, so one day when I dropped Meagan off for a play date at the Hill house, I ventured downstairs for a look at Lisa's scrapbook design center. A huge rectangular table served as the assembly center. Bins and drawers were stacked neatly under the table and labeled with labels, stickers, scissors, and every imaginable shade of paper. Each time Lisa developed a roll of film, she painstakingly created pages just for that event: vacations, birthday parties, holidays, and so on. I stared agape at the rows upon rows of neatly organized scrapbooks on the shelves on the wall by the table and just shook my head. "You are absolutely amazing!" I exclaimed. It *was* amazing, but I could *never* in a million years find the time, energy, or excitement to organize my photos in this way. I tried scrapbooking and went crazy by the third page. It's just not my "thing." My solution? To purchase cardboard videotape boxes (the kind you can find at Target or Wal-Mart) to store my photos. I purchase one for each year and use twelve sturdy index cards (some boxes include these) to mark the months of the years. As I get my photos back from the developer, I simply file them behind the appropriate month. I write dates, comments, and occasions on the front of the index card, marking the photos that come behind it. This method is fast, simple, and organized. Although I'll never have the beautiful scrapbooks Lisa does, I'll still have the memories—and the ease of being able to find the photos! When people give me random photos they think I'd like, I might jot a note on the back, and then I roughly identify the month and file it. Close enough!

PUT KEEPSAKES IN TREASURE BOXES. When each of my children was born, I wanted to save all the little things from the hospital: the name tags on their cribs, the bracelets from their wrists, and their "going home" outfits. Add to that their first pair of shoes, their favorite (now cast-away) blanket or stuffed animal, their first lost tooth—what a bunch of stuff! So I got three of those sturdy plastic bins with a lid and designated one for each child. I keep each treasure box on the shelves in their closets and add to them as I come across a "must save" keepsake. From the Lillian Vernon catalog, I also purchased a cardboard "chest of drawers" that holds papers, schoolwork, and special craft items. I limit my collection to one treasure box and one set of drawers, so I can keep the kid memorabilia from becoming a tidal wave.

COLLECT YOUR CHILDREN'S ART PROJECTS. Lillian Vernon's cardboard "chest of drawers" mentioned above is perfect for storing your kids' art projects. The trick is to make sure you're only keeping the most special papers: original creations, "firsts," and items that weren't mostly created with the help of an adult. You could also get a three-drawer rolling storage cart from Target or anywhere plastic storage bins are sold. Each of my children has one of these craft chests in his/her closet. Or you can use an art portfolio, which stores flat and can only hold so much. Just remember that you can only keep as much as the chest, bin, or portfolio can hold. When you run out of room, you have to purge. Fawn over your child's projects as you should, but then, once they've moved on to other projects and concerns and won't notice, secretly throw most of them out. I have a single large envelope of very special art projects I created as a child that my mother saved; as an adult, I wouldn't want to own any more than those. Remember, you're saving for your children, so select the best for them and don't burden them with unnecessary clutter.

SET UP A BABY BOOK FOR EACH CHILD. Ideally, you would have started each child's book upon becoming pregnant, kept up with it as the child reached milestones, and completed it before you forgot everything that happened. If you didn't, don't despair. It's not too late to get a baby book, fill in the blanks, and gather as much information as you can. For me, my baby book is a real treasure. I love feeling the lock of my baby hair and looking at the little bracelet that had been placed on my wrist at birth. Your kids will certainly love to know the details of their births as they get older, especially when it's time for them to have kids of their own.

CREATE A SCHOOL MEMORIES BOOK FOR EACH CHILD. Again, I found an excellent book from Lillian Vernon. It has two pages for each grade K through twelve. In addition to giving lines to record activities, signature, friends, dreams, and vital statistics, the book has a pocket for each grade to store the most important documents: report cards, photos, letters to Santa, and small samples of artwork. To keep up, I wait until the school pictures come in from that school year. I paste the photo, fill in some of the blanks, and (here's the trick) give it to my child to fill out the rest. I keep them handy on the bookshelf in my office and throughout the year, I put important items (report cards, a special drawing, some writing) in the keepsake pockets.

POSSESSIONS quiz item 46

46. _____ Keep kids' toys, clothes, and books organized.

Toys Are Us!

When our kids are infants, toys are large, safe, and unbreakable. Tiny pieces are absent due to the potential chocking hazard, so it's easier to organize toys when kids are young. However, when your child hits three years of age (the magical age when children supposedly no longer put things in their mouths), toys with tiny pieces suddenly emerge—lots of them. My editor Trish Medved of Broadway Books and I both have boys named James around the same age, and we also both have older daughters. Trish expressed dismay at the tiny Polly Pockets shoes, clothes, and accessories that end up all over the house or get picked up by the vacuum cleaner. She asked me for reassurance that boys' toys don't have quite as many pieces as girls' toys. Unfortunately, I couldn't give her that reassurance: boys' superheroes have lots of weapons, ammunition, and clothes. Any family with children inevitably fights the battle of the messy toy monster. Having toys around is inevitable, but clutter is not.

Here are some organizing ideas to keep you sane:

KEEP WHAT GETS USED; GET RID OF THE REST. As you know, when your children grow, their toys change. At least twice a year, go through every inch of your kids' playroom or bedroom, sorting and organizing their playthings. Infinitely easier to do when the kids are *not* around, this chore should be done without their help because you're getting rid of their things. Your child may not have touched a toy in a year, but the minute you put it in the pile for charity, a wail rises up. Evaluate each toy individually for age-appropriateness, usage, and function. If your kids have outgrown it—*out*! If they never play with it—*out*! If it's too complicated—*out* (or stored away for when they get older). If you absolutely must keep a toy for memory's sake, limit yourself to a few precious objects and place them in your child's treasure box.

ROTATE TOYS. It's difficult for a child to find something to play with when faced with toys he or she has outgrown or simply too many toys. Make it easier on them and yourself by eliminating the least desirable choices, boxing them up for a sibling or cousin, or rotating boxes of toys each month. When a toy is out of sight, it's out of mind. When you take out "new" toys each month, it will be like a birthday! And you'll keep the volume down.

MAKE THE PLAYROOM EASY TO PLAY IN. Now that you've pared down the toys you keep, design a plan for these toys to actually get played with. If your kids can't see a toy, they don't think to look for it, and will soon forget it exists (and you'll probably discover forgotten treasures in the sorting process). Take advantage of any available vertical wall space in a dedicated playroom or on one wall of a bedroom by installing adjustable shelves. Leave more room between the floor and the first shelf to accommodate large items. Place the other shelves about eighteen inches apart. For the odd areas under the windows, purchase bins, carts, and storage units. Once you have your organizing equipment, group the toys in a logical order based on type. Invest $30 in a high-grade labeler so you can print and stick custom labels to the edge of the shelves, indicating what goes there.

We have large bins (we actually toss the lid, because they are hard for children to open and aren't very useful) for the following:

- Construction equipment
- Large animals
- Dress up
- Balls and outside toys

We have medium bins (no lid) for the following:

- Toy weapons and vehicles
- Superhero accessories
- Hot Wheels track and accessories
- Musical instruments
- Legos
- Books stacked vertically as in a bookshelf (I find that bins keep books from falling over)
- Blocks
- Dinosaurs
- Stuffed animals

We have small bins for the following:

- Plastic play dolls and animals
- Scratch paper
- Stickers
- Markers
- Crayons

- Colored pencils
- Craft items
- Blocks
- Pegs
- Puppets
- Electronic games
- Electronic books

We have two large rolling carts with three drawers each. One contains:

- Large superhero characters
- Medium superhero characters
- Small superhero characters

The second set of drawers contains:

- Small superhero pieces (discs, small plastic weapons used by superheroes)
- Sets of small items in individual sandwich baggies (Ninja Turtles with their weapons, wrestlers with their folding chairs and champion belts, etc.)
- Lace-up sets

We used to have a third set of drawers in a rolling cart that had Barbie dolls, Barbie clothing, and Barbie equipment. But when Meagan announced she was too old for them, I secretly bagged up her well-worn dolls and put them in the crawl space. When she's sixteen, I will give her the chance to keep (I hope) her old Barbies. If not—*out*! We keep larger toys, such as spacecraft, electronic games, and musical instruments on the shelves. Puzzles and games are kept in the box they came in. Don't toss the original box—you'll simply end up substituting bags with twist ties or other less durable options.

KEEPING TOYS IN BEDROOMS. Many homes don't have a separate playroom, and children keep toys in their rooms. The key is to take advantage of unused vertical space. Select one wall away from the bed and install shelves from the floor to the ceiling. Keep toys that are played with frequently (such as favorite dolls or superheroes) in plastic bins that can be stored underneath the child's bed. Use a chest at the foot of the bed with a lid that opens to conceal additional toys; this also doubles as extra seating.

ORGANIZE ENTRYWAYS. Make it easy for your children to keep their shoes, gloves, and jackets organized. We installed cubbies vertically up a wall in our mudroom, which is right off the garage, and assigned the highest to the tallest child. As each kid walks through the door, sunglasses, mittens, and hats are immediately deposited in the cubbies. Each child also has three hooks for jackets, coats, and backpack. Shoes are placed underneath the cubbies, so they are out of the way.

PUT LIBRARY BOOKS IN THEIR OWN TOTE. How many times have you brought your child home from the library with books that were then accidentally combined with their own books and hence forgotten? When you finally discover and return them you may end up paying late fees. Simple solution: Keep a separate tote for library books. The next time you go to a conference, keep the cheesy bag you get gratis to carry around your materials. Take it to the library with you and immediately put your checked books inside it to transport home. Train your kids to always put library books they've finished reading back into the special book bag. Meagan has a separate compartment in her school backpack just for school library books that need to be kept separately and returned. Using these methods, you'll never again have to rummage through a hundred books on your kids' shelves to find the borrowed ones.

SORT CLOTHES AND HAND-ME-DOWNS. My two boys are far enough apart in age that when the oldest grows out of something, it will be another season before my youngest can wear it. So I have designated a "future" area in each of their closets: hand-me-down for the youngest, James, and clothing I purchased on clearance for the oldest, Johnny. I purge their drawers and closets once a season, move anything now ready to wear into drawers, and move anything that's too small into a charity bag. Goodwill and other charities will often call once a quarter and pick up giveaway items from your porch. When they call, just say yes, and use the deadline as encouragement to get the task done.

POSSESSIONS quiz item 47

47. _____ Set up and maintain my kitchen in an organized fashion.

Man Is a Cooking Animal

I believe the kitchen is the most essential room in the home to organize. We spend so much time putting groceries away, preparing meals, and doing dishes, it's important to maintain an organized space.

Can you easily prepare a meal without having to empty an entire cabinet to get to your pan? Can you find your paprika? Do your drawers look as if a tornado has ripped through them? Don't despair. You can whip your kitchen into shape using a few simple tips.

BE PICKY ABOUT WHAT YOU KEEP IN THE KITCHEN. Items you use once a year (such as the punch bowl, ice cream maker, popcorn popper, and the deviled egg tray) shouldn't be kept on counters and might not even need to be in the kitchen at all! I keep mine on top of the cabinets in my laundry room, adjacent to the kitchen, so they are out of sight of guests and don't take up space in my kitchen, but aren't too far out of reach if I need to get one down. If you rarely use cookbooks, don't display them proudly on the countertop where they take up valuable space. Can they go on a bookshelf in your office?

TOSS, TOSS, AND TOSS AGAIN. Attempt to move, throw away, give away, or recycle whatever you don't need or use. How many plastic grocery sacks do you really need? Your seven-year-old no longer needs the lidded sippy cup and plastic elephant circus cup. How many cheese graters do you need? Toss any unidentifiable doodads and gourmet gadgets you never use. If you have ten knives, but you really only like three because they are sharp enough and easy to hold, get rid of the other seven.

SEPARATE OUT FREQUENTLY USED ITEMS. Your fried eggs are burning on the stove, and you can't find a spatula in your utensils drawer because you're pawing over the pastry blender, wire whisk, and apple corer for the hundredth time. Keep the drawer closest to the stove reserved for frequently used utensils—spatulas, ladles, and slotted spoons. We keep our top five utensils in a ceramic jar right on the counter next to the stove. Keep the corn-on-the-cob holders, potato masher, and eggbeater in a different drawer.

CORRAL POTS AND PANS. You need the big Dutch oven to make your world-famous chili. It's in the back of the cabinet, behind the skillets. You take everything out, including the other pots you were storing in the Dutch oven. You put everything else back, make the chili, wash the pot, then do it all over again in reverse. No wonder the chef is cranky! Convert your cabinet shelves into pullout shelves that are actually modified drawers. Or use expandable shelves to fit the width of your cabinet, such as Closet-Maid's large expanding shelf (www.closetmaid.com for store locations). You could also use sliding baskets like a filing cabinet (I like the mesh sliding cabinet baskets at www.organizes-it.com). Or install a chef's pot rack that hangs down from the ceiling to give you easy access to your cookware. Other systems let you use the inside of a pantry door, such as the Elfa door and wall rack (www.containerstore.com).

FREE UP COUNTER SPACE. Install a shelf to hold smaller, infrequently used items such as salt and pepper shakers, canisters, and coffee cans. Also consider installing small under-cabinet appliances such as a can opener and toaster. Create new counter space by purchasing a cutting board that spans and hooks on the sink. If you have enough floor space, you can purchase a wheeled cart with a butcher-block top. Hang a wall grid for utensils and a pot rack from the ceiling like professional chefs do.

DON'T SAVE WHAT YOU WON'T EAT. One of my pet peeves is people who cook something they didn't particularly enjoy and box up the leftovers! If you didn't care for it much the first time around, you'll like it even less the second time. Throw it away! But you say, "It's too good to throw away," and you put it back into the fridge—until it turns *what* color? If you do save something, use disposable containers, so you don't have to wash double dishes or mess with plastic wrap.

CLEAN OUT YOUR REFRIGERATOR REGULARLY. Know the shelf life of different foods. Soft cheeses (like cream cheese), lunchmeat, milk, and fresh meat are good only three to five days after opening. However, yogurt, eggs, hard cheeses, and ice cream can last two to three weeks. Frozen items, condiments, and pickles can last several months. Every few months, do a complete overhaul by taking out all items on one level and washing the shelves thoroughly.

ALWAYS PUT THINGS IN THE SAME PLACE. Designate different areas of your refrigerator by food category. We keep the open bottle of milk on the door for accessibility. We have two beverage shelves, one for tall items such as unopened milk, juice containers, and bottled water. We have another shelf for sodas, juice boxes, V8 cans, and other small beverages. Then we have a dairy section for butter and eggs, a drawer for lunchmeat and cheese, a shelf for condiments, a leftovers section, plus the vegetable bin. The kids have their own drawer for yogurt in a tube, applesauce containers, Jell-O, pudding, fruit packs, etc. They know where everything goes, so they can get themselves a snack without asking for my help. Buy children a small Tupperware milk container and keep it full, so even young children can pour their own milk and get cereal independently.

POSSESSIONS quiz item 48

48. _____ Keep my car organized and clean.

A Two-Ton Trashcan on Wheels

I never pictured myself driving a minivan. As a kid, I thought I'd rather die than drive one of those ridiculous-looking station wagons. They definitely weren't cool. But, alas, I'm a minivan mom.

Granted, it's a *cool* minivan, because it has so much storage space and the doors open automatically. With three kids, often their friends, and all their junk, I've decided a minivan is an essential piece of organizing equipment. Because it's *so* big and roomy, the three kids have managed to trash it by the time a trip to the zoo is over. Food wrappers and used Kleenex litter the floors, and empty juice boxes and toys cover the seats. When the car pulls into the garage, the kids know to grab as much as they can; no one is allowed out of the car empty-handed. If the car still has junk in it, additional trips are required until it's once again clear. If you let the mess go, it soon becomes overwhelming and requires a much bigger effort to clean. Don't allow yourself to settle into your home until your car is clear of clutter. Even when babies are infants, you can grab the carrier in one hand, throw the diaper bag over your shoulder, and grab whatever you can manage in the other hand. Then one extra trip out to the car (before your child starts to protest) goes a long way. Get your kiddo settled then run out to grab any last remnants. Systematically clearing one area at a time will give you a sense of completion and help you feel calmer.

Believe it or not, you can actually organize the clutter! Especially on longer trips, you need lots of stuff, so having the right organizing tools makes cleanup so much better. The latest car models have many neat organizing gadgets built right into them: center consoles for sodas; underseat drawers for CDs; large glove boxes for maps, tire gauges, and car care books; remote-control holders or preprogrammed buttons. Still, many things that are "homeless" in your car just end up getting tossed about. The solution is to create a home for every type of item you need in the car. Over the years, I've discovered great accessories that will keep your car from looking like a hurricane went through it.

You could do a Google or Froogle search for these items, and

I will give a specific recommendation where applicable. Check these out.

BACKSEAT ORGANIZERS. Kids want to bring coloring books and markers, handheld games, water bottles, and superheroes or dolls with a million tiny pieces, etc. They either end up all over the seat or strewn about the floor. The simple solution is a back-of-seat organizer by Case Logic (www.stacksandstacks.com). Put it on the back of the seat in front of your child's seat. You'll be amazed as little fingers take their things in and out of the pockets. Adults can use them to stash the umbrella, ice scraper, camera, maps, and so on. If you'd rather have a cooler hanging over the seat, try the Lewis N. Clark insulated seat-back cooler (www.ebags.com). If your little ones like to draw, get the Axius backseat travel tray (www.axius.com) with a fold-down tray, just like on airplanes, for activities requiring a sturdy work surface. That way, your budding artists won't lose their markers under the seat when you have to slam on your brakes.

CENTER CONSOLES. If your front seat has one long seat or doesn't have a newfangled organizing console between the seats, buy one! Center consoles come in handy in the backseat between two warring children who typically fight over the extra space between them. Try the canvas High Road kids backseat organizer (www.ajprindle.com). It straps into the backseat between the kids and has different-sized pockets, outside drink holders, and a top that can be flipped over for playing travel games. In the front seat, it can be used for extra sodas as well as the garage door opener, sunglasses, cell phone, or anything you use frequently and don't want to search for as you drive.

PASSENGER SEAT ORGANIZER. This is my favorite. When I'm loading up for a trip, the front passenger seat is usually the catchall for my directions, apple, protein bar, the CD I want to hear, and my extra water bottle. Whenever I would hit the brakes, my apple used to roll under the seat and my water bottle went flying. Enter the handy Lewis N. Clark seat caddy organizer (www.ebags.com), which straps into the front passenger seat and keeps everything you need in a pinch readily accessible and organized.

TRUNK ORGANIZATION. The trunk is typically "clutter's last stand" and serves as a catchall for homeless items. We realized we had a problem when soccer balls were on the loose, a milk jug toppled and spilled milk everywhere, and my new potted plant overturned and created a milky mud mess. So I went on a search for a way to systemize that vast trunk. Although having the big space is great (thanks, Honda), it's difficult to secure loose items. My solution is twofold. The Axius Easy Access trunk organizer (www.axius.com) neatly corrals the jumper cables, flashlight, first aid kit, and coolant. In front of that, the Highland three-pocket storage net (www.cargogear.com) restrains sports equipment, groceries, and plants. It's big enough for a small cooler as well. If you'd rather have an organizer that's portable, the Creekside Cargo Mini (www.drivewerks.com) might do the trick. With its firm sides and adjustable section dividers, it keeps groceries firmly upright.

DRY CLEANING. If you pick up your dry cleaning rather than having it delivered, install your own clothes rack. The adjustable LoadMaster car bar (www.containerstore.com) mounts quickly between any two outside walls to create a hanging bar and stores away when not in use.

DOG DIVIDER. If you want to keep your pooch out of the front seat, use the Bauer Doggon' pet barrier (www.stacksand stacks.com) to keep Fido in the back of your minivan, SUV, or wagon. It is safer for your dog and your family.

CDS AND TAPES. I like using my CD carrying case I picked up at Best Buy. My friend swears by her visor CD holder by Case Logic (www.casedirect.com). It quickly converts your sun visor into a handy, quickly accessible storage space for twelve CDs. There's also a mesh pocket for receipts or toll money. Or if you own a mounted DVD or VCR, you need a full-blown organizer with more space. Try a backseat model like the High Road entertainment organizer (www.thebusywoman.com) with pockets for videos, CDs, and tissues.

TRASH. I used to simply use the side pocket on my door for trash, but it was so small, filled up too quickly, and looked bad. Now I use High Road's bottom-weighted collapsible wastebasket (www.thebusywoman.com). I keep it on the floor in the middle between the front seats. It doesn't tip over and has a Velcro top that prevents spills. For backseat riders (e.g., children) who have larger garbage needs, the High Road TrashStash may be perfect (www.containerstore.com). With its three-gallon capacity, it won't fill up quickly. Whenever I'm stopped for gas and hanging around waiting for it to fill, I dump the trash. Find an automatic car wash in your area that has vacuums available, so you can keep your car neat, inside and out.

POSSESSIONS quiz item 49

49. _____ Set up an effective office space in my home.

Have Bunny Slippers Will Travel

I've worked full-time from my home since 1992 and can't imagine doing it any other way. Whether you work full time out of your home, occasionally telecommute, catch up on work in the evening, or run a household, you need some sort of dedicated office space in your home. Offices can serve as the family computer center, a place to do paperwork, and the occasional work-at-home office.

The first big question is where to locate your home office. Until recently most builders hadn't caught on to the popularity of a built-in home office. If you have a computer, you probably need more than an antique writing desk in the living room. But if you only use your office to pay bills, write letters, and return phone calls, you can get away with a corner of the kitchen.

In most homes, extra space is difficult to come by, so you'll need to get creative. I've seen people attempt to use a hallway, part of a bedroom, and even a closet. However, it's difficult to work while children are running around, when you see your bed and think about napping, or when you're too cramped. So I've always commandeered the formal dining room or living room—no one ever used it anyway so it was wasted space. Or perhaps you can steal the guest room or space in a finished basement or attic.

SET YOURSELF UP FOR SUCCESS. If you are going to be working from your home full-time, use this checklist to ensure you're set up for success and maximum productivity.

- Where will you set up your home office?
- How will you modify the space to meet your needs?
- Can you lock the door? Can you lock the windows?
- Do you have sufficient lighting for that area?
- What office supplies will you need?
- Where are the electrical sockets located? Will you need additional power sources?

- Do you have enough storage space, such as a file cabinet, bookcases, credenza, closets, etc.?
- Where will you store backup disks? Is the storage area safe from fire, flooding, etc.?
- If your home office is in the basement, and if the basement tends to get damp, do you have a dehumidifier?
- Do you have a personal computer that you already use at home? Will you need different software or to upgrade the RAM? Will others need to stop using it for personal purposes?
- Do you have sufficient office equipment for your home office?
- Do you have a desk? Is it large enough to do office work?
- Do you need to have a modem installed on your home computer?
- Are there sufficient phone jacks in the area you've designated for your home office?
- Do you need a separate fax line, Internet line, and business line?
- Do you have voice mail or an answering machine?
- Do you have a smoke detector in your home office area?
- Do you have a fire extinguisher located near your home office?

Regardless of whether you work from home full time or a few times each month, your home office has some common requirements.

Furniture and Storage

- A professional office desk and worktable
- Sturdy filing cabinets and drawer space for files. Invest in quality pieces that won't fall apart

- An ergonomically correct chair
- Bookcases or shelves to hold binders, trays, phone books, and reference manuals
- Stackable storage units that maximize your space vertically
- Large wastebasket
- Supply caddy/accessories
- Stackable trays for "in" and "out" boxes
- A large, standing document sorter with slots for envelopes, fax paper, letterhead, etc., that fits under your desk for easy access

Computer and Peripherals
- A computer with lots of RAM, a large hard drive, and a DVD burner
- External backup system (like www.godaddy.com or an external drive)
- DSL or cable or satellite Internet connection (dial-up is too slow)
- High-security remote access to your offsite office computer (like www.GoToMyPC.com)
- USB hub such as Linksys 2.0, which has seven easy access ports to plug in your keyboard, iPod, PDA docking station, digital camera, USB flash drive, etc.

Software
- Spam filter, such as *McAfee*
- Internet security and virus protection, such as Norton Internet Security
- Spyware protection, such as Webroot
- Integrated contact management, such as ACT (my favorite) or Goldmine

- Fax within the computer, such as WinFax Pro
- Postage, such as www.stamps.com, www.pitneyworks.com, or www.dhl.com
- Accounting, such as QuickBooks Pro for business or Quicken for home only
- E-mail software, such as Microsoft Outlook
- Calendar, such as Microsoft Outlook, or a paper planner, such as the ones available at www.franklincovey.com

Other Technology and Equipment

- A separate business phone line and fax line if you conduct business from home, so your clients don't get voice mail saying, "You've reached the Smith residence."
- Wireless headset (I use GN Netcom plus receiver lift)
- Cell phone and PDA, which can be separate, but optimally a SmartPhone, which includes PDA and e-mail access
- Pager or text pager (only if you're required to carry one)
- High quality laser printer, copy machine, and scanner (separately or all-in-one)
- Telephone with voice mail

Who knows? Setting up a clean, organized, productive office space at home might allow you to consider more work-at-home time or other home-based business opportunities.

POSSESSIONS quiz item 50

50. _____ Keep my house neat and tidy up daily.

An Empty Room Signifies an Empty Mind

I want to begin this section by making a distinction between "neat" and "organized." For example, the Denver Water Board, one of my clients, brought me in to organize a National Clean Off Your Desk Day (yes, there is such a day!) contest. This "holiday" falls on the second Monday in January each year. We had three categories: most organized, most improved, and messiest office. I took "before" photos of each person's office. Next, I gave a seminar on getting organized and putting systems in place. Contestants had one week to get organized. Then I took an "after" photo. We posted the before and after photos on the employee cafeteria wall, and employees voted on the most improved.

I, however, was the sole judge of the most organized and messiest office categories. I went to the office of a woman who was competing for the most organized office. Wow! There were no papers on her desk—or anywhere for that matter. Files were out of sight, and everything looked neat and tidy. I remember thinking, "Is this the right office? Does *anyone* work here?"

I walked over to her overhead bin and opened it . . . and a pile of papers came crashing down upon me! She had simply taken her piles of papers and stuffed them into cabinets and files. Her coworkers peeked in and began to tell on her. "She's really not like that!" "She just cleaned up for the contest!" Cleaned up? The title is for the most organized, not the tidiest office. There's a big difference, isn't there? Just because it's neat doesn't mean it's organized.

But it is important to keep an area neat. Eliminating items from surfaces forces you to get the area organized. Putting things out of sight gives your home a peaceful, rather than chaotic, feeling. Cluttered surfaces quickly remind you what requires your focus in order to maintain your systems. Here are some ideas for keeping an area neat and free from clutter.

PUT AN ITEM CLOSER TO WHERE IT BELONGS. John puts his credit card receipts in my office in-box, and I give them to my bookkeeper once a week. The kids know to put their school papers or nifty artwork on my office desk for safekeeping. They've learned that if it's on the kitchen counter, it's eligible to be tossed, so if they want Mommy to look at it, they put it on her "safe zone." If I see toys out of place, I'll toss them in the playroom as I wander by. The second time I have to touch a toy, it goes into time-out for twenty-four hours. After all, the kids have an entire room for their toys; they know how to throw them in there and put them back on the shelf. They also know not to expect Mommy to do it.

USE A STAIR-STEP SYSTEM. Our three kids have bedrooms upstairs. If I had to run up and down the stairs each time I wanted to return Johnny's stuffed elephant to his room, I'd have fabulous thighs but a lot less time. So we've designated the bottom stairs as our catchall place, and we all put things on the stairs that are headed up. As the kids leave various items around the house—books, stuffed animals, socks, or anything that belongs in their rooms—I place them on the stairs. Each time I must go upstairs, I grab something and toss it in the right room (that each person must keep clean). The children check the stairs before they go up and take anything with them that's theirs. I've been known to withhold a dollar of allowance because an item ended up on my living room floor instead of the stairs. Because the kids know it's an interim place, they are less resistant to putting things there. It means they don't have to run up both flights of stairs—at least for the moment.

NEAT DOESN'T MEAN FANCY. When John and I were first married, I was a single mom. I only had to worry about Meagan's schedule, my speaking career, and the house. I actually had much more discretionary time than I do now with a husband, a bigger house, and two more children. In those days, I made up my bed every day with eight (no exaggeration) pillows. After marrying John, life got more complicated, and I no longer had time to maintain my pillow ritual. "What happened to the fancy pillows?" John asked one day. "Oh, they're only kept around for pillow fights," I replied as I threw one across the room at him. Making the bed doesn't require fancy pillows to make it look neat. Now I stick with a comforter and a couple of pillows, and I can toss up the bed in no time.

DON'T PUT THINGS DOWN "JUST FOR NOW." How many times have you put something down "just for now," and that item still sat in the same place a week later? Temporary places too often become permanent places. It's better to put something away while it's in your hand than to allow large piles of clutter to accumulate. If clutter does build, take a moment to straighten rooms as you leave them. It sounds simple, but if you devote a few minutes each day to putting stuff away room by room, it will prevent a whole-house de-cluttering session later.

CHAPTER SIX

Mastering the Sixth Pillar—

PAPER

WHEN PEOPLE MOVE, one of the first things they do is arrange to receive their mail at the new location. No matter how technologically savvy we become, we can't eliminate paper. In fact, various studies estimate we generate up to ten times more paper than we did before the advent of the computer! Whatever happened to the promise of a paperless office? And how much of that paper is sitting in stacks on multiple surfaces all over your home and office?

I met my husband, John, at a friend's barbeque and volleyball party. John knew my friend's roommate. When I first saw John, I thought he was the most handsome man I'd ever seen. So I approached him (duh!) and started chatting. When I asked him what he did for a living, he replied, "I'm a mailman." I was instantly smitten . . . my grandfather, God rest his soul, was a career letter carrier. Now I tell people I married the mailman! People always look at me knowingly and say, "The mailman always knocks twice, eh?"

I loved the image my Grandpa Herbie created in my mind of his work ethic when he would repeat the mail carriers' mantra, which is a paraphrase of a quotation from Greek historian Herodotus: "Neither snow, nor rain, nor heat, nor gloom of night, stays these couriers from the swift completion of their appointed rounds" (which appears carved over the entrance to the Central Post Office building in New York City). Unfortunately, Herodotus never gave us guidelines on what to *do* with all the paper those devoted mail carriers bring. John couldn't tell me, either. He was only responsible for delivering the piles of mail.

This chapter provides solutions on what to do with the mail that ends up in your home and the mountains of paper that seem to appear out of nowhere. Read on, and learn to make your bill paying, filing, reading, tracking, and scheduling more manageable.

PAPER quiz item 51

> 51. _____ Consistently purge my files without fear.

This Is My CYA Paper File

Before you embark on an overhaul of your filing systems, you must first purge all the old junk. Why spend time dealing with paper you're just going to toss anyway?

If you don't purge regularly, you will have to buy more filing cabinets, look for a home with a dedicated "office" space, or add a room to your home—none of which are exactly attractive options. Any unnecessary duplicates, outdated draft copies or otherwise outdated materials can and should be thrown away *before* you clutter your life with more file cabinets!

You can purge your files in one of two ways: either purge as you file or during mega-sessions a few times a year (my preferred method). At the beginning of each calendar year as I'm preparing for tax time, I remove all files I want to keep for history (bank statements, credit card statements, charity donations, etc.). I put the files in white cardboard archive boxes and label them with the year. I keep the previous seven years' worth of records stored in my basement. I create new hanging files to replace these purged files (if I get audited, I don't want my papers jumbled together). At midyear, I go through my files and do another purge, removing and tossing the items I haven't used in a year.

Getting your files organized is actually a five-step process, which I call my 5-P System:

1. Purge: get rid of outdated information
2. Plan: map out your new system and equipment
3. Purchase: get what you need
4. Place: get the new stuff ready and in the right place
5. Put: file the papers into their new homes

Here are some guidelines on what to eliminate or move:

- Old newspapers (they contain old news!)
- Catalogs you didn't request (if you want to buy something, look for it online)
- Financial records (anything older than a year should be moved out and stored in cardboard archive boxes)

- Business cards from others (input the data into your contact management software and toss the cards)
- Old college term papers (how often have you referenced these?)
- Outdated policies (if you no longer hold the policy, you don't need it)
- User's manuals for items you no longer have and warranties that have expired
- Old calendars with "pretty pictures" (donate to a school or nursing home)
- Greeting cards (those that serve no sentimental purpose or plain-vanilla variety)
- Filed cartoons (if you file them, you won't be able to laugh at them)
- Stacks of magazines you haven't touched in years (enough said)

Unfortunately, some people have a fear of dumping. They hoard things because of a Great Depression mindset. You likely have a Depression mindset if your mother always told you:

- Don't throw anything away.
- Everything has value.
- You can use it again.
- Waste not—want not.
- Eat everything; the children in [a poor country] are starving.

These instructions may have been valid during the depression of the last century, but old tapes like these playing in our heads have actually created a society of pack rats, who during the Digital Age, desperately need to throw things away. Strike a balance between saving everything and recklessly throwing everything away. My husband will say I err on the side of reckless tossing. Keep in mind, however, how much you toss that you never need again. If about once a month I say, "Hmmm . . . that's maybe one I could have kept," I think I'm doing a great job. I'd rather err this way than keep too much, wasting time, energy, money, and space hanging on to things.

How do you get over the fear of dumping? Have you ever said, "I'd better keep this because you never know . . . it might come in handy sometime," or "I threw something away once, and don't you know, I needed it again the very next day?" We've all had this experience. However, consider these:

- How often does that happen, compared with the times papers are discarded and never needed again?
- If you have not reorganized your things in a long time and your backlog is severe, you probably wouldn't have found it again anyway.
- Almost everything is replaceable and you could get another copy if you really needed one.

Perhaps you've lived in the same community for eighteen years and receive the cultural arts calendar for a local community center. You have never once attended an event there, but someday you intend to. Instead of throwing out the calendar, you put it down randomly, not sure where to store it.

Ask these tough questions:

- Why should I keep this? (Not "Can I throw this away?") You can always think of a possible reason not to toss something. "I might need it someday" is not an acceptable answer.

- Can I get another copy? If an organization or another person tracks this information as well, let them be the librarian and refer others to the appropriate person.

- Do I have time to ever read this? If it's been gathering dust for two years, you're probably not going to use it, try it, or do it. Get rid of it!

- How often will I refer to the information? Believe me, you're not destroying the past. You are not erasing the history of your company by throwing out a memo or report. You are simply making a decision about whether an item has enough value to warrant the time, energy, and cost of saving it.

- Does it exist in an electronic copy? With computers, much of what we create exists in soft copy. Why also keep a hard copy? No need to have duplicates of everything (assuming you have a proper computer backup system in place).

Save it only when it is (1) the only copy, (2) you will need to refer to the information in the near future, (3) you are required by law to keep it, or (4) it is a necessary part of a project file you're working on. If the community calendar doesn't fit into one of these categories, toss it.

And if it's simply "too good" to part with, recycle it or give it away. Those beautiful cards you get all year from fundraising organizations can be given away to a grade school for craft projects rather than dumped. If you have an old pile of magazines you won't have time to read, take the whole lot to a doctor's office or take it to work for others to read. One friend uses cards and unread magazines to make collages with her daughter. While her daughter is snipping away, she can find that worthwhile recipe or bit of information she needs.

---

52. _____ Create and maintain a filing system that allows me to find papers easily.

I Filed It So Well, I Hid It From Myself

There are three types of papers you must file:

1. "Action" papers you need to see or do something with on a certain date.
2. "Project" papers related to redecorating projects, PTO, kids sports, committees, etc.
3. "Reference" papers you don't need to actively use but need to refer to periodically.

Creating a filing system encompassing all the different types of paper that come into your home seems like a daunting task—one that many people put off for as long as possible. Your personal productivity will come to a halt if you have no idea what happens to a document or piece of paper after you read it or finish with it.

USE THE TICKLER FILING SYSTEM FOR ACTIVE PAPERS. A tickler file is the single most important thing you can do to organize your papers. Think of the tickler file as a calendar for paper. It is a well-sorted and well-managed in-box. It is an essential ingredient for running any household. It allows you to pace yourself better, eliminate piles from surfaces, and keep all your reminders in one place. After you adjust to this system, you gain confidence that items you've filed out of sight will pop up again.

To create it:

- Get forty-three hanging (Pendaflex) files. Thirty-one of them are labeled for the days of the month (1, 2, 3, 4, etc.) and twelve are labeled for the months (January, February, March, etc.).

- Hang them in a file drawer, a hanging file box with a lid and handle, or a rack that sits on a surface.

- Put the current month's folder first, followed by the day. So if today were May 17, the May file would be first; behind that the number 17, then 18, 19, etc. through 31. Then June would come next, then 1 through 16, because the 17 is behind May (you're only rotating thirty-one days). Anything beyond the thirty-one days is put in a monthly file.

- Each day, you look in that day's numbered file for the items you need to handle that day. Then you rotate that file to the next month, so May 17 would go behind the 16 in June and become June 17.

Let's walk through an example, with today being May 17:

- You purchase a birthday card for a friend whose birthday is May 28. You want to remember to send it in time, so you file it in the 25 folder. When you look in the file on May 25, you will take out the card, write in it, and put it in the mail.

- Your family is going on vacation over the Fourth of July weekend. You file the plane tickets in the July folder, because the numbered folders stop on June 16.

- You're attending a wedding on June 6, so you file the invitation with the directions in the 6.

- A friend wrote you a letter; you're going to be very busy the next few days and won't have time to write back until the weekend, so you file it in the 22.

- You pay bills twice a month on paydays, which are the first and fifteenth of the month. You file bills in either of those days, depending on when the bill is due.

- You returned a sweater to the department store and want to make sure the credit is applied to your credit card. You file the receipt in the day you typically receive your credit card statement to remind you to check it.

- Your son has show-and-tell at kindergarten on Wednesdays, and you always forget to send him with something. You file the flyer from the teacher on the following Tuesday, so you see it in time to pack his bag.

- You pull a page from a catalog to order a really cute Halloween costume, but your daughter might change her mind, and it's only May. So you file it in the September monthly file, so you remember to think about it then.

- Your church is changing the room locations of the Sunday school classes and e-mails you a new map with class assignments. You print it and put it in the tickler for the next Saturday, so you remember to put it in your purse to take with you.

- You ordered a part for your broken washing machine online and printed out the receipt. The company promised to send it in seven business days. You file the receipt in that date, so if it comes up, and you haven't received the part, you remember to contact the company for status.

If you're going on a trip, review activities for the days you'll be gone before you leave. Knowing you have covered everything gives you peace of mind and helps you enjoy your travels. Customize the contents of your files to fit your needs. Find a system that works for you. For example, you can use two calendar files (one at work and one at home), or you can transport personal papers from home and incorporate everything into your work file. Frequent travelers often use an expandable accordion file that fits in a briefcase.

USE THE STEP FILING SYSTEM FOR PROJECTS. Buy a metal step file, which is a vertical file with each level a little higher than the other (thus, it looks like steps). The step file holds file folders (not hanging) in a way that allows you to see the name of each file, one above the other. (I don't like stackable files, because it's harder to retrieve and add information.) Every time I start a new project, it gets a new folder. Then you can add information directly to it, rather than creating little piles of paper on your desk. For example, I currently have files titled:

- Artwork for Grandpa
- Bedroom redecorating
- Bible Blast
- Girl Scouts
- PTO Committee
- Newsletter
- Receipts (to be processed)
- Soccer club—James
- Soccer club—Johnny
- Taxes 2006
- T-Ball

For larger projects, with many things happening at once (such as sitting on boards of directors), I create a binder with tabbed sections, rather than having a file folder bursting at the seams.

USE THE MARKER FILING SYSTEM FOR REFERENCE ITEMS.
Doesn't it make sense to group files of the same type or category together? Rather than repeating the word "insurance" every time you label an insurance file, create a marker in your files to indicate that all files behind it will be related to insurance. To begin, get a bunch of hanging files (like Pendaflex) and different colored plastic tabs (I use yellow and blue, in addition to the white that comes in the box). To create the marker, cut some hanging files apart along the bottom fold (lengthwise), so you're left with two halves. The marker itself doesn't hold any information. To designate the marker, use a yellow tab in the first position (most hanging folders have five tab placement positions). In the example above, the yellow tab would simply have the word "Insurance." All the actual files related to insurance (using a white tab in the middle position for the main file and a blue tab in the fifth position for a subfile, if needed) would be filed behind the marker.

Think of how your computer's operating system organizes files with this folder-within-a-folder scheme—breaking out levels and groupings—getting narrower as you go. You can do the same with your paper files! File alphabetically by the markers, which are so broad you never forget what you called them. Once you set up your system, make a list of all the titles for reference. You can check the list before making a new file to see if it already exists or trigger your memory about where to file existing information.

PERSONAL FILE DIRECTORY FOR LAURA AND JOHN STACK. Here's my template you can use to begin creating your filing system. All the words on the left margin, in capital, bold letters are the markers (yellow tab, first position, on a half of a hanging file). The files themselves are listed underneath (white tabs, middle position), and any subfiles are indented (blue tabs, fifth position).

CAR

AAA

Honda

Infiniti

CATALOGS

CHURCH/CHARITY

Cherry Hills Community Church

Compassion International

Young Families Group

EDUCATION

Bright Beginnings

College Planning

Primrose

University of Colorado

University of Phoenix

Washington & Jefferson

Wildcat Mountain

ENTERTAINMENT

Colorado Ideas

Gymnastics

Holidays

    Halloween

    Christmas

Ocean Journey

FINANCIAL

Bank Statements

    TCF, business

TCF, personal

Credit Cards/Statements

    American Express

    Discover

    Express Toll

    JCPenney

    Norwest

    Sears

    USAA MasterCard

    United VISA

Credit Report

Financial/Retirement Planning

Flexible Spending Account

Insurance

    Automobile

    Business Insurance

    Claims

    Homeowners

    Life

    Medical

    Personal Articles

Investments

    American Century

    Salomon Smith Barney

    Thrift Savings Plan

    Waterhouse

Merchant Accounts

    American Express

    Discover

    National Processing Company

Mortgage

    Burberry

HOUSE

INTERESTS

LEGAL

MEDICAL

Dental (multiple)
Diet (multiple)
Eye (multiple)
Osteopathic (multiple)
Physical Therapy (multiple)
Stack, James C.
Stack, John J.
Stack, Johnny K.
Stack, Laura
Stack, Meagan

TRAVEL

Brochures
Frequent Flyer
 American
 Continental
 Delta
 Northwest
 United
 US Air
Hotels

UTILITIES

Cable
Electric/Gas
Phone
 Lightyear
 T-Mobile
 Qwest
Trash
Water/Sewer

WARRANTIES/INSTRUCTIONS
(this alone takes an entire file drawer!)

Appliances, Large

Appliances, Small

Baby Items

Burberry

Cordova

Cottoncreek

Computer

Electronics

Exercise Equipment

Furniture

Jewelry

Miscellaneous

Tools

Once you have your system set up and loose papers filed in the appropriate folders, make sure you maintain it by filing every week. If you don't keep up with your system, you'll soon have a two-foot pile of papers that will take you hours to organize again. When you are going through the 6-D System (see quiz item 53, below) and you come across an item to keep, take a second to write the title of the proper file on the upper right-hand corner of the document. When you go to file it, you don't want to have to reread each piece of paper in order to determine where it should go.

PAPER quiz item 53

53. _____ Follow a daily processing system for staying on top of the mail and paperwork.

I'm Drowning in a Sea of Paper!

When I was a young girl, I didn't get any mail and got along quite well without it. The first time I felt excited about getting mail from my parents was on my first sleepover summer camp. Then came the magazine subscriptions and letters from friends and family. As high school ended, the trickle increased with college materials, catalogs, and magazines. Getting mail became a constant after entering college, with newly acquired bills to pay. The floodgates opened fully after I became employed for the first time and paper obligations increased, worsening with business ownership. Parenting made the deluge bigger yet with warranties on baby gear, school rosters, take-out menus, health plans, etc. Finally, as my mother-in-law Eileen tells me, the mail dwindles at retirement—just at the point in life when I'd enjoy getting friendly letters!

Here are some tips for dealing with the daily deluge:

COLLECT ALL YOUR PAPERS. Wherever you are in your home when you bring your mail inside—the side table by the front door, the washing machine by the garage door, or the kitchen counter—that will become your trouble spot. So buy a wire bin and designate it as your collection point or in-box. Mine is located in my home office; my friend Melissa keeps hers in the kitchen; others use the dining room table. Drop the mail there; instruct kids to unload backpacks with permission slips and school papers there; ask your spouse to leave credit card receipts there, etc. Train your family members that *any piece of paper they want you to see* must be put in this bin.

GET THE COLLECTION TO YOUR "OFFICE." The key is to take this bin to your office area (see quiz item 49) for processing (see below), ideally on a *daily* basis. If you don't visit your office area daily for the most part, it's okay to let it build up for a couple days. Going much beyond that, however, will make the task too daunting.

USE THE 6-D SYSTEM. As you process your mail, remember this: There are only six things that you can do with any piece of paper:

1. **DISCARD.** Get rid of it, permanently, by tossing or recycling. Sort your in-box over a trash can and throw away, shred, or recycle as much as possible. Be ruthless. Most mail is junk. Toss catalogs without reading them and throw out junk mail envelopes without opening them. I keep a small paper shredder handy near my desk so I can quickly destroy any credit card offers and checks that come with promotional offers.

2. **DELEGATE.** Route each item to the appropriate person. No routing system at home? Make one! Determine the best spot in your home to locate mail folders. Buy a vertical file bin. Use a different color file folder for each member of the family: for example, Mom is red, Dad is blue, and the kids are green, yellow, and purple. File mail in the appropriate person's folder. If you need to give an instruction or make a comment, jot it down on a sticky note and attach it to the item before filing it. It's also a good idea to keep plain envelopes (stamped and labeled with a return address) nearby. Then, if you discover an article that might interest your sister, you simply cut it out, place it immediately in an envelope, address it, and put it in your "out" bin.

3. **DO.** If you have the time to complete, review, sign, or reply to an item in less than three minutes (such as an RSVP to a party), do it immediately. Get it done the first time you process it. Investing the time now will save time in the long

run because you won't review that item over and over again. Paying a bill actually takes more time, since you have to gather all the pieces and might not have the cash in your account that day, so it makes sense to batch that a few days a month. You might not want to toss the coupon mailer in step 1, because there might be something good in there, so immediately open it and spend three minutes figuring out what's worth keeping and toss the rest.

4. **DATE.** For items you can't work on immediately, ask, "*When do I need to see this again?*" and file in your tickler file on that date (see quiz item 52).

5. **DRAWER.** File items you want to save that don't require any action. You can file items in an action file, such as "to be read," "to be copied," "to be faxed," "computer entry," or "to be filed." Or you can put the paper in the appropriate project file. Or place it in your "to be filed" bin to be filed in your reference files. You can also have a "to create a file for" folder for items that don't yet have a home in your filing system.

6. **DETER.** Halt the information; keep it from getting to you in the first place. You can stop junk mail, e-mail, and faxes by visiting the Direct Marketing Association at www.the-dma.org. If you don't have time to read that magazine, cancel the subscription. If you never order from that catalog, call the company and ask to be removed from the list. Curtail any unnecessary flow of paper into your home.

OHIO—ONLY HANDLE IT ONCE. You've heard the old adages;— don't shuffle paper ... touch it one time ... immediately put it back where it belongs. If you pick up a piece of paper and read it, your brain formulates a response or reply. If you put it down again without doing something, you have just wasted time. The next time you go to pick it up, you'll have to read it again, think about it, and decide what to do—what a huge opportunity cost! Do you ever review the same piece of paper three, ten, or twenty times before you do anything with it? Instead, use the OHIO principle to force yourself to make a decision about the item, using one of the options from your 6-D System.

PAPER quiz item 54

> 54. _____ Handle bills in a timely fashion and keep up with recordkeeping.

Oops, Where Was This Hiding?

In the Denver area, where I live, and in most major metropolitan areas, road construction is a reality. Because of the heavy traffic volume, new light rail stations are being constructed and highways are expanding. The funny thing is that the construction experts estimate that by the time these projects are completed, capacity will have already outgrown this new infrastructure. Additional cars will quickly fill in the newly painted lanes, and we'll be back to gridlock!

Do you ever feel this way about your bills—that it doesn't matter how hard you work paying bills and reducing the volume of paperwork on your desk, it always builds up again. But instead of building a bigger road to keep up, I suggest dealing with the sources of the problems rather than the symptoms.

Here are some typical problem areas:

- More than one checking account in the family. Even married couples have been known to keep separate accounts. People try to explain it's simpler that way, but it's not that simple. If you get divorced, half belongs to the other person anyway.

- Multiple credit cards. This is a sure way to get into financial trouble. John and I use a single United Airlines mileage credit card: one bill, one payment, one account to track, and lots of miles to earn free tickets for family vacations.

- Having a poor filing system. I've often heard people say they find bills buried in a pile somewhere, long after they've come due.

How can you deal with these problems? Here are some ideas:

GET THE RIGHT PEOPLE ON YOUR BUS. You don't have to handle your finances alone! Depending on the level of complexity of your situation, you may need one or all of these people to help you:

- Financial advisor/broker
- Banker
- Accountant
- Bookkeeper
- An online bill-pay service
- Someone who manually pays bills

USE AUTOMATIC OR ONLINE BILL PAYING. Online bill paying has revolutionized the way I pay my bills. I resisted this for a *long* time because what if, for some reason, the money wasn't in my account at the scheduled day? I realized that my bank's online bill-pay service didn't have the flexibility I wanted. Then I found www.paytrust.com. For around $20 a month, they pay all my bills for me: I receive an e-mail when they receive a bill. I click on the link and specify when I want it to be paid and from what account (personal or business). I can change my mind and the date any time. Once it's paid, I receive a second e-mail with the notification. I can print the bill if I want to, but I usually don't to reduce filing and because I can easily access my accounts through the company's computer. I no longer have to open, organize, write, and mail my bills. The investment each month is definitely worth the time I save. You can also pay bills through your bank's online service, but it generally takes a lot more work on your end to set it up. PayTrust did it all for me. I haven't found a downside yet.

PROCESS PAPER-BASED BILLS EFFICIENTLY. Granted, some people don't want to use online bill-paying methods. Unless you're extremely organized, I wouldn't recommend paying them as they come in, simply because of the time it takes to gather the necessary supplies to pay a bill. It's much easier to pay eight bills at one time than pay eight one at a time. So when you receive a bill, start with the obvious: open the bill. Do *not* put it back in the envelope. (I see people folding and unfolding, reading and rereading things, and putting bills in and out of envelopes. This is a waste of time and space.) Instead, toss the envelope and any little inserts that came with it. Rip the ad off the envelope flap and toss it (do *not* bother to look at it). Rip the payment portion of the bill off the statement and put it in the payment envelope. Only pay bills twice a month (usually around your paydays), let's say the first and the fifteenth. File the bill in your tickler file on one of those two days, depending on the due date. Staple the rest of the statement together and file it in your "to be filed" bin. The entire process of processing a bill in this manner should take no more than one minute. I don't bother writing check numbers on bills; I've rarely ever needed to know a check number. In the case of an error, you can always go back and look at the duplicates (you do have duplicates, don't you?) of your checks.

USE ACCOUNTING SOFTWARE. Instead of manually figuring your checking account balance, you could enter the check numbers, recipient, and amount in an accounting system like Quicken. Then you can look up the company in the accounting software and instantly find all related bills, amounts, dates, and numbers.

PAPER quiz item 55

> 55. _____ Know where to put every piece of paper I receive.

Where the Heck Does *This* Go?

Along with the many categories of paper handled elsewhere in this chapter or book, I'd like to mention special areas of paper clutter. Entire books have been written solely on the subject of paper management (I like Barbara Hemphill's *Taming the Paper Tiger*), so I'll only cover a few highlights here.

COUPONS. Most coupon cutting is a waste of time. Cutting coupons limits you to a small discount for a specific item. I find most grocery store loyalty programs have a better in-store value on similar items. By the time you cut, organize, store, transport (and remember to use it before it expires), you're better off signing up for their discount card. At checkout, you automatically are entitled to the discount listed on the shelf pricing.

Let's say I want to buy canned green beans. I go to our local King Soopers, which carries five or six different brands of green beans. One or more of those brands is almost always on sale. This week it's the ABC brand that is regularly $.79, and this week it's $.49. Let's compare that to cutting a $.25 coupon for Green Giant vegetables. Green Giant green beans are $.89 minus $.25 for a total of $.64. Not only is the other brand cheaper with the in-store discount, but I had to find, cut, and organize that coupon, and then remember to bring it, all before it expired.

By shopping for your entire list this way, you'll save 25 to 30 percent off your entire grocery bill. Your tape will be twice as long because of all the discounts! So by being a little more flexible in the brand you select when shopping, you are able to save a great deal of money. When you find something on sale, buy more of that item, so you have enough until another item is offered in-store at a discount.

Before you leave for the grocery store, also check that store's "online specials" and print out coupons on a timely, as-needed basis. When you arrive at the store, grab the flyer by the door and do a last-minute quick scan for products you might want to purchase.

RECEIPTS. What do you do with all those receipts? You saw in quiz item 52 where to file the actual warranty or instruction manual in the reference filing system. But what about the receipt for the item? I recommend that every home needs an inexpensive copy machine (you can get them for as little as $50). When you purchase something, say a bicycle for your child, put the receipt in the "Receipts" project file until you have reconciled your credit card or entered it into your accounting software; then make a photocopy of the receipt and staple it to the inside of the instruction manual; then file all of your receipts in your reference file in an envelope behind "Receipts," starting a new envelope every two weeks. If you need to return something, you can easily find the original receipt. Some people just staple the original receipt to the instruction manual, but I like to keep my financial records separate from the warranty information, so a copy works for me.

IDEA FILES. Do you tear out and keep articles and little scraps of paper on projects you may implement in the future? I have another step file on my credenza with manila folders dedicated solely to ideas: Book, Booklets, Business Issues, Consulting, Marketing, Presentations, Products, Publicity, Technology/Equipment, Vendors, and Web site. As I tear out or print out material related to my speaking career, I simply drop it into the appropriate idea file. When the time comes for me to update my Web site, I just grab the folder and review all the great ideas I've captured in the past year. You could keep idea files on gardening, computers, bathroom redecorating, etc. The difference between an idea file and a project file is you are not currently working on idea files. When you decide to plant the garden, it becomes a project folder and gets filed with your other projects.

SUBJECT FILES. What about all those trade journal articles, magazine tidbits, Internet studies, and statistics you find that are handy for personnel issues, procedures, and reference information? I have a paper system and an electronic system to handle these items. Again, I use folders, but now I use expandable Pendaflex folders in a filing cabinet to accommodate the more voluminous material I gather. For example, I have folders marked "Time Management," "Information Overload," "Life Balance," "Stress Reduction," etc. I file hard copy information here, generally from magazine articles and newspapers. You could keep subject files on Child Care, Gifted Education, Discipline, Communication, Travel, Business Start-ups, etc.

MEETING RECORDS. By putting this point in writing, I run the risk of being flogged by a few people, but it must be said. If you happen to sit on a board of directors (as I do with the National Speakers Association and NSA Foundation) or sit on a committee or attend a regular association meeting, you'll be inundated with information including minutes, agendas, task force reports, committee reports, schedules, policies, new business, old business, financial data, and more. Because of my NSA commitments, I receive no fewer than six big three-ring binders each *year*. And with a three-year term, renewable for two terms, that adds up to a lot of shelf space. I know some of my colleagues have saved these troves from the beginning. I just toss them out after the meeting is over and transfer actions to my master list. I have no desire to keep binders for posterity or pomposity. They only serve the purpose of guiding the group in the discussion process. I take notes in my planner on anything requiring my action or memory. If I ever need anything, I call the association directly and ask questions of the competent staff (whose job is to retain and store all that information). The only exception to this rule would be to keep binders if you're the incoming president, so you can carefully monitor the year prior to your being president. To that end, I have created binders for other NSA board members to help them carefully track the information they'll need.

56. _____ Handle phone calls and voice mail productively.

Don't Call Me: I'll Call You

Rrrrrinnnng! Should I answer the phone or let it go to voice mail? That's an important consideration—one that deserves exploration. What you want to avoid is the proverbial telephone tag—you leave a message, I call you back, you're not there, I leave a message, you call me back to leave a message . . . Sometimes the most efficient thing to do is to pick up the phone when it rings. Issues can often be handled in one minute versus the ten minutes you'll spend thinking about calling back and leaving voice mail messages. Other times, however, you are flowing nicely on a high-priority project and know if you break your concentration to answer the phone, you'll get sidetracked. Perfect time to let voice mail take over.

Here are additional telephone timesaving tips:

- When leaving a message, give the person a specific time you will be available for a return phone call.

- Shorten the social niceties. Although you can't launch right into, "Hey, I need you to . . ." when someone answers the phone, you also don't need to spend ten minutes chatting on the front end before you state your business.

- Remember, it takes less time to speak words than to write them. A one-minute phone call can deliver the same message it might take ten minutes to compose in e-mail. Pick up the phone instead.

- Reduce travel by experimenting with three-way calling and teleconferencing, if you've never tried it, even from home.

- Use a wireless headset. I love my wireless headset. It allows me to answer my phone from any room in my home. I'm not tethered to the base of the phone, and my hands are free to pull a file, water the plants, or get a glass of water.

- Plan your message before you call. There's nothing more frustrating than a stream-of-consciousness voice mail. Before I make a multi-issue call, I take a few seconds to jot some bullet points about what I need to discuss. Then I go through the list in an organized fashion.

HANDLING VOICE MAIL OR ANSWERING MACHINE MESSAGES. My phone company offers voice mail as part of our phone service, so we use that; others use answering machines to pick up their messages. If you're concentrating on a task, trying to get out the door, or if the baby's screaming and knocking peas everywhere, it's a good idea to let your calls go into voice mail. Now the trick is organizing the messages. You could keep a phone in your office area, retrieve messages there, write a note, and put it in your tickler file for action. Or you could keep a list of phone calls separately on your daily to-do list, logging them as you receive them. I use my Franklin Planner to list them. Some of my seminar participants have had success with a phone log. It's a spiral notebook that allows them to keep all phone information in one place and maintain a historical record should they need it—such as providing "proof" that you notified someone.

To create a phone log:

1. Get an 8½ × 11 spiral notebook.
2. Put the date you started using it on the front cover. When it's full, add the ending date, so that you can see the range of messages contained within it.
3. Date a new page each day.
4. Number (starting over each day) and code the calls as they come in or out:

   I = Incoming call (live)

   O = Outgoing call (whether you get them or leave them a voice mail)

   V = Voice mail message (your personal voice mail)

   M = Message given to you by another person (pink slip, sticky note, etc.)

   Laura = message for Laura

   John = message for John, etc.

5. Include all pertinent information, including the name, number, and summary of the message. If recording a message from another person, throw the scrap of paper away after you've transferred it. Any corresponding action required on your part will be written on your to-do list.
6. Cross out the messages as you handle them.
7. Use a large fastener to clip completed pages together and bind them to the front cover. This way, you can open right up to the current day.
8. Keep the log near your telephone.
9. Keep the notebook as a record for future reference as long

as required by your organization, or until you're comfortable that you won't need the information again.

10. If the kids are old enough to answer the phone, they are old enough to take a message and note to whom it is addressed. No message—no answer.

VOICE MAIL 6-D EQUIVALENTS. The 6-D System I outlined in quiz item 51 can also be applied to voice mail. When you are first listening to a voice mail, do one of six things with it:

1. **DISCARD.** Delete it.
2. **DELEGATE.** Forward it or write a phone message for another person and put it in his/her mail folder.
3. **DO.** Reply or call back if you can respond in less than three minutes. If your voice mail system has an automatic reply feature that sends a message right to the person's voice mail, you don't have to speak voice-to-voice.
4. **DATE.** There are several options when dating a voice mail message:

- Make an entry in your phone log as described above.
- Write a note in your planner on the day you need to respond.
- Write the information on an index card and file in your tickler file.
- Create a new task in Outlook or your electronic to-do system, noting the person's name, number, and information in the text field.

5. **DRAWER.** Transcribe the information (only if no action is required) and file in the appropriate project or reference file.

6. **DETER.** Contact the caller and remove yourself from the distribution list. To keep others from leaving a voice mail, turn off your answering machine or put a vacation greeting on the recording.

PAPER quiz item 57

> 57. _____ Use technology to reduce paper and complete tasks quickly.

My Brain Has a Loose Wire

At home, do we spend more time in front of our televisions or our computers? If you guessed television, you're wrong, according to an Insight Express survey of 500 home PC owners, 57 percent of Americans are likely to point and click, rather than channel-flip; 62 percent expect to increase computer use over the next year.

However, the study did not break down computer time into *what* people are specifically doing while using it. My guess would be that most of that time is spent surfing the Internet and using e-mail. Most people don't take full advantage of the wonderful software programs available to help them automate what would normally be a paper-based task or activity.

PLAN THE YEAR BEFORE. When you receive cards, tear off the return address labels and tape them to a piece of paper. Put the sheets in a file marked "holiday card list," and that will be your card list for next year. If you use a Rolodex or address book, put a small red check or mark next to those who sent you a card. At the same time, you can add any new names and update your information. Next year, you simply flip through your list and address a card for people who have a check by their name.

CONTACT MANAGEMENT SOFTWARE. Better yet, consider putting your old handwritten address book into a contact management package such as Outlook or ACT. Add all your names to a database with a field called "card." Put a "Y" for Yes in this field when you receive a card. Then instead of hand-addressing the envelopes, run a report for the individuals whose "card" field equals "Y," and print self-stick labels for those records. Or code them as "friends" or put them into a group called "Holiday Card." Learn the technical aspects of the contact management software, and you can send a mailing with a few clicks.

BREAK THE PROCESS DOWN. Now, let's say it's holiday time again. Many people take one look at that mound of Christmas cards and can suddenly think of three or four other things that require their immediate attention. If you love getting cards but hate the prospect of sending yours, you may be tempted to procrastinate until December 22 and pull another 2:00 a.m. shift to get them in the mail by Christmas. Instead look at sending your cards as a process and break the project down into smaller pieces to make it seem more manageable.

Traditionalists will cringe at my next suggestion of creating a newsletter and doing a mass mailing, thinking it's much too impersonal. If you love handwriting the same message to people because it adds a personal touch, then of course do it. If this is important to you, efficiency in your case is irrelevant. I personally cannot stand handwriting cards, but my more remote friends and family do expect an annual update of family happenings. Here's how I automate my holiday mailing: First, I create the labels. Second, I stick them on the envelopes with a return address label and stamp. Next, I write the family newsletter and get it copied onto special holiday-themed paper. Finally, I set up an assembly line: (a) add a salutation to the card such as "Dearest X Family," (b) sign our names, (c) enclose the newsletter and a picture, and (d) seal the envelope with a sticker. No licking for me! If you prefer to handwrite your cards, the trick is to write five each day, starting the day after Thanksgiving. Take some with you wherever you go, in case you find some free time: at the doctor's office, waiting for a meeting to begin, or picking up your child from a lesson.

WORD PROCESSING SOFTWARE. I've done a holiday newsletter for five years. I've even signed my cat's name by tracing her paw prints at the bottom. My son James added his signature last year with a few crayon scribbles. Buy special colored paper with a pretty border and copy your newsletter onto it.

ACCOUNTING SOFTWARE. If you use a bookkeeper, he or she will insist that you use an accounting software program like Quick-Books or Quicken (nonbusiness version). If you don't use a bookkeeper or accountant, you should learn to use the software anyway. Imagine being able to print checks right to your printer with a few mouse clicks; being able to look up payments by name, date, amount, or number; balancing your checkbook without doing any math; never forgetting to enter a purchase in your manual bookkeeping system; or having automatic tax reports generated at the end of the year. All this is possible, and more! Take a deep breath, buy the software, install it, and go through the Wizard that pops up when you load it. You'll be on your way in no time. You'll be so relieved that you'll never look back!

RESEARCH. The Internet is great for conducting research on brands and prices. When I left my laptop computer on a plane (yes, I really did . . . the lady two rows behind me was having a heart attack), John turned the loss in to the insurance company and went shopping for a new one. He didn't drive around to every store in Denver; he just surfed the Web for the best price. He found a $750 coupon to boot (www.techbargains.com), and we got a brand-new computer for less than the original one I'd lost! John also uses the Internet to check on library books, make hotel reservations, and find the cheapest airline tickets.

REDUCE TIME AT THE MALL AND POST OFFICE. Make use of catalogs that will gift-wrap and mail the present for you. Buy gourmet gifts from an online bakery or specialty store to have on hand as hostess gifts when you attend parties—nuts, jams, teas, dried fruits, and candies make excellent gifts. Wrap extras for a guest who shows up unexpectedly and gives you a gift. Send a hard-to-buy-for individual a gift certificate from a nice restaurant or tickets to a theater or special event. Teens especially love cash and gift cards so they can purchase what they want (which saves you time). Also, order your stamps online instead of standing in line.

E-MAIL. You can use the 6-D System I discussed for paper for your e-mail as well. Here are the equivalent action steps:

1. **DISCARD.** Delete it.
2. **DELEGATE.** Forward it.
3. **DO.** Reply immediately if it will take you three minutes or less.
4. **DATE.** There are several options when dating an e-mail message:

- For e-mails that require action (assuming you use Microsoft Outlook), drag them to Tasks, which will open a new task window and automatically move the e-mail message to the text portion of the window.

- For time-sensitive e-mails (meetings or appointments), drag them to Calendar, which will open a new calendar item and automatically move the e-mail message to the text portion of the window.

- If you'd rather work with a paper copy, print the e-mail and file it in your tickler folder. Create a personal folder called @Tickler and drag e-mail that requires follow-up there. When the paper copy comes up in your tickler file, you know the original is in your @Tickler folder. That will save you from having to retype the e-mail message when you respond to it.

- Copy the e-mail into the contact's record in your contact management software and schedule an activity to follow up.

5. **DRAWER.** If no action is required, but you'd like to keep the e-mail for reference, create a personal folder for the project or reference type and drag the e-mail to the correct folder. Or you could create a Word or other word processing document and save it on your hard drive.

6. **DETER.** Unsubscribe from e-mail lists and tell your friends to stop sending you their "joke of the day"! Or use Alerts (under Tools) or other rules to automatically move e-mail from particular people to certain folders (or just delete them).

CREATE A THROW AWAY E-MAIL ADDRESS. Spam can be annoying and time consuming. In a test, Northeast Netforce investigators seeded 175 different locations and monitored the fake addresses over the next six weeks for spam; 100 percent of e-mail addresses used in chat rooms received spam; 86 percent of posts in news-groups received spam. So what can you do to help reduce it? Bottom line: Don't use your work address or personal address for open, public forums, where spammers are harvesting your e-mail address. Create a screen name that isn't associated with your e-mail address, or a dummy e-mail address. Your ISP can automatically forward the dummy address to your real address. When spam builds up, delete the decoy. For $9.95 a year, you can get a block of 500 disposable e-mail addresses to use from www.Spamex.com. You can also purchase spam-filtering software for your computer, which grabs junk e-mail and files it in a special folder, separate from your real e-mail in the in-box (my favorite is McAfee Spamkiller, www.McAfee.com).

AUTOMATE PERSONAL ACTIVITIES. Another fun computer project is creating automated electronic birthday greetings from the Internet. Perhaps you'd enjoy creating a family calendar, adding soccer games, birthday parties, PTO meetings, doctor's appointments, vacations, or anything else that affects the schedules of multiple people. You can print it out and post it on the refrigerator, so people can write in new events. You can periodically update the calendar, tossing notices as soon as they are entered. Some software packages allow you to create customized, automated grocery lists and recipes. Any of these activities can be both fun and productive; in addition, you will experience measurable results from your investment of time.

> 58. _____ Keep insurance, medical documents, wills, and important papers up-to-date and easy to locate.

If I Die, Can Anyone Find the Marriage Certificate?

If you die tomorrow, will your loved ones be able to manage your estate and affairs quickly and easily? Do they even know what you have and where things are?

They will be grieving and stressed enough by their loss, so make organizing easy on them by creating a document called "Important Personal Information and Locations for (your name)." Make sure to keep any passwords separate, and inform your loved ones of where you will locate these items (safe, hidden area, filing cabinet, computer, bank, etc.). To get started, here's the template I created. You can find the electronic version at www.TheProductivityPro.com at Free Stuff under the Resources menu.

Personal Data

FULL LEGAL NAME

Name on Birth Certificate:

Other Name(s) Used:

Birth Date:

Birthplace:

Country of Citizenship:

State of Residence:

Home Phone:

Work Phone:

Present Address:

MOTHER

Name:

Birth Date:

Birthplace:

Date of Death If Deceased:

Present or Last Address:

Phone Number:

Spouse:

FATHER

Name:

Birth Date:

Birthplace:

Date of Death If Deceased:

Present or Last Address:

Phone Number:

Spouse:

BROTHERS AND SISTERS

Name	Age	Address	Comments

SPOUSE

Name:

Name on Birth Certificate:

Birth Date:

Birthplace:

Citizenship:

Date of Marriage:

CHILD (REN):

Present Name:

Name on Birth Certificate:

Birth Date:

Birthplace:

Adoption Date (If Applicable):

Present Address (If Living Apart):

Name of Spouse:

Name(s) of Children:

GOVERNMENT IDENTIFICATION DATA

Social Security Number:

Medicare Number:

Medical ID Number:

Veterans Administration Number:

PERSONAL ASSOCIATIONS ADDRESSES

Closest Friend and Confidant:

Clergyman and Church:

Attorney:

Physician:

Accountant:

Bookkeeper:

Tax Consultant:

Stockbroker:

Banker:

Insurance Agent:

Business Associates:

IMPORTANT ITEM LOCATION DATA

Safe Deposit Box Number:

Safe Deposit Box Key(s) or Password:

Original of Last Will:

Copy of Last Will:

Original of Trust Agreements:

Copy of Trust Agreements:

Original of Contractual Papers:

Copy of Contractual Papers:

Power of Attorney:

Driver's License Number and State:

Birth Certificate:

Death Certificates:

Marriage Certificate:

Citizenship:

Adoption Papers:

Real Estate Deeds:

Mortgage Papers:

Financial Records:

Retirement and Pension:

Social Security Records:

Tax Records:

Titles, Licenses, and Deeds:

Insurance Policies:

Military Service Records:

Government Papers:

Medical Records:

Directive to Physician (Living Will):

Other Legal Papers:

Retirement Papers:

Survivor Benefit Papers:

OCCUPATIONAL AND EMPLOYMENT DATA

Occupation:

Name of Employer:

Address (If Different from Self):

Phone of Employer:

Position Held/Duty Title:

Date First Employed:

Prior Address Data

From	To	Number and Street	City	State	ZIP code

Insurance (life, medical, auto, long-term care, disability)

Name of Insurance Company:

Policies carried:

Address:

Effective Date of Policy:

Property Insured:

Type and Amount of Coverage:

Policy Number:

Asset Data

CHECKING ACCOUNT

ID Number:

Location:

Type of Ownership:

Present Value:

SAVINGS ACCOUNT

ID Number:

Location:

Type of Ownership:

Present Value:

CERTIFICATES OF DEPOSIT:

NOTES AND ACCOUNTS RECEIVABLE:

SECURITIES:

BONDS:

STOCK:

MUTUAL FUNDS:

REAL ESTATE:

INSURANCE—CASH VALUE:

Personal Property

AUTOMOBILE(S):

VIN Number:

FURNISHINGS:

Item:

JEWELRY AND HIGH VALUE ITEMS:

Item:

Liability Data:

CURRENT LIABILITIES:

Monthly Rent Payment:

Average Monthly Utilities:

Average Monthly Phone Payment:

Average Monthly Credit Card Payments:

Average Merchant Credit Account Payments:

Automatic Savings:

Other:

LONG-TERM LIABILITIES:

Home Mortgage and Other Real Estate:

Secured Notes and Loans:

Unsecured Notes And Loans:

Life Insurance Loans:

Contingent Liabilities (Suretor/Cosigner):

Legal Judgments:

Other:

Financial Statement Data

CREDIT REFERENCES

Name:

Address:

Phone Number:

Account Number:

Information (date)

Signature

Store important originals of papers such as wedding photos, birth certificates, and wills in a fireproof box or move them into a safe deposit box. Ask, "If my house burned down, what can I not replace?"

PAPER quiz item 59

> 59. _____ Use a calendar system to track family members' schedules.

Where in the World Is My Family?

People often ask me how to track and sync other people's schedules with their own. The important thing to remember is to use *one* calendar that contains *all* your personal, family, and work commitments. If you attempt to use one calendar for work, one for family, and one for school, for example, you'll inevitably have conflicts. You try to schedule a late meeting at work. You vaguely remember that you have a conflict that day for your daughter, but you've left the weekend calendar at home. Bad outcome. If you use a daily planner for your work activities and a wall calendar at home for your family plans, make sure that every family event that affects your personal time also gets recorded in your planner.

Make these suggestions work for you:

COMMAND CENTRAL. Designate one place in your home as "command central" for your family. Assign each person a color. Each person has a corresponding pen color to write in appointments on the family calendar that will affect more than that one person. If your child needs a ride, for example, that time is listed on the family calendar in that child's color or with colored dot stickers of the type used at garage sales. Each week, keep your personal calendar updated with anything that will affect your time.

WORK/HOME CALENDAR. Make sure to write personal activities or children's school events on your work calendar as well, so you don't have conflicts. I know one man who kept a detailed schedule in a handsome leather diary. Unfortunately, it only contained his work commitments Monday through Friday. At home, he used a family wall calendar his wife maintained. That was all fine and good, except the personal commitments that affected his life never got transferred into his work diary. One Saturday, his son had a regional championship soccer game. The Friday before, the boss called an emergency meeting for that Saturday and asked team members what time would be most convenient. Of course, because his weekend calendar was at home, he vaguely remembered he had something going on but couldn't think of it. Inadvertently, he scheduled the meeting right over his son's soccer game. He said that one of the hardest things he had to do was tell his boss he couldn't meet at that time after all and needed to reschedule. (You thought he'd choose to miss the soccer game, huh? Fat chance!) Because the line between work and home blurs so much, it's critical to have the ability to see your entire schedule at one time.

CALENDARING SOFTWARE. Some families prefer a large, paper wall calendar to track their various schedules and commitments. Others don't have the wall space or have more technological savvy and can use calendaring software. Software programs like Microsoft's trusty $50 Works 8 gives you all the features you need for a calendar without the triple-digit price of its bigger sibling, Microsoft Office. A noteworthy feature is the ability to let up to four family members create and merge their own color-coded calendars, so everyone is up to speed. If different people are maintaining separate Outlook calendars, you can share and synchronize your calendars with groupware programs such as www.familyscheduleronline.com, which allows family members to access the family calendar from any Internet connection. ShareCalendar (www.4team.biz) allows your family members to receive updated Calendar items (appointments, meetings, events) by regular e-mail. It lets you update and manage all your shared Calendar folders offline or using any Internet connection.

In my case, I have multiple people who need to be aware of my travel activities, including my employees, my husband, my family, and my clients. But they all work virtually in different locations. Our solution to this particular dilemma is a Web-based calendar. Many different versions are available on the Internet; we use one specifically designed for professional speakers and meeting professionals at www.eSpeakers.com. Each day, these individuals can pull up my schedule on the calendar and know exactly where I am and when I'm available.

PAPER quiz item 60

60. _____ Organize and keep up with my reading.

So Much to Read, So Little Time

According to the January 2003 edition of *Publishers Weekly*, several indicators from the last six years offer some pessimism about the long-term prospects for books and reading. First, Americans are spending less time reading, down to 109 hours a year in 2001 compared with 123 hours a year in 1996. Second, the number of households buying at least one book a year has dropped, falling from 60 percent in 1996 to 56.5 percent in 2001. Lastly, consumer spending on books rose 16 percent between 1996 and 2001, but unit sales dropped 6 percent (meaning readers laid out more money for books, but actually bought fewer of them). Here are alternatives to books that people are finding.

LISTEN TO AUDIO RECORDINGS. Your local library probably has a books-on-tape section. Instead of purchasing a book and trying to find time to read it, you can listen to the audio version in your car or in your home while you work. If not immediately available, most audio books can be located on interlibrary loan or ordered from your local bookstore. Or if you're really hip, you can download audio magazines and books onto an MP3 player or PDA and listen to them while you're on the treadmill, on a plane, in a taxi, and so on. I find them less clunky than books on tape, plus I don't have to return anything. The listening options are expanding nicely. Sites like www.audible.com, www.mediabay.com, and www.audiofeast.com are uploading hundreds of new hours of content each day, ranging from *Forbes* magazine and the *Harvard Business Review* to books ($21.95 a month for two books). If you're not quite ready for managing electronic audio files, you can get audio books in CD or DVD versions and listen to them on your computer.

SUBSCRIBE TO E-MAIL NEWSLETTERS. Many consultants, speakers, trainers, and authors provide a weekly or monthly e-zine, designed to educate and inform subscribers about subjects of specific interest. If you want ongoing tips about being more productive, for example, please sign up for my free monthly newsletter, *The Productivity Pro*®, by visiting my Web site at www. TheProductivityPro.com.

CANCEL HARD COPY SUBSCRIPTIONS. Evaluate your subscription list on a regular basis. If you find yourself falling behind in reading the magazines you're paying for, let selected subscriptions lapse. Instead, use your local library and the Internet to locate information on an as-needed basis. Many books, magazines, and newspapers are also available in electronic and audio formats. You can read them on your PDA, listen to them on your iPod as an MP3, or tune in on CD or tape as you drive.

If you enjoy reading the old-fashioned way, here are some tips.

USE A READING BASKET. When you first receive new reading material, scan the table of contents. If nothing appeals to you, toss it. If you're a ripper (like I am), tear out the interesting articles and toss the rest. Put your articles (or entire magazine, if you must) in a large wicker basket with a handle that can be picked up and moved easily. Keep your reading supplies—a mini stapler, pens, paper clips, highlighter, stamped envelopes, etc.—inside your reading basket.

FIND A CONVENIENT, QUIET PLACE TO READ. I absolutely cannot read with my three children running around like banshees, so I usually give up my attempts and join them. When I can, I like to read on airplanes or in my bedroom retreat area in my comfy rocking chair.

DITCH THE DULL. If you find something boring, stop reading it! There's no law that says you must finish every book you start. If you don't like it, I give you permission to *not* finish it. You'll hear your parents' voices saying, "Finish whatever you start." Nonsense! Or if you come to a tedious part of the book (where it takes two pages to describe the lobby of a hotel), you can skip it without guilt.

CREATE A TABLE OF CONTENTS FOR JOURNALS. Some people receive beautiful, expensive trade magazines or journals they simply can't bear to tear apart, but they don't always have time to read. I'd recommend photocopying the table of contents each time you get one and keeping a master reference binder of all the volumes. Number the sheets chronologically as you place them in the binder and label the journal with the same number. (Make it simple and start with 1 the first time you receive a copy.) Then use a knife to cut out the metal hanger from a Pendaflex file and thread it through the spine of the journal. Hang the volumes in chronological order in a filing cabinet and shut the drawer. When you need to find something, simply pull the binder with the copies of the table of contents and do a quick scan. That's more efficient than taking out and opening each individual journal, one at a time, to locate a particular article or volume in your cabinet.

CHAPTER SEVEN

Mastering the Seventh Pillar—

POST

WITH THE EXCEPTION OF military families, no population moves more frequently than employees of Fortune 500 companies. These people relocate, on average, once every four years.

The transition to a new house may be exciting. But unless you do the proper work beforehand, the process of moving can be overwhelming to everyone in the family. I think they should create a new reality TV show called *Moving*—it would be scarier than anything they've shown on *Fear Factor* (although the food would certainly be better).

In the military, your job or position is known as your "post." As a military wife, my mother's post was to pack and prepare the house each time we moved. I remember the first time she let me help her pack the basement. My dad had been given a new assignment, and we had four days to move up, move out, and move on.

"What is all this stuff down here, Mom? We'll never get it packed in time."

"Of course we will, Laura. Start over there. Just focus on boxing one shelf at a time."

In no time, Mom had a household of boxes lined up in precise formation, exactly in the order they needed to be moved out, and ready for the Colonel's inspection.

Mom ran her house like a well-oiled machine. Although her post didn't involve working outside the home, I know she worked harder than many who did. In addition to moving, her post included shopping, cleaning, laundry, errands, and child care. Watching the way she completed her day-to-day tasks, chores, errands, and responsibilities taught me a lot.

You may not be in the military, but you have your own post and set of responsibilities, inside and outside the home. When this pillar is strong, other things in your life fall into place more smoothly. When this pillar is weak, your personal responsibilities seem to get in the way of *life*.

POST quiz item 61

61. _____ Hire out tasks requiring a level of expertise I don't have.

Wow, You're Smart!

Interdependence is an important productivity concept. We're wise to rely on other people to do things that we don't have the time, talent, or wherewithal to do ourselves. That's why we can eat bananas in the middle of the winter in Denver!

So if you work full time outside of the home, you don't have the time to do many of the things a person working from home would. Period. If you have a life partner, the tendency is to think the solution lies simply in divvying the duties better, as I described above. However, getting others to pitch in isn't always the solution. More often, it's outsourcing, which involves being *interdependent* on others. Service providers rely on you for their paychecks, and you rely on them to free up your time.

Increasingly, Americans are hiring others to do traditional and nontraditional homemaking functions, driven mostly by three factors: women working outside the home almost as much as men; an older population; and a growing affluent class. We are taking the principles of business to the home: Individuals do best when they focus on activities in which they can add the most value and outsource other activities to specialists or laborers. The implications of extending the services industry into the household will be huge.

So take a deep breath and join the millions of people who spend some of their hard-earned money to buy a life. Yes, money does buy time! You can outsource just about anything these days, so when you're thinking about what to hire out, it's useful to think of tasks in two categories:

1. **SOPHISTICATED**—tasks having high decision-making responsibility and requiring a high level of expertise you don't possess (doing tax reports that are complex, for example) or that would take you a significant amount of time and energy to learn. These are specialties.

2. **LABOR-INTENSIVE**—tasks having little decision-making responsibility and requiring a low level of expertise you do possess and *could* do but *should* not (mowing the lawn, for ex-

ample). Given where you could invest your time, these activities are time wasters—for some people, but not all. Service providers can make a significant income providing services other people categorize as timewasters.

When I started my business in 1992, I had just graduated from the University of Colorado with an MBA. Boy, I thought I was hot stuff! Out of necessity, I was the Jill-of-all-trades in the company, trying to do every little task myself. "My MBA taught me all of this, didn't it?" I rationalized. But I quickly discovered after almost burning myself out that I didn't learn nearly enough to keep things going by myself long term. So I slowly started building my team of specialists to help me do tasks I didn't do well.

Today, here are the sophisticated tasks I hire out that I wouldn't dare attempt myself:

CAR. I used to giggle (privately, of course) when my husband tried to play auto mechanic. There he was in the garage, swearing, banging his head, cutting his hands, getting angry because he didn't have the right tools, running to the auto store two times to get something and spending two hours of his time to do a stupid oil change . . . and all to save thirty bucks. Enough said.

BOOKKEEPING. Even though having a bookkeeper is essential since I own a business, I know several people who use one to help with all the receipts, bank and credit card statements, and bills. After work is complete, bookkeepers often file papers and complete tax paperwork. Some people would much rather hire someone to take care of the bookkeeping than do it themselves.

ACCOUNTING. If you have a semicomplicated life like we do with two working parents, child-care expenses, and investments, it's definitely worthwhile having a specialist do your taxes. Add in a few rental properties, a business, and education costs, and it's a no-brainer to hire an accountant. As we've concluded, it's simply not worth the time and brain damage trying to manage on our own.

HOME REPAIRS. Trying to fix the dishwasher? Install a new hot water heater? Fix the holes in the sprinkler system? Forget it! Unless you are already skilled in these areas, it's not worth the headache, hassle, and energy to learn to do these things yourself. Hire an independent handyman to work on all these projects once at a daily rate, which is often cheaper than having a skilled trade person come out for each job. Keep looking until you find someone whom you trust to do it right.

COMPUTER WORK. My husband actually built his computers and he's darn good with them, considering that, when I met him in 1998, he had never surfed the Internet or sent an e-mail. He handles many technical tasks himself. But when I have a complicated technical issue, I don't hesitate to pick up the phone and call my IT guy, who has been studying computers for most of his adult life. I'm sure John could probably learn to program, code, write in HTML, post video clips to Web sites, and more, but it's just not worth his time. As the COO of our company, John's time is much better spent elsewhere. Leave the expertise to the experts.

FINANCIAL MATTERS. Ditto on working with a broker who counsels us on picking stocks. Unless it's a hobby, and your savings and retirement don't hinge on market gains, don't try this one yourself, kids.

Lastly, since I'm a small business, I've had to learn that I can't do it all. I surround myself with a team of experts: graphic designers, printers, editors, public relations specialists, and marketing communication writers, all of whom I am more than happy to pay because they get it done in less time, for less money, and with less stress than I could have done myself.

POST quiz item 62

> 62. _____ Hire out simple chores to helpers.

At Your Service

It's far harder for most people to cough up money for the second category: labor-intensive tasks. Most people get that it doesn't make sense to try to tinker with your car if you're not a mechanic. But you *know* how to do the laundry, so you feel guilty for paying someone else to do it, almost like you're being lazy. Well, for goodness' sake, what are you working so hard for? To earn a bunch of money, just to work hard again at home? When do you get to raise your children? Volunteer? Spend time on yourself?

I believe the money we spend on services is far better than any other stuff we could have bought with that money. If you work all day in a job outside the home, and then come home to work a second shift in your home with your family and children, and also try to do the housework and chores, you may feel as though you have the equivalent of three full-time jobs! In bygone days, one spouse would work outside the home, and one would work inside. With both partners often working outside the home, there's often not enough time to get the inside work done. The solution is hiring out labor-intensive chores.

TRADE TALENTS. Perhaps you're reluctant to part with the cash. I believe you'll change your mind as soon as you realize the money was well spent. Cut out a few restaurant meals and pieces of clothing a month, and you've covered the cost. However, if you absolutely don't have the money, find someone who loves doing what you hate and vice versa, and exchange your services for theirs. For example, if you hate to wash windows, trade it with your neighbor to steam clean his/her carpet. If you hate gardening, find the best green thumb in the neighborhood and offer to watch her kids several times a month in exchange for fresh tomatoes and flowerbeds. Two seminar participants told me their story: One loved to do crafts and the other loved to bake. At holiday time, one wraps the other's presents beautifully and decorates her home, while the second woman bakes all the holiday goodies for the other and prepares her holiday meals. What a great exchange!

Here are some services to consider outsourcing.

FILING AND OFFICE HELP. My assistant Jenny does the filing in our office, which also happens to be our home. Of course, not everyone is lucky enough to work from home or have an administrative assistant. However, it's quite easy to hire someone. Post an index card at your church or local community center and advertise for a stay-at-home parent, college student, or retiree who would like to work a few hours a week while children are in school. Pay ten dollars or so an hour. After making sure he or she is trustworthy, give that person a key. Leave a list of duties to complete, such as filing, writing (not signing) checks, and paperwork. This kind of job is much better work than flipping hamburgers, and you'll love the time you free up. Who wouldn't pay $10 for a free hour of time!

IRONING. Simply, don't iron. I don't buy cottons or linen or any other fabric that wrinkles when I sit on it or has the slightest hint of needing to be ironed. If you must purchase clothes that require ironing, send them to the dry cleaners for laundering or pay your kid a buck an item.

ERRANDS. That watch needs a new battery, that zipper needs to be replaced, those library books need to be returned, those clothes need to be donated to the church or dropped off at the dry cleaners, the shirt that doesn't fit needs to go back to the store, your son needs a piñata for his birthday party, and on and on and on. Keep a list of all these menial errands and the corresponding items in one central place. Our assistant maps out her path, completes these errands all at once, and does them most efficiently.

HOUSEKEEPING. We've had the same housekeeper for years. She comes every other week and spends about five hours in our home working like the Tasmanian Devil. We keep up with the light tidying and she does the heavy-duty cleaning like bathrooms, floors, and dusting. In most areas, an average-sized house will cost around $50 to $100 a session to have cleaned (we pay $80). This may sound like a lot, but do the math. Let's say your housekeeping took about five hours a week, which is about normal for a family with kids. That's approximately 20 hours a month or 250 hours a year. If you value your time at $10 an hour, you'd be willing to pay $2,500 to outsource this duty. If you can pay $1,800 a year for this service, it is a better deal! On the other hand, if you don't outsource it, you may find weeks go by when you don't find time or energy to do it yourself. A dirty house definitely becomes a source of stress. Have a family meeting and figure out where that $100 to $200 a month will come from. Can you avoid replacing your car for a few more years? Can you cut back on the number of times you eat out? Can you reduce your clothing or entertainment budget? I find that people who are motivated enough to get their lives back manage to find the money to buy more time.

LAUNDRY. Next to housekeeping, this is the absolutely best thing you can outsource. Find a retired person or stay-at-home parent who wants a side job. Ours happens to be my awesome mother-in-law Eileen Stack (yes, we pay her). For eight to ten dollars an hour, you can outsource the most tedious of chores. Each week, my children take a big black lawn bag and empty their dirty clothes hampers into it. We drive the bags and laundry baskets over to John's mom's house. Alternatively, you could have your laundry person pick them up or do the laundry at your home. My mother-in-law prefers to do our laundry in the comfort of her own home, so we buy the detergent and softener. A few days later, she brings the laundry baskets back, now full of clean, folded, and sorted clothes and puts them away in the drawers. If you can't find someone to hire, many laundromats will offer this service by the pound.

YARD WORK. You can get the kid down the street to mow, bag, and trim your lawn once a week for around twenty bucks. Considering the fifty bucks you can easily drop when you eat out at a restaurant, that's money well spent. Or you can have a service that comes once a week. Lawn services can often charge much less, because they can do three houses in a row in under an hour! You can also have them handle tree trimming and fall/spring cleanups.

CLEANING. For big annual cleaning projects such as washing the outside of upstairs windows, cleaning the upholstery and drapes, and steam cleaning the carpets, hire someone. By the time you get all the necessary equipment together and do it—and after factoring in the stress—it would have been worth it to pay someone who does it for a living and can finish the job in half the time. If you see a company servicing a neighbor's property, ask your neighbors afterward if they were satisfied and which company they used. Many companies go door-to-door and leave flyers. Or you can find someone in the yellow pages or church directory.

DOGGY POOP SCOOPING. Yes, unbelievably, in addition to pet sitting and doggy day care, you can hire someone to clean up Fido's mess as well. Our family has really wanted a dog or two, but we've had lots of reasons not to get one. Our kids were too young to help walk a dog, I'm allergic, and there's always the poop issue. Now that our kids are older, and I've been getting allergy shots— and we've found someone to come to our house for $6 a week and clean up the yard—we got a dog! (Thinking ahead, it's smart to schedule this service the day before the lawn guy comes, so we don't make enemies.) Drop me a note at Laura@TheProductivity Pro.com, and I'll e-mail you a photo of our new Bichon Frise!

Remember, spend some of your hard-earned money and give yourself the gift of time! The next time you have a birthday, anniversary, or holiday, purchase a few months of housekeeping for yourself instead of clothes. Purchase a gift certificate to a restaurant so you don't have to cook. Have the veterinarian or a groomer bathe your dog instead of getting soaked and making a mess when you do it yourself. Hire a teenager to do the major cleaning required before houseguests arrive. You get the picture.

If you're having a hard time deciding what to hire out, it's simple: delegate the tasks that don't involve repeated decision-making. You make the actual decisions—when, how often, at what level, which things, etc.—and delegate the labor itself. You do *not* want a clone of yourself—stick to what you're good at and separate the labor from the decision. Beware: If you delegate the decision-making to someone else, you'll pay "sophisticated" rates for "labor-intensive" tasks.

POST quiz item 63

> 63. _____ Have goods delivered to avoid unnecessary time at the store.

Can You Bring Me More Time?

If you think about how much time you spend, say, driving to the dry cleaners, dropping off the bag, driving back, and picking it up again, you've used a lot of precious time. Today, anything you normally have to shop for or pick up can be delivered.

DRY CLEANING. Send clothes made of fabrics that can't be washed and dried, or that would require ironing of any kind, to the cleaners. But don't drive over yourself—find one that picks up and delivers. Most large metropolitan areas will have this service if you check the yellow pages. I compared the pricing of one in my area to the drop-off facility I was currently using, and then I called and asked for a 10 percent discount so the pricing would be comparable. A company rep leaves a recorded message on my voice mail the night before the cleaning gets picked up to remind me to put out the special bag they provided on the front porch. The driver picks up the bag before 10:00 a.m. on Thursday and returns it after 5:00 p.m. on Friday.

MILK SERVICE. The milkman does still exist! I used to swear up and down I'd never pay such ridiculous prices for at-home service. Instead, John and I were constantly running to the grocery store to pick up another three gallons for our three children, who went through it every three days. Whew! What a waste of time! Our refrigerator can't hold the amount of milk required along with the rest of the stuff we need—and we have the biggest refrigerator possible! It was making us crazy to run out of milk every few days simply because we didn't have enough room to buy what we needed. Now Royal Crest Dairy delivers our milk on Tuesday and Friday. We never run out, and the milk *does* taste better because it's hormone-free. For the few extra cents it costs for delivery, we get *fresh* milk (within hours of milking), brought to us on a regular basis. We have saved far more in time than we've ever paid. Plus, once I stopped being a cheapskate on principle, I eliminated yet one more thing to think about. This dairy figured out how harried parents might also benefit from home delivery of other essentials, so now we can order our bread, coffee, cream, and many of the important little things we tend to run out of.

PACKAGE PICKUP. Similarly, my husband John used to complain loudly about the $3.00 pick-up fee DHL charges to fetch packages off our front porch. When we had a large box to ship, he would get in the car, drive to the local Office Max, drop off the package, and drive home again to save the $3.00. For the half-hour round trip this took him, doing this proved to be an incredible waste of his time and company time. Factor in not just what he's paid to drop off the package, but also the opportunity cost of what he *could* have been doing back in the office.

MEAL DELIVERY. Never mind pizza and Chinese food; you can have real meals delivered to your door at less than the cost of buying the ingredients. You don't even have to spend time shopping or cooking or planning—you just pop a homemade frozen meal in the oven and violà! Or if you own a deep freeze, buy a month of frozen food in bulk from a personal chef. Look in the yellow pages under Chefs for services in your area.

GROCERY SHOPPING. Many people have discovered the ease of online grocery shopping. Check out www.peapod.com or www.safeway.com. Shopping this way, you'll have fewer impulse buys. The prices are the same as or similar to a supermarket's, and the ten dollar delivery fee is well worth the time it would take you to shop and drive—plus the delivery people will often bring your bags inside. You can often get good prices buying toiletries on drugstore Web sites like www.drugstore.com.

ONLINE SHOPPING. You think of the perfect gift. By the time you get around to buying it and getting it in the mail, the occasion has arrived and you're too late. Why not shop for kids' clothes, electronics, shoes, and gifts via the Internet? By the time you get around to getting to the store, the stuff you wanted "right away" could be delivered right to your home. For gifts, an online store will wrap it and include a gift card for the recipient. You might pay a few dollars for shipping, but it's definitely worth the time and hassle (see quiz item 64 for more ideas). I also love www.eBay.com. I can search for anything I'm looking for and pay a fraction of the full retail cost. It's also easy to set up an account and sell things you want to part with that are too expensive to give away.

POST quiz item 64

64. _____ Complete shopping efficiently.

The Faster I Shop, the Faster I Eat

If I can't find an item online, I have to purchase it the old-fashioned way, which involves driving. Shopping is one task that must be done on a regular basis, whether you have time for it or not. You have to go to the grocery store and make periodic trips to the mall for kids' school clothes, the department store for household goods, and the mall for gifts you want to hand-select yourself.

Streamlining how you approach your shopping can give you more time to do what you really want to do. Try these suggestions.

PLAN AN EFFICIENT ROUTE. When your route is not mapped out properly, you'll find yourself driving by a department store and stopping in to grab one thing, like fish food. As you pull into your driveway, you remember your son needs baseball socks for his game next weekend. But because you didn't have your list with you and hadn't sequenced your activities, you now have to make yet another trip. Instead, think carefully about your route and how you can knock out several errands most efficiently. Even if you don't *need* gas, fill up when you pass a station and have a minute. When picking up a take-and-bake pizza, drive through the car wash while waiting. When you're mapping your route, plan the order of your stops in a clockwise direction, so you can avoid time-consuming left-hand turns. One of my friends keeps a cooler in the back of his SUV so he can put perishable food in the cooler and doesn't have to rush home immediately after shopping at the grocery store.

CHANGE YOUR PACE. If you normally do your grocery shopping on Saturday, pick a weeknight to go instead. Set your mind all day long that you are going to the store after dinner. Better yet, go straight there after work. The stores are much less crowded on Wednesday evening than on Saturday when most of the world shops. The feeling that you want to get home, instead of feeling like you have all day, will keep you clipping down the aisles.

DON'T TRY ON CLOTHES. That's right—*don't* try them on. The dressing rooms are noisy, crowded, and often have long lines . . . not to mention horrible lighting that makes everyone look like Frankenstein. It's much easier to buy what you like and try it on at home where you have the time, space, and lighting to size each item up appropriately. You'll be back at the store again and can return the items that don't fit. Of course, if you're the type who would buy an item and never get around to returning it, you might want to stick with trying things on in the store. Or send your new chore assistant out to return the item for you.

CREATE A SHOPPING CHART. I know this one will sound really crazy, but it saves time! On your next trip to your grocery store, take a pad of paper with you. Write down the aisle numbers and all the items you purchased while in it, as well as other foodstuffs you purchase frequently. Or go online to see if your grocery store has done this for you already. After you get home, unpack, and get settled, create a matrix on your computer using word processing or spreadsheet software with the aisle numbers and contents of each. Then reduce the size, so it fits handily on the refrigerator and in your purse. Print it out, make photocopies, and post it on your refrigerator for everyone to see. As you need things, simply circle the item instead of writing it over each week. When you go shopping, take down the list and carry it with you, starting another one in the process. Here's a sample:

PRODUCE	DELI	1	2	3	4	5	6
Apples	Ham	Lunchables	Kid bread	Shampoo	Yogurt	Salad dressing	Spaghetti sauce
Oranges	Turkey	Bologna	John bread	Deodorant	Go-gurt	Olives	Spaghetti
Grapes	Beef	Chix nuggets	Laura bread	Band-Aids	Drinkable yogurt	Gherkins	Soups
Celery	Provolone	Steaks	Bagels	Lotion	OJ	Dill pickles	Tomato
Carrots	Muenster	Chicken	Raisin bran	Cotton	Lemonade	Catsup	Chix noodle
Potatoes	Salami	Roast	Buns	Toothpaste	Cheese	Mustard	Clam chowder
Lettuce	Tuna salad	Hamburger	PB	Tylenol	Eggs	Mayo	Ramen
Bananas		Pork loin	Jelly	Cold med	Sour cream	Miracle Whip	
Salad		Hot dogs		Pantyhose	Butter, tub	Relish	
Tomato					Butter, stick		

7	8	9	10	11	12	13	14
Rice	Cake mix	Cereal	Cookies	Juice	Napkins	Tide	Lean Cuisine
Instant Potato	Frosting	Oatmeal	Crackers	Apple	Plates	Clorox	Frozen Waffles
Can fruit	Crisco	Pancake mix	Snacks	Cranberry	Silverware	Clorox II	Pancakes
Pear	Oil	Syrup	Roll-ups	Bottled water	Cups	Dish Det.	French Toast
Peaches	Flour	Coffee	Candy	Soda	3 oz	Dishwaher	Scrambles
Mandarin	Choc. chips	Tea	Gum	Diet	5 oz	Fabric soft	Pizza
Applesauce	Pie crust	Creamer	Peanuts	Coke	TP	Soft scrub	Ice cream
Gravy	Br. Sugar	Hot Choc.	Doritos	Caff-free Sprite	Paper towel	Bar soap	Cool Whip
Chicken	Sugar	Cat food	Popcorn	Fresca	Puffs	Hand soap	Popsicles
Beef	Spices	Dog Food	Pop tarts	Kool-Aid	Hand-wipes	Kitchen spray	
Boxed pot	Jell-O		Pretzels		Baggies	Dish-washer tablets	
Canned veg.	Pudding		Cheetos		Ziploc		
Green Beans	Evap. milk				Straws		
Corn	Cond. milk				Toothpicks		
Peas					Trash bags		
Cranberry							

BUY IN BULK. Stocking frequently used items such as toilet paper, paper towels, lightbulbs, and bottled water makes good financial sense because it lowers your cost-per-item significantly. Many household items such as dishwasher detergent, kitchen garbage bags, spices, and liquid soap are sold in large sizes; check the bulk aisle of your grocery store or look into joining a shopping club. If you have the storage space, buying in bulk helps you avoid repeat trips to the store for the same items over and over again! In addition, if you are a small business owner, shopping clubs like Sam's open early to business members, so you can get your shopping done before the public arrives.

POST quiz item 65

65. _____ Run errands efficiently.

If I Drive Faster, Does It Count?

It's too bad my daughter can't drive yet. Friends tell me not to rush these last six years, because it will come soon enough. But I would love for her to be able to run little errands for me throughout the week. Instead, each evening, she completes one of the seven tasks required each week to earn her allowance. Whether it's emptying the trash containers around the house, bagging up the newspapers, or gathering the laundry from the bedrooms, she performs one task. When Saturday arrives, she's already finished with her weekly chores and can enjoy the weekend. Adults should use the same logic with running errands throughout the week.

DIVIDE AND CONQUER. Weekends are supposed to be relaxing. Rather than running all your errands on the weekend, divide up your errands and complete one or two each evening. After working hard all week, you need a period of time to take a deep breath, recover, and get ready for another hard week. Unfortunately, many people complain that their weekends are more stressful than their workweek. Instead of relaxing or having fun, they cram weekends full with chores and errands, leaving no time for leisure.

I've found that by planning for my work to get done during the week, I can rest easily and enjoy the weekend once it arrives. If it's part of your plan to spend the weekend watching your son play in his soccer tournament, you must make the time to fulfill that goal without staying up until 2:00 a.m. each night and returning to work a zombie.

CONSOLIDATE YOUR ERRANDS. A nice thing about living in the little city of Highlands Ranch, Colorado, is that most of the businesses I frequent are all in the same place. I can drop off a prescription, pick up the dry cleaning, deposit checks, get gas, and buy a few items at the grocery store without going more than a mile. Others aren't quite so lucky. If you don't live next door to the supermarket, it doesn't make sense to run all the way out there for a few items and then drive all the way home. The next day, you dash off to the post office (which, by the way, happened to be on the way home from the supermarket yesterday, but you weren't prepared). This is why you want to consolidate your errands.

DO ERRANDS WHILE DRIVING BY. Why go to the bank on a Saturday to deposit checks when I drive by it on the way to picking up the boys from day care? Why put off refilling my prescriptions when Walgreens has a twenty-four-hour drive-up drop-off service one minute from my home? If a DVD is due at the library, I could give it to my assistant and pay her to do it, or I could simply change my route to day care and drop it off on the way.

DESIGNATE AN "OUT" SPOT AT HOME. Designate a place to gather your errand-related items that is somewhere on the way to your car. As I come across errand-related items during the course of my day—letters to be mailed, a prescription to be dropped off, a CD to put in the car—I put them on the dryer in the laundry room. That way, as I walk through to get to the car, I can grab everything all at once.

POST quiz Item 66

> 66. _____ Function effectively as the social, child, and family coordinator.

If It Weren't for Me, Honey, We Wouldn't Have Any Friends

I'd love to hear from the men on this one. Why does it seem that, at least in my circle, the woman is the social coordinator in the family? I'm not kidding when I say my husband wouldn't have any friends if it weren't for me. We wouldn't have any couple friends, either.

I've tried to sit back and see if John would reach out to our couple friends to schedule a get-together. But even when he and the man in the couple are close, no dice. Though he's perfectly willing to be told, "We have a dinner date tonight" and go with the flow. Kind of makes me crazy, but I do get to see who I want, when I want, so I'm not exactly complaining. *But* being social coordinator does put an extra responsibility onto my already-full plate.

Here are a few ways I handle these responsibilities that might be helpful to you.

SCHEDULING TIME WITH FRIENDS. I make sure I connect with good friends in a meaningful way about four times a year. I'm not suggesting rigid scheduling ("Ooops, you've had your designated visit this quarter"). To the contrary, scheduling actually helps you make sure a year doesn't go by without a visit. If you're not careful, good friends can accidentally slip away. Each time a visit ends, look ahead on your calendar and schedule the next visit if possible. My friends have honestly told me they appreciate my being proactive in nurturing our friendships. They even ask jokingly, "Hi! Are you calling to schedule our next play date?" If I don't call, they wonder why, and call me. Be careful that you're not doing all the work, however; if your friends really want to hang out with you, they should take the initiative once in a while.

PLANNING FAMILY GATHERINGS. Similarly, I often wonder if I didn't make the calls and coordinate holidays and family activities, would we ever see each other? About a month before a big day, I look at the upcoming holidays, if any, and e-mail the entire family (done easily with a distribution list in Outlook or a group in ACT). I suggest a date and time that would work best with my schedule and get input from my family. By now, they're used to keeping holidays open until Laura dutifully sends out her family communication. If something comes up early for one of them, I actually get a call requesting a particular day. It's pretty funny at this point. And honestly, I don't mind doing the planning. For all I joke about it with them, I always get to schedule it the way that it's most convenient for me. My family members are pretty good about saying, "It's my turn to host," but if you've had them over too many times, don't hesitate to suggest a get-together at another house.

COORDINATING SCHOOL ACTIVITIES, SPORTS, AND SOCIAL PLANS. Children lead busy lives, don't they? I've heard the phrase "You ain't seen nothin' until you have teenagers," so I know future years will become even more complicated. Even though John and I share activity-coordination duties, I've found it's easier if one person takes responsibility for divvying up the jobs. Each Sunday night, we bring our calendars to the family powwow and review the upcoming week: who has a birthday party and who is driving to and from; who has a Bible study class and will need the other to watch the kids; when do I have a speaking engagement that will prevent me from picking up the children from day care; what work is due at school; who needs a permission slip and money for a field trip; when is show-and-tell and who will cover getting the item in the backpack; where do we have dinner plans and when will we ask Grandma to come over and put the kids to bed. You get the idea. We review and plan anything and everything that's likely to happen and cover our bases. We also do some advance planning at this point and discuss what's come up since last week: vacation plans, airline tickets to purchase, etc. The kids only need to be involved for the first part of the powwow. John and I connect for another thirty minutes or so over a glass of wine (which always makes it fun).

GETTING READY FOR GUESTS. The holidays usually bring with them family members and friends from out-of-town, who usually want to bunk with you and have you play tour guide. For many, hosting guests can be stressful because it changes your routine and can put a strain on your time. In part, however, stress gets created because you rush around at the last minute pulling things together, making beds, cleaning the house, and shopping for food. If you're proactive, you'll start getting ready for a visit weeks before they roll into town. Buy extra supplies, make plans for entertainment, and set up the guest room. My favorite idea comes from my own Daddykins and his wife, Naamah, who, when my children are visiting for a sleepover, pretend their home is a bed and breakfast. The children are greeted at the door, sign the register, receive their keys and guest amenities (usually small water bottles, snacks, bars of soap, and toiletries), and check into their rooms, which are (temporarily) labeled with the corresponding room number received at check-in. Imagining your home as a B&B in this way will help you think through what would make your guests most comfortable. If your in-laws tend to be flaky and don't decide until the last minute whether they are coming, simply explain that you will be excitedly preparing for their visit and will need to know by X date whether they are coming or not. If you don't have a firm answer by then, let them know your family will be making other plans. Take a deep breath, follow through on this a few times, and they will be more cooperative in the future, once they discover you *are* really serious.

POST quiz item 67

> 67. _____ Do routine chores on a regular basis and keep my house clean.

The Domestic Diva

As you struggle to keep your house clean and in working order, it might benefit you to think of your housekeeping duties in two categories: routine and maintenance items.

Routine tasks are required to keep the household humming along smoothly—they are your needs. We all need to eat. We all need clean clothes to wear. We need to pay the electricity bill so the power isn't shut off.

Certain maintenance tasks, however, aren't *required* for you to function. Your windows might be dirty on the outside but, hey, you can still see out of them. You want to organize your photo album, but you don't *have* to. It would be helpful to organize your CDs by genre and your books by author, but you're getting along just fine without doing it. Let's discuss routine tasks first, and we'll tackle maintenance activities in the next section.

Handling routine items on a regular basis keeps them from getting out of hand. If you let a routine activity go for too long, it becomes a maintenance activity. Do you avoid doing certain chores because you dread the task so much?

If you perform routine tasks too infrequently, they will become more of a chore than they need to be. Here are some suggestions.

CLEAN IT WHEN YOU SEE IT. I don't have time to clean the house all day, but there's something comforting about walking through a sparkling room, so try to clean as much as possible as you go. Spray your glass shower walls with no-spot cleaner after showering. Wipe up kitchen spills immediately so they don't harden on the counter or the floor. Wipe up coffee drips on the counter, so they don't leave a stain. Do a quick vacuum if you see a mess on a high-traffic carpet. Keep a container of disinfecting wipes in each bathroom and quickly wipe down surfaces and toilet seats every few days. Wait for the housekeeper to do the rest.

WASH CLOTHES INFREQUENTLY. My kids know that jeans can often be worn more than once if they didn't roll around in the mud that day. Even the little ones look at their clothes for spots before proclaiming them "dirty." I like going to hotels where I can have clean towels for my shower, but at home, I'd rather use them a few times and save on the laundry. Unless it's summer and you're sweating quite a bit, the sheets can make it for two weeks before washing. Unless you're mucking out horse stables, your jeans can probably make it for three wears instead of one. Using things twice or more drastically cuts down on laundry volume, not to mention lengthening the life span of the clothes themselves. Remember, there's more to doing laundry than just throwing it in the hamper!

USE TELEPHONE TIME TO DO CHORES. I take advantage of the time I chat with friends and family by wearing my wireless headset and wandering around the house doing chores that don't engage my mind. You can dump a glass of water in a plant before you notice it wilting. You can clean leftovers out of the fridge or take the kitchen trash into the garage. As you talk, collect the newspapers and put them in the recycle bin or unload the dishwasher. The number of little tasks you can accomplish this way will surprise you! It's well worth the cost of the headset.

KEEP CLEANING SUPPLIES WHERE YOU USE THEM. I stock our bathrooms with disinfectant wipes to clean up after my little boys. I also stock disposable dust cloths, fresh hand towels, and spare toilet paper. Storing needed supplies in each of the bathrooms keeps me from running around from one to another to use them and put them all back again.

CLEAN ONLY WHAT YOU NEED TO, WHEN YOU NEED TO. My mother used to make me clean the shower in the guest room, even when we weren't expecting any company. I remember thinking how futile it was and what a waste of time. I still think that. Don't vacuum if no one's coming to visit. If you splash your soda can on the floor, use a dishrag to spot clean it; you don't have to mop the entire floor. Having a sticky floor is a nuisance but your family can function with a little dirt. Give yourself a break and remember every "A" doesn't require a "plus."

DO A LITTLE BIT EACH DAY. If you hack at tasks daily (routine), you won't end up with seven hours of cleaning to do on a Saturday (maintenance). Here are some tips.

- **LAUNDRY.** John laments that his mother still does his laundry, but it's a feigned annoyance, since he's incredibly grateful. Mom will be the first to say it's wise to do a load each day. The machines do most of the work, so it only takes a cumulative ten minutes to toss clothes in the washer and put them in the dryer. The folding and sorting take the longest amount of time, but you can do that while chatting or watching your favorite TV show. With five people in our household, if we didn't keep up with it, the laundry would soon pile up to the ceiling. When certain things can't wait for the weekly laundry pickup (soccer uniforms, horse jodhpurs, potty accidents), we become more aware of the need to work at it daily. If you sort, wash, dry, and fold seven loads of laundry on Sunday, change up. Instead, toss in a load each evening.

- **DISHES.** We have a housekeeper, yes, but she only comes every two weeks. Unfortunately, the dishes can't wait that long! Because John does all the cooking, I do the dishes. (It's actually evolved into "picking up" the kitchen, which means putting all the things away that have been strewn about by the family.) If there's one thing I've learned about dishes, it's not to leave them overnight. Mashed potatoes and eggs, for example, are difficult to get off dishes after they've dried. Scraping dishes is such a waste of time! When you wash a dish right away, the food comes right off, giving you more free time when the chore is complete. If you do the dishes right after you eat, you never have to look at unsightly dishes in the sink, you don't feel behind, and you have a clean kitchen the next time you need to cook. In between meals, I just leave single cups and plates from snacks in the sink and load them all into the dishwasher at one time after a meal.

- **BATHROOMS**. If you wait too many days between the times you tidy up, the cleaning becomes a lot yuckier. To avoid water spots, keep a dry hand towel hanging near your sink to immediately mop up spills and splashes. Use disinfectant wipes to do a quick clean of sinks and counters every few days or when you notice stuck-on toothpaste. Spray shower floors, walls, and doors with a daily cleanser (such as Tilex Fresh Shower) right after you shower.

Lastly, here are some **cleaning tips** to cut the time you spend cleaning.

- **GRAB YOUR CLEANING SUPPLIES.** Get a five-gallon paint or spackle bucket and tie a carpenter's work belt with pockets or a ready-made cloth carryall around it. You can keep cleaning supplies inside the bucket and put brushes, sponges, and other necessities in the pockets outside. That way, when you're ready to clean a room, you don't have to waste any time gathering and regathering your equipment.

- **DECLUTTER BEFORE YOU CLEAN.** It's difficult to vacuum the dining room floor if the kids' toys are strewn about. I grab a big laundry basket and toss all the toys in it, then deposit the basket in the playroom with instructions for my kids to tidy up.

- **CLEAN IN A PATTERN.** Work from left to right and top to bottom around the room, leaving the center of the room for last. Always start by dusting from the top down. When the dust falls, it won't land on something you've already cleaned.

When the weekend finally comes, you can hit the slopes or bike trails without guilt because your house looks great.

POST quiz item 68

68. _____ Conduct preventive maintenance on my home.

Cobwebs in the Corners?

I went to see a new friend's home and was repulsed by the filthy washrag in her sink. I thought, "I wonder how long it's been since she's washed that? And is she wiping down her counters with it?" The dish scrubber had different colors of old food stuck in between the spines. It's probably not a shock to you that the next time I invited her to come to my house to eat, and the time after that we met at a restaurant. I've never been able to eat at her home again.

Even though your house is tidy, you may inadvertently be spreading germs with these often-neglected areas:

- Dishrags should be replaced every day. Put the scrubber in the dishwasher every time you run it and replace it frequently. Sponges should also be washed in the dishwasher regularly and replaced every two weeks.

- Refrigerator doors and the edges of the dishwasher collect food and grime. Because they're in contact with your food and clean dishes, make sure to wipe them down with a bleach and water solution once a month.

- Trash cans. If you toss a soda can that's not quite empty into your office trashcan and it spills, clean it up right away with a bleach solution or disinfectant wipe. If you leave it, bacteria will quickly form. Wipe the outside of the kitchen trash can when you mop the floor.

- Vents. Heating vents and cold air returns gather dust particles and can make allergies worse. Vacuum these once a season and have a professional duct cleaning company inspect and service them once a year.

- Welcome mats and throw rugs are meant to keep dirt out of the house and catch grime once inside, but they don't work if they're filthy. Buy throw rugs you can toss in the washer periodically. Shake outside rugs, hose them off, and replace them occasionally.

Once in awhile, whenever I think about it or happen to notice it needs attention, I do the maintenance tasks. You could also drop slips of paper into your tickler file if you want to remember to do them on a regular basis.

Kitchen

- Clean behind the refrigerator (my housekeeper staunchly refuses to do this)
- Wipe down refrigerator shelves and drawers
- Toss chipped or ugly dishes, unused plastic kids' cups, and stained plastic storage containers
- Wash chair pads
- Disinfect children's booster seats
- Clean out the toaster

Bathroom

- Replace burned-out bulbs
- Wash throw rugs
- Replace shower curtain liners
- Wash valences
- Organize under the cabinets
- Toss unused toiletries

Bedroom

- Flip the mattress
- Vacuum windowsills
- Wash windows

Laundry room

- Clean off spilled soap from inside the washer lid
- Vacuum inside the dryer duct to prevent clogging
- Vacuum behind appliances

General

- Wash walls from the bottom up. Drips are easier to clean off a wall that you've already cleaned.
- Be frugal with cleaning liquids; you'll spend less time wiping off the excess.
- When washing windows, wipe horizontally on the inside, vertically on the outside. If you end up with streaks, you'll know which side they're on.
- Use your vacuum's attachments to get big chunks and dust off windowsills and blinds before using a liquid cleaner.
- Freshen washable, dusty curtains and valences by tossing them in the dryer with a damp towel on the air-dry cycle for about twenty minutes.
- Every couple months, put your prize houseplants in a luke-warm shower for one minute and soak them thoroughly. Dry completely before putting them back.

POST quiz item 69

69. _____ Prepare meals quickly and systematically.

Boxed Macaroni and Cheese for Dinner?

I look back on meals with my family with great fondness. We ate dinner together every night, with no exceptions, no television, and no phone interruptions. My mom was a great cook. She somehow always seemed to make a meal I liked: sweet and sour chicken, chili, spaghetti, or one of twenty-seven other tempting meals. When I was old enough to help her in the kitchen, I discovered her numbered meal plan taped to the inside of a cabinet door. I found out there were thirty things she cooked—all of them loved by everyone. When we returned from school, my two brothers and I would look at the list and know what we were eating for dinner.

My mother's shopping system may be a bit more organized and extreme than some families can handle, but I want to encourage you to think big! To ensure she had the right ingredients on hand, Mom had a three-ring binder with each recipe numbered and copied on a piece of loose-leaf paper. She also had a photocopied chart of the grocery store, with multiple columns that corresponded to the aisles and individual items listed beneath the heading. She kept a grocery store map on the side of the refrigerator. If we were out of milk, the person who drank the last bit was responsible for finding the "milk" entry on the map and circling it. Each Sunday, she would review the upcoming seven days' menu plans and add the items she didn't have on hand. When it came time to shop for the week, she simply took the completed "list" (the map) to the store and bought the circled items. If we didn't circle the item we wanted, we didn't get it. She never bought cheese curls or anything extraneous that wasn't requested. Of course, circling something didn't always mean you would get it, either.

I guarantee these actions will make meal preparation much easier:

MAKE A MEAL PLAN. When I had my own family, making a meal plan didn't seem like an unusual practice. But I clearly remember my new husband laughing and laughing about how anal I was. Now that he's our primary cook, he isn't laughing quite as loudly. Try it! Sit down with your family and interview them to find out their favorite recipes. Either make a list or have each person submit his or her top five to seven (depending on how many are in your family) main dish meals. When you build your master list, make sure to space each person's favorite recipes fairly each week. This way, your family will never again ask you, "What's for dinner?" And there will be no complaining because they all created the plan.

USE A COOKING KITCHEN. More and more convenience cooking facilities are cropping up all over town. Our current favorite is Dinner and Dish. If you're not familiar with these cooking services, check out www.dinneranddish.com or www.suppersolutions.com. Unless you live in Colorado, you might not have these particular facilities, but you'll have similar offerings in your area. Our $175 purchases twelve meals for six people. John goes to Dinner and Dish once a month. In his registration materials, he receives instructions on how many baking dishes to bring (they provide the Ziploc bags). When John arrives, he moves from station to station, assembling the meals we'd selected online. The kitchen is very sanitary and under strict regulation by the health department. It's not like a shared salad bar! Ingredients are already chopped and assembly instructions are listed. John mixes the spices and materials in the pans, affixes a label with the cooking directions, and packs it all in a laundry basket to bring home. He receives a printed checklist to hang on the refrigerator, with the meals purchased, cooking directions, and side dishes listed.

Each night, when John is planning our meal for the next day, he makes his selection and removes it from the freezer. His favorite recipes are the ones he can throw in a crock-pot and leave all day to cook. We have a leftover night only once or twice a month (the meals are *big*), we order out a couple of times, and visit a restaurant on the days we feel brain-dead. That pretty much takes care of the meals for the month. What a bargain, considering the amount of time we'd spend reading recipes, making a list, shopping, paying for the ingredients, chopping, mixing, and fixing them ourselves!

DON'T MAKE LUNCHES FOR YOUR KIDS! Every month, Meagan brings home the school lunch menu and hangs it on the refrigerator. The cooks at her school are diligent in creating a balanced meal, including protein and vegetables (their lunches are healthier than mine). Each night, she looks at what's being served at school the next day. If she wrinkles her nose at the offering, she packs her lunch that night and puts it in the refrigerator. Generally, though, she likes what's being served and buys her lunch. She has a spending account I fill up once or twice a year, so I never waste time looking for change in the morning. Meagan simply gives her account number to the cashier and takes her food. When it comes right down to it, the cost of purchasing at school (national average: $2.00 per day) is minimal. When you factor in the cost of the food (juice boxes, deli meat, precut and washed vegetables, apples, etc.) plus the time (ten minutes a day equals fifty minutes a week) and hassle to prepare it (priceless), the extra few bucks a week spent in hard cash is worth a panic-free morning.

POST quiz item 70

> 70. _____ Expect family members to do their fair share of the housework.

What? Your Five-Year-Old Doesn't Cook Yet?

I chat with people—both men and women—who have unequal and unfair distribution of chores in their families. The most common behavior is to silently fume until one item left out of place triggers the building geyser and a huge fight erupts. Needless to say, it's imperative to develop an understanding with your partner about how to divide household chores. Emphasize fairness. Don't imply that it's your responsibility and you need help (that is, your partner is your assistant).

Pick a time to sit down together and calmly discuss home responsibilities and time spent on chores. If one person's standards are higher, they might spend more time on a particular task than you would, which is fine if you agree to let them handle it at that level. You're not counting the number of tasks: Each person does the same work in *time* spent, not how *many* things are done. The nonpicky person might have a higher quantity of chores because the picky person cares about doing something just so, as long as the time spent is equal. Also consider if one person must work more hours outside of the house, the other spends more time working inside the house. Talk through all of these issues. I've seen couples even create a spreadsheet to ensure time was divided equally.

Divvy up the duties daily, weekly, and monthly.

DAILY. John doesn't like tidying the house and I hate to cook, so John does the cooking and I do the tidying. Technically, I am responsible for the dishes, but our daughter, Meagan, generally does them during the week, and I do them on the weekend. Each night, the dishwasher is humming, and each morning we unload it while getting breakfast together before beginning our workdays. You may discover, as many people have, that dishes can be used directly from the dishwasher. Amazingly, when I'm out of town, John manages to survive without always putting things away.

WEEKLY. We tend to trade off grocery shopping. Whoever has some time and realizes we have no cereal typically goes without much argument. Or you could implement a formal system where you trade off every other week. When the groceries arrive home, however, that's another story. I have a certain place I like food to go in the pantry and refrigerator, and John doesn't much care. So he unloads the car, and I unpack and organize the groceries. Similarly, I hate to pack the large trash cans in the garage and bring them out to the curb. What if it's cold outside? Yuck! I'll let John do that. I'd much rather toss out the trash as it fills up in the kitchen and replace the liner over a week's time, rather than drag the trash to the curb on Mondays. There is no right or wrong system, as long as you both are content with the arrangement and follow it consistently.

MONTHLY. On the rare occasion, my mother-in-law is ill or has a toothache and doing the laundry is up to us. John and I still maintain somewhat traditional roles around this area (even though we're nontraditional in others), and I end up doing everyone's laundry that week. To be fair, however, I still think dealing with cars falls into the guys' territory. Not that women aren't capable of pumping gas or taking the car for an oil change, but it's just not "princess-like" to have the smell of gas on your hands. I think trading laundry for car maintenance is a good deal. Now, if I can just get him to dust my dashboard . . .

Keep these principles in mind when you do divvy up the chores.

IF YOU LIVE HERE, YOU CLEAN. Even my four- and five-year-old boys have chores. I went to the grocery store and bought a big poster board. In the left-hand column, I listed a due date for chores. (Each chore may actually be completed any day during the week, but it *must* be done by Saturday.) Across the top row, I listed the chores. Each child has his or her own chores posted. When one gets completed, the boys put a sticker on the corresponding column (Meagan uses checkmarks; she's much too cool for stickers). The last column is for "bonuses": extra chores done that weren't required. We pay one dollar for each year of a child's life as an allowance. If something isn't done or gets done incorrectly or with whining and complaining, the child's allowance gets docked.

DON'T PLAY THE MARTYR. I like the commercial for Rice Krispy cereal where viewers see a family in the dining room impatiently waiting for the mother who is painstakingly making Rice Krispy treats in the kitchen. Break to the kitchen where the mother has her feet up, reading a magazine, and is leisurely eating a Rice Krispy treat. She looks at her watch, sighs, gets up, reaches into the flour bag, tosses flour on her face, grabs the tray of goodies, and dramatically swoops out of the kitchen looking victorious, but exhausted. I laughed hysterically when I saw that because it rings so true of some people today. They concoct similar dramas, simply for effect, so that people feel sorry for them. If you enjoy doing a task, do it. If you don't, stop complaining to everyone about how overworked you are and delegate it, eliminate it, or hire it out.

PICK AGE-APPROPRIATE CHORES. As the boys grew older, I let them start taking over some of Meagan's chores. I'm sure she initially thought she'd have less work to do, until I explained that responsibilities shift as people grow older. Fathers and mothers of other animal species only feed and shelter their babies until they're old enough to fend for themselves, at which point they deliberately stop helping them. Teach your children to be self-sufficient, and you will give them important life skills, while at the same time reducing your own workload. Accept the fact that hard work and responsibility are actually good for a child. Allow them to complete the chore their way, as long as they achieve the result you want. Consider complaints a part of raising a child and, rest assured, parents across America are hearing: "Well my friend Boo-boo doesn't have to do this."

We know from experience that, at ages four and five, children can:

- Put away silverware from the dishwasher.
- Set and clear the table.
- Empty small wastebaskets around the house into a big bag.
- Put dirty laundry from the hamper into a black lawn bag and haul it downstairs into the laundry room.
- Pick up the playroom (especially if you've made it easy for them to know where things go).
- Keep their bedrooms clean.
- Brush their teeth.
- Get dressed on their own (you'd be amazed how many people still dress their four-year-olds). By the way, if you wet your child's shoelaces before your child ties them, they won't have to be retied all day. Better yet, get shoes without laces.

At age ten, children can:

- Clean the cat litter.
- Gather Mom and Dad's laundry.
- Wash the dishes.
- Load and unload the dishwasher.
- Wipe off kitchen counters.
- Pack lunches for school.
- Tidy the living room.

- Do homework without being asked.
- Get out of bed and get ready for school while parents sleep in.

Remember, parents are not servants; they are teachers. You won't be around forever. Being slaves to children when you can teach them independence undermines both your life and theirs. Stop it as soon as possible.

MAKE IT EASY FOR CHILDREN TO SUCCEED. Keep a stepstool in the kitchen so they can reach the drawers and lower cupboards. Use paper plates that can be thrown away at the end of the meal, and to save on breakage of your dinnerware. The time saved is far worth the extra money spent on the paper plates. Ditto on plastic cups. (Of course, when we have company, we do use regular dishes.) We buy milk in gallons and pour a small amount into a small Tupperware container within easy reach, so the children can pour their milk themselves.

It's important for you to instill the values of hard work and fairness in your children. As they gain responsibility and perform chores at home, they learn it's important for everyone to pitch in and do his or her fair share and to share the burden.

CHAPTER EIGHT

Mastering the Eighth Pillar—

PLAY

UP TO THIS POINT in the book, you might have been thinking, "Great! This is all wonderful! Now how in the world am I supposed to make time to do all of this, since I work twelve hours a day?" Are you working your life away? Yes, you, the one working six days a week, twelve hours a day. Oh? So you rest on the seventh day? Hey, even God rested on the seventh day. *You*, however, put in a few more hours. When did you confuse your job with your life?

If you have a hard time kicking back, this chapter is for you. We will explore the importance of leisure, wellness, fun, and stress reduction. Helping you find time for the activities you enjoy is one of this book's main goals. Play is more than something extra—it's the final pillar on which your life rests. You know you desperately need this chapter if you feel anxious and guilty when you play or go on vacation.

When you wind up back in your home office each night, every night, hitting the e-mail that could just have easily been done the next morning, you are depriving yourself of needed leisure time. And at what cost? Stress-related health problems? Your relationships? A nagging sense of dissatisfaction? A tug from your soul that something's vaguely wrong, asking, "Is this *it*?"

It's okay to love what you do. It's okay to have passion for your work. But you are not defined by what you do professionally. Your tombstone will not say, "Productive, hardworking employee."

If you have a hard time leaving the office on time and are spending too much time at work, I would unselfishly recommend you read my book *Leave the Office Earlier*. Use productivity as a tool to help you accomplish your results in less time, so you can get out of work on time, and get home to the people and the life you love. You have to do this selfishly, without guilt. You must truly understand the importance of balance for yourself and those around you. You don't "have to" work long hours. Most employers are happy for you to think that way, but in reality, once you draw a line, they are usually okay with it, even if they aren't thrilled. If your boss is not okay with it, read quiz item 15 on finding a new career.

There's a temptation every day for every one of us to be workaholics. I feel it, too. After all, aren't we all busy? Ask people today, "How are you?" and you will most likely hear, "Oh, I have been *so* busy." Hey, who's not? Busy is the new normal. Even people who aren't at an office get caught up in busyness. I encourage you to fight this addiction, this desire to live and breathe work, every day. Eventually your house will topple over and crash if this play pillar isn't firmly rooted in the ground.

PLAY quiz item 71

> 71. _____ Close the mental office door and turn off work each day.

Hopelessly Devoted to Work

Many workaholics are in denial, says Bryan E. Robinson, Ph.D., a professor of counseling, special education, and child development at the University of North Carolina at Charlotte. "Listen to what your friends and family members say about your work habits and then look at the cues: Do you have other things going on beside work such as hobbies or interests or intimate relationships? Are your personal relationships faltering?"

Robert J. Filewich, Ph.D., a clinical psychologist and director for the Center for Behavior Therapy in White Plains, New York, puts it this way: "Workaholics get their sense of worth, value, and importance from work. This has nothing to do with whether or not they like what they do."

How can you learn to separate your sense of self-worth from work? Start by slowing down. As Filewich says, "Workaholics need to take a look at the fact that their life is not balanced, and learn how to make time for relaxation, education, culture, friends, and family that are neglected because of their work habits."

RECOVERING FROM WORKAHOLISM. Start by challenging the social acceptance—even society's encouragement—of these common phrases: "Look how productive you're being. You are accomplishing great things." "You need to earn a living, after all, to clothe your children." "The economy is bad, and it sure isn't easy in competitive times like these." "After all, you possess that strong work ethic your father instilled in you. Hard work is good for you, and you're not about to become a slacker." "You just love your work; it is your hobby, in fact, and you're doing great things for people. You're having so much fun that it just doesn't feel like work." Yeah, yeah, the rationalizations abound. Is there incongruence in these words or simply denial?

This workaholic syndrome is socially sanctioned, and in many cases, it's revered and rewarded. Robinson calls workaholism "the best-dressed problem of the twenty-first century." Tony Schwartz, author of *What Really Matters: Searching for Wisdom in America* (Bantam Books, 1995), said, "Any culture inevitably pulls people toward its norms. Ours elevates those who work relentlessly and disdains those who are more laid-back. Those who embrace long hours and devotion to the workplace not only earn a special place in the ranks of the company, but they also frequently earn more money, which translates into even more approval in our culture."

Here's how to leave work at work so you can get approval from the people at home, the people who matter most.

USE DRIVE TIME TO DECOMPRESS. Leave voice mail messages to yourself at work as reminders of things to do in the morning during your drive time. If you don't capture your thoughts, you'll continue to think about them at home. Or listen to books on tape or music you enjoy to decompress.

DON'T GO IN THE HOUSE UNTIL YOU FEEL CALM. Coming in and taking your hard day out on your significant other, kids, or a dog is certainly counterproductive. These are your loved ones—those whom you most want to see and least want to irritate. If you must, vent to someone outside your family. Or agree on a specific time and amount of time in which to discuss work with your partner—let it out and then move on.

PUT SOME TIME BETWEEN WORK AND HOME. If you face doing a stack of household paperwork and chores, then going straight to the gym instead of home might give you the energy you need to get through the evening's work. Perhaps you could go to the grocery store, pick up the dry cleaning, or get your nails done before going home to put you in a better frame of mind.

PUT WORK-RELATED ITEMS "OUT OF SIGHT AND OUT OF MIND." One danger of working in a home office is the temptation to sneak back in after hours and check e-mail just one more time. Instead, figuratively close the door on your work each day and be completely present with your family. If you're going to attack a pile of paperwork or read for a few hours, keep materials in your briefcase or behind your office doors until you're ready to work on them. If you're half-working throughout the evening, you won't be giving your complete focus to your work or your family, thus decreasing the quality of your efforts on both.

PLAY quiz item 72

> 72. _____ Leave work on time, so I can get home and enjoy my personal life.

If I Leave My Computer On, Will People Think I'm Still Here?

"Now what should I do?" a reader laments. "I've instituted many of your productivity techniques, and now I'm getting out of the office on time. I arrive before my boss does in the morning, so she doesn't see how hard I work when I start my day. Now that I'm leaving by 5:00 p.m., she thinks I'm slacking. But I'm actually getting more work done than ever before!"

Although some companies understand the realities of time constraints due to day care, most still measure employees the old-fashioned way—by the clock.

According to a study conducted by the Families and Work Institute called "Ask the Children: Youth and Employment," 81 percent of girls and almost 60 percent of boys said they would reduce their work hours if they have children in the future.

You might be thinking, "How cute. But get real. Wait until they grow up and see how hard that is." But these children might be smarter than you think. A May 2003 study by the same organization, titled "Leaders in a Global Economy," challenges conventional assumptions made about what it takes to be a successful male or female executive at companies such as IBM, Dow Chemical, and Eli Lilly.

Many people believe executives have to be more work-centered in order to succeed; indeed 61 percent of the executives surveyed were, in fact, work-centric. However, 32 percent were "dual-centric," meaning they placed the same priority on their lives at work and their lives outside of work.

Of particular importance is this: Executives who are dual-centric feel more successful at work, are less stressed, and have an easier time managing the demands of their work and personal lives than work-centered execs.

Do you think women in particular have to sacrifice career aspirations in order to have a family? On the contrary: The study showed that women who are dual-centric have advanced to higher reporting levels and feel more successful in their home lives than those who are work-centered.

Looks like those kids who said they'd reduce working hours when they are parents are pretty smart after all! To experience real success, I suggest you strike a good balance between your career and your personal life.

Here are some ideas on how to draw attention to the work you do in the early morning hours.

SPEAK UP. If you have a conflict that forces you to leave earlier than most people each day, talk to your supervisor. Have an open conversation, explaining how important it is for you to be productive and do a good job, and why you must leave on time each day. Point out that you're the first one to arrive each day and how much you get done without people interrupting you. Certainly, one hour of uninterrupted work can equate to three hours with frequent interruptions.

COMMUNICATE INSIDE THE BOX. Drop completed work in your boss's in-box by 8:00 a.m. with a message and the time written on a sticky note.

JUST SAY JOE. Start the office coffeepot before others show up, and then slyly ask your boss if she enjoyed the special Kona coffee you brewed. After all, you are the first one in to the office each day, so you have to get the Joe going.

TRACK YOUR TIME. Use a time log consistently, so you can prove how much you're getting done in the early-morning hours. Track your accomplishments as you go, so that you have good material for your performance review.

BECOME INDISPENSABLE. Just because someone works longer hours than you doesn't mean that person is more productive. The more indispensable you are, the more you can distinguish yourself—and the more likely you will gain flexibility and still move ahead.

STAY VISIBLE. Volunteer for special committees, especially those involving other departments. Make a point to talk about the value you add to the committees you're on and the projects you're doing with your boss. Soon, people will look to you when new projects come down the pike.

FOCUS ON DESIRED OUTCOMES. Write out a list of the top ten responsibilities you have and rank them in order of priority. Have your boss do the same for your position. Compare the two lists. Are you working on activities and tasks that aren't valued by your boss? Are you spending too much time on tasks that don't move the company's main agenda forward? If something has to drop off your plate, make sure it's something less important. Once you're completely focused on outcomes, face time becomes less important.

SHOW DEDICATION BY NOT SOCIALIZING. Politely let chatty friends know that you have a limited time to talk today because you must leave the office on time. Show your manager how committed you are to your job by working hard all day and not engaging in excessive socializing. When you demonstrate that kind of clear-cut dedication to getting the job done, coworkers are less likely to question your productivity.

USE TECHNOLOGY TO YOUR ADVANTAGE. Clearly communicate, "I leave at 5:00 p.m. every day to go pick up my child from day care. However, that doesn't mean I'm out of touch. If you must reach me in an *emergency*, my cell phone is on until 6:00, or you can leave me a voice mail or e-mail." Be willing to do what it takes to stay on top of business that's conducted after you leave the office. But if people call even when it's not an emergency, remind them of your boundaries, because this type of thing can get out of hand.

In the long run, the workplace will inevitably move away from the concept of face time to a more flexible, results-oriented workplace. The more indispensable you become and the more you can distinguish yourself as a talented contributor, the more likely it is you can gain some flexibility. Until then, try one of the tips above to allay the clock-watchers.

PLAY quiz item 73

> 73. _____ Keep my stress levels low.

My Middle Name Is "Zen"

Kids say the funniest things! When my daughter Meagan was four years old, John and I took her to church dressed in a beautiful red dress with a big matching red bow in her blond hair. We ran into one of my friends in the lobby who has a daughter about the same age. She exclaimed to Meagan, "My, Meagan, what a pretty dress! Where did you get it?" Meagan replied promptly, "From my closet."

If my stress levels were too high, that precious little moment might have passed me by. Just thinking about her sweet face makes me laugh (and tear up a bit). We can learn a lot from children. They remind us to lighten up and laugh at life's absurdities. Remember, the lower your stress level, the higher your appreciation of life and ability to care for yourself and others.

VISUALIZE. Take a minute to turn away from your task and stare out the window. Picture your favorite vacation spot. I like to see swaying palm trees and the rolling ocean of Hawaii. Using the power of your imagination, go back to that place. Smell the salt in the air and see the puffy white clouds. At one time, such imagery likely had a healing effect on you; allow it to do so again.

COMFORT YOURSELF. In moments when you feel like you're suffering, put your hand over your heart with one hand and touch your cheek with the other hand as you might touch the cheek of a child you love. Then simply say, "I understand." In that moment, you're helping yourself feel loving kindness and compassion.

BREATHE. Catch your breath. Close your eyes and breathe deeply for one minute. Then take a deep breath and gently exhale through your mouth as if you were blowing out a candle (making the exhale slightly longer than the inhale). This helps you increase the amount of oxygen in your system, which aids in concentration.

REST YOUR EYES. Try this one for instant stress relief. Anytime your eyes are tired, like when reading or working on the computer, pause to give your eyes a rest. Rub the palms of your hands together in a vigorous fashion to generate energy and heat. Then quickly place your hands one over each eye socket, so that your eyes are at the centers of your palms. Let your eyes relax in this warm darkness for one full minute. Instant relief.

LAUGH. People will wonder what you're up to. How long has it been since you've had a rolling-on-the-ground laugh? A *true* belly laugh, one that rises up uncontrollably when you're completely tickled? Too long? Laughter is good for your soul, your mood, and (as some studies have shown) your immunity. People who laugh a lot have more robust immune systems than those who don't. So look for funny things around you and take the opportunity to laugh.

I was teaching a seminar for First Premier Bank in Sioux Falls, South Dakota. My hotel didn't have good cell phone reception, so I gave my husband the phone number of the hotel. My youngest son, James, wanted to talk with me before going to bed. When the phone didn't ring in the room, I figured he got caught up doing something and would call me back soon. Still not having heard from him an hour later, though, I called home using my calling card. The conversation with my husband went something like this: "Hi!" I said, "I've been waiting for you to call so I could talk with James. Everything okay there?" "What?" he said. "James just talked to you." "Huh?" I said intelligently. "Uh . . . no . . . I haven't talked to James." "Noooo . . ." Silence. Silence. "Oh, my gosh!" my husband exclaimed. "I forgot to ask for your room. James just talked with the front desk clerk!" We laughed and laughed.

Apparently, John had just dialed the number of the hotel and handed the phone to James. When the clerk answered, he proceeded to tell her all about his hangnail! Then he babbled on about his day, said "Bye Mommy!" and hung up. He went to bed *totally* believing he had just talked with his mommy.

I picked up the fruit basket I had been given as a gift, left my hotel room, walked down to the front desk, and smiled at the clerk. "Did you just talk with a little boy?" I asked. "Oh, yes, he was adorable! Was that your son? He sounds like mine." I smiled through my tears as I handed her the fruit basket. Then we enjoyed a great laugh together as we shared this story. Laugh often, at everything. Life is just too funny to miss!

BREAK YOUR FOCUS. When you're stressing out over something, force yourself to stop thinking about it.

- Say or write the alphabet backward.
- Close your eyes and hum a song.
- Drink a glass of water in exactly twenty-seven sips.
- Close your eyes and think of a color. Now picture seven things that have that color.
- Try to recall all the objects in your purse, wallet, or briefcase. Write down as many things as you can in one minute.
- List six things you've enjoyed most in the last week.
- Picture a room in your home and write about it as if you're describing it to someone else.

These techniques won't eliminate your stressor, but they allow you to step back, clear your mind, and deal more effectively with the pressing situation.

PLAY quiz item 74

74. _____ Rest, relax, and play daily.

Recreation Means to "Re-Create"
Are you fun-challenged? Do you have difficulty allowing yourself to have a good time? Have you forgotten how to play? A recent Harris Interactive poll found that 40 percent of people surveyed say they don't spend enough time enjoying leisure activities. The biggest obstacle to play? Ourselves.

Give yourself permission to have fun and try these ideas:

TAKE A BREAK. Find little ways to play; no one can concentrate every minute of every day. In fact, you would experience a point of diminishing returns if you tried. You have to stretch your body and your brain every so often. When I'm writing, when my brain begins to wander and my body begins to ache every hour or so, then I know it's time for a break. I do a few quick stretches and refresh my glass of water. Then I spend just a few minutes doing something fun. I'll call a friend, check my book's rankings on Amazon, or make a cup of tea. These breaks absolutely *do not* replace a real vacation, but they are necessary for getting through the day. And you don't have to hide your break! As long as it doesn't become excessive and take too much time, you're not wasting time. Taking a sanity break should not make you feel guilty.

GO ON A MINI-VACATION. One of my friends keeps a putter and electronic golf hole in his office and takes several putts when he needs a quick break. Another seminar participant said spending five minutes reading her trashy novel does the trick for her. On sunny days, I like to take a leisurely five-minute walk around the neighborhood and slowly enjoy the sights instead of going at my usual power pace. Warming up my beanbag neck roll in the microwave is always sure to give me a mini-vacation. I suggest saving up pleasant tasks (like telling someone about a promotion) for when you need a break. Then make a point of leaving your office to go do that task. The combination gets your mind off what you were working on so that you're refreshed and ready to concentrate again when you return.

FOCUS ON SIMPLE PLEASURES. When your day's work is done, make time for yourself with simple pleasures. Playing in the park with your kids takes less time, costs less money, and can be done more often than going to Disneyland. Certainly relaxing doesn't have to be expensive or complicated. Think bubble bath versus spa; a cup of really good coffee versus going to a four-star restaurant. Yes, the more extravagant occasions are nice, too, but when you focus on simple pleasures, you'll get more for less, in less time, more often.

ENJOY A STEAM. Not from your ears, but while standing in a hot shower. Let the hot water run over you and loosen the stiff muscles in your neck. Lean over and feel the water pound on your back. Breathe in the steam, which carries moisture to your airways and your skin.

It doesn't matter what you do as long as you relax on purpose. Keep a journal. Play an instrument. Play with your pet. Take a walk. Work in the garden. Take a catnap. Find a new recipe. Meditate. Pray. Stretch. Dance. Listen to quiet music. Put your feet in hot water. You get the idea.

PLAY quiz item 75

75. _____ Go on a long vacation each year.

I Have Fourteen Weeks of Saved Vacation!

Families need a change of pace and scenery and to have fun on a regular basis. Vacations offer the restorative power many people desperately need. *Everyone* needs an extended break—not just a rest period. Without the ability to recharge your batteries for a longer period of time, you're on a slippery slope to burnout.

Yes, I know you generally love your work. You don't mind working hard because you get recognition for it and they need you there. I've heard all of that before. The fact is you can get another job more easily than you can get another family. You might work yourself to the bone, only to turn around and get handed a pink slip. At some point, your job can turn on you and throw you into chaos, at which point you may find that your family and friendships have been neglected and your usual support system is in shreds.

In the United States, there is no law on the books that gives people the right to paid vacations. A May 2004 study by the online travel company Expedia.com found that at least 30 percent of workers would give their vacation time back to the company. In all, they estimate that workers will return 415 million days in a year. Some people have proudly told me they have surplus vacation time they can't use because they work so much and don't have time to take off. I don't admire their dedication; I marvel at their foolishness.

Not you! Each year, have a family meeting, break out a calendar, and block time off for your next vacation. If you don't plan for it to happen in advance, something *always* comes up that prevents you from going. Sure, you'll have some occasions when you've planned a vacation and an emergency prevents you from taking it—there's not much you can do about that—but be proactive and try to schedule everything else around it.

Here are some ways to make your vacation more enjoyable and less stressful:

TRY TO BE GONE FOR TWO WEEKS. Know that it will take a few days just to unwind and forget what day it is. I always encourage people to vacation longer than an extended weekend. If you're only gone one week, your colleagues will "hold your work for you until you get back." If you're gone a couple of weeks, you will probably have someone covering for you, and less will be piled up for you to deal with when you return.

VACATION WHEN EVERYONE ELSE IS NOT. Conference planners have known this secret for ages. If you plan an event in July in Phoenix, Arizona, you can get a killer deal and the resort won't be crowded. If you go to Hawaii in the winter, expect beaches to be crowded. Go to Disney World when kids are likely to be in school, so the lines will be much shorter and less frustrating to deal with.

BE A TOURIST AND STAY CLOSE TO HOME. Sometimes the best vacations of all can be those when you don't go anywhere. You can lounge around the house, catch up on projects you've been meaning to start, and discover new, fun activities around town. These "stay-cations" can lower your stress and shift your perception. It's important to have some framework in mind on what that time will look like, so your week doesn't go by without you doing anything.

LEAVE THE LAPTOP BEHIND AND DON'T CHECK VOICE MAIL. It's becoming more acceptable for people to leave extended absence greetings or automated e-mail responses that say, "I'm out of the office on vacation until X and will not be checking e-mail or voice mail. In my absence, please contact . . ." If you team up with a colleague to cover for you, then you can return the favor. If you must work, limit the time to an hour a day and set boundaries around the exact time you will be available for questions via cell phone.

USE TEMPORARY MESSAGES FOR YOUR OFFICE. To avoid returning to utter chaos when your vacation trip is over, create your temporary voice mail greeting and e-mail notification. Inform people when you'll return and who to contact in your absence. For this person, make a reference sheet of needed information and places where current project documents have been filed. Sit down with that person before you go and provide a rundown on what you're currently working on. Promise to return the favor, acting as the contact person in the future. Ask your contact to sort your e-mail and check your tickler file each day to ensure nothing important falls through the cracks. When you do this, you'll feel much more at ease while lounging on the beach.

PREPARE YOUR HOME FOR YOUR ABSENCE. Back up any important software or turn off your computer completely, just in case there's a power problem or sabotage that could wipe out your hard drive. Put your mail delivery on hold. Find someone to water your plants and bring in the paper. Clear your in-box of papers, so you can distinguish the old from the new upon your return.

GET PREPARED MENTALLY. Especially with young children, vacations don't always equal relaxation. I remember a trip our family took to Orlando in December 2002. I had a speaking engagement there, after which we set sail on a Disney cruise. I was told, "Oh, yes, those are wonderful for children!" But no one told us the cruise was only wonderful for children who were potty-trained. At the time, Johnny was three years old and James was two, and neither one had such discipline. So the trip turned into a nightmare of babysitting two small children in a tiny, cramped room, and praying for the nursery to open for the standard two hours twice a day (which, of course, cost extra). I'm still desperately trying to block that memory from my subconscious, but I keep reminding myself that a vacation is meant to be spent with the ones you love.

RELAX WHEN YOU'RE WITHOUT KIDS. When we go on vacation without our children, John and I have learned the hard way not to schedule every single minute of the day. We've had the luxury of visiting an island in Hawaii once a year since we've been married. Excited to be there, we wanted to get the most out of our time on our first time there, so we crammed every available minute with activity. We went from historic site to the ocean to swimming pools to shops to tourist attractions and back to the hotel. When we finally had a minute to relax, we were back reading the brochures again, planning the next activities. By the time we returned home, we felt exhausted and in need of . . . a vacation! But the last time we went, we got smart. We slept late and only planned one activity for each day. When John asked me, "What would you like to do next?" I replied, "Nothing." And we just enjoyed being there together, sans kids, doing nothing. Even when you have the kids with you, make time to do nothing by rotating child-care duties or finding a kiddy camp.

PLAY quiz item 76

76. _____ Create fond memories with the people I love.

Do You Remember When?

Experts on child memory and child psychology agree that we tend to remember things that stir our emotions and forget about things that don't. Painful or traumatic experiences are the exception to this—they are sometimes repressed and pushed below a child's level of awareness as a defense against their frightening qualities. So the question becomes: How can you create positive experiences for your children that stir their emotions and will therefore impact them, so they will remember?

CREATE MEMORIES. The home I grew up in was just a few hours from several national parks and camping spots. Our family loved to backpack, fish, and camp. We did it the old-fashioned way. No RVs and fancy trailers for us: just a tent, sleeping bags, and a hole in the ground. If you haven't ever roughed it, you're wondering, "What's the hole for?"

We had a 1968 VW Bus. It was kind of a reddish-orange color. Okay, it was white with a lot of rust. Daddykins had specially modified it just for our weekend camping adventures. He would take out the middle bench, leaving the backbench for the three kids to sit on. The big wooden toy box would go in next, bolted up against the sidewall the long way. A portable refrigerator bolted behind Mom's seat contained hard-boiled eggs and sandwich fixings.

I somehow always managed to get the prime seat—the one next to the window but in front of—the porta-potty. Now you're probably thinking, "Laura, I didn't realize that the 68 VW vans came with an optional porta-potty." No, you won't find that on the list of available options. This was Daddykins' invention. It was the wastebasket from the den, a ring on the top to sit on, and a Hefty bag! We'd all get real religious whenever Daddykins took a sharp corner. When we stopped at a rest area, we all knew we had better take advantage of facilities there because Daddykins only made one pit stop, no matter how long the trip was. If we didn't take advantage during the pit stop, we'd have to settle for the side of the road and the porta-potty.

Now, these were the days before seat belts so Daddykins rigged his own version. He suspended a large board over our laps and then bolted it to the sides of the van. It was like a combination child restraint/craft desk.

I remember so clearly the excitement taking off on those

trips. Mom would be smiling and humming and Daddykins would shake his belly and sing "If I Were a Rich Man" from the movie *Fiddler on the Roof*. You know, we didn't care that he wasn't, but he was definitely goofy.

This memory is so etched in my mind that I can easily re-create it again and again. I don't remember much of the day-to-day activity spent with my parents, but I do remember the camping trips. It takes time, planning, and preparation to create events such as these, but it will be worth it in the memories you're cultivating in your loved ones. They will later fondly recall these stories with your grandchildren and great-grandchildren.

EVEN WORK CREATES MEMORIES. A child is never too young to learn that cooperation and team effort make many jobs easier and speedier—and often more fun: "Let's all pitch in and finish raking the leaves so we can go in and bake cookies," or "Let's clean up the kitchen quickly, so we don't miss the movie." Family activities and group chores can develop into pleasant rituals that enrich a child's life and create fond memories.

GREET THE HOLIDAYS AS JOYOUS FAMILY EVENTS. For every holiday task, try to engage the entire family. Turn tasks into fun family events. For example, enjoy a family-wide card-sending event. While adults write, young children can draw pictures on the back of the envelope. Brainstorm the shopping list as a family. Children often have perfect ideas for gifts for relatives and family friends. Cook together. Each family member can help in the kitchen, from chopping to washing. Hold a whole family cookie-baking event or experiment with different recipes and have the family vote at a tasting party. Sing along with seasonal music and chat while everyone helps wrap presents, and the packages will be ready in no time.

ALWAYS ASK ABOUT YOUR CHILD'S DAY. Even if you get a grunt for an answer, your child will come to expect the question and know you care. I try to ask my kids questions that require more than a yes or no answer. "What did you enjoy about your day today?" or "What was the most interesting thing you learned in class?" This small investment of time shows your love and concern and keeps you informed about upcoming events and assignments, as well as important experiences and relationship problems.

READ TO YOUR CHILD DAILY. Ever since my children could hold their heads up, we've read to them every night. This ritual not only instills a love of learning but also establishes a meaningful and intimate relationship with your child. Reading allows you to snuggle with your child, experience physical closeness, and build fond memories that both of you will treasure for a lifetime.

PLAY quiz item 77

77. _____ Have a regular family time with loved ones.

Remind Me What Your Name Is, Again?

The traditions you share with your family are important ways to nurture and express your love for the important people in your life. A tradition can be as simple as buying a too-large holiday sweater for your little girl and photographing her in it every year for ten years until she can actually wear it. (I cried when I packed up my daughter's wonderful sweater and added it to her memory box.) Here are a few other ideas.

DINNER. It's a standing rule in our home that we eat dinner together every night—no excuses. All school, work, sports, and friendship activities must be completed by dinner or done following this special time. We don't watch television, answer the phone, or get up until everyone has finished eating. We hold hands around the table and pray before anyone can eat. Then we chat about our days, talking about things important and not so important. But the main point is we're together, and we can all count on this special time.

SUNDAYS ARE FAMILY DAY. Growing up, we knew never to plan anything personal on Sundays; that was family day. As we got older, we would roll our eyes at the indignity of having to spend time with our *parents*, for heaven's sake, but we secretly loved these days. My two brothers and I rotated taking turns to select the activity. We would bowl, go to a movie, eat at a restaurant, or visit a museum. With limited income on a military salary, our parents only spent money on amusements on this one special day.

Now, as a parent myself, I gladly continue this tradition with our family, knowing how much our children will come to treasure these times. Our Sundays consist of visits to Chuck E. Cheese, playtime in the park, and Chutes N Ladders on the floor. Our activities aren't always glamorous, but we're creating memories nonetheless.

A PARTICULAR DAY WITH EACH PERSON ONCE A MONTH. If you can't eke out one day a week, try devoting one day a month to each member of your family. This practice creates intimate moments and special memories with that family member. When I mark out a "Johnny" day, for example, we might go to the pool, have a special lunch at his favorite restaurant, and play at the park. It doesn't have to be an entire day, but it must consist of activities the *other* person finds memorable, not necessarily what you would choose to do, and must be one-on-one.

SATURDAYS ARE DATE NIGHT. Every Saturday night, John and I go out (barring an illness or holiday). It's written in pen, not pencil, on our calendars. My wonderful mother-in-law always comes over to stay with the kids. John and I trade off who plans the evening's activities. We'll get together with friends or go out alone to putt-putt golf, a dance club, or a nice restaurant. We rarely talk about the children. Rather, we spend time talking about personal topics including our marriage, life plans, and goals for the future.

BIRTHDAYS. In our house, when it's *your* birthday, you get to be the king or queen for a day. You don't have to go to school on your birthday, and we make no apologies for it. You can do whatever you want all day long. You can sleep in, eat out, go boating on a lake in the mountains, go to Six Flags, hang out at Chuck E Cheese, or do anything your heart desires. When you reunite with the rest of the family, we have cake and presents. You don't have to do any work on your special day and you get to dictate how the time goes. You get to eat all your favorite foods and get waited on with great fanfare. It's even better because you know when it's coming and you can plan your own perfect day well in advance. This ritual is quite a luxury for our children, and I'm sure it will become a cherished memory.

A RITUAL TIME. With my husband, John, and two sons, Johnny and James, the males outnumber my daughter, Meagan, and me in our home. So when Meagan and I have the occasion to spend time by ourselves, we begin by chanting together in a singsong voice, "Meagan and Mommy time . . . Meagan and Mommy time." Thus begins our ritual and marks this special time. We shop, get our nails done, or attend one of her Girl Scout meetings, which I lead. When I'm going to be away from the house, I attempt to take her with me whenever I can. If I'm traveling on business over a weekend, I often bring her with me. Right now, I'm typing this page on a three-day writing retreat at an AmeriSuites in Denver. (I find that getting out of the house for an extended period of time helps me concentrate better.) John dropped by with the kids for a quick hug and kiss and a piece of chocolate. The boys jumped on the bed for five minutes, then the males left and Meagan stayed here. She's now reading quietly in the easy chair next to my desk. I'll take a break and drive her to school in the morning. We're not talking, but we're together and smile at each other occasionally. This time with her serves to balance both of our lives better—even though we are doing separate activities, we're together.

PLAY quiz item 78

> 78. _____ Make time for a favorite hobby.

You Collect What?

Having a hobby is a great way to reenergize. Whether you like to knit, create scrapbooks, or design clothes, do something regularly. Make time for it. Hobbies are a wonderful outlet for creative expression often missing in many people's lives. The very act of creating, and the joy of putting your time into something lasting and tangible has the power to take you off the hamster wheel. Hobbies such as book clubs or art classes also allow you to socialize with like-minded people. If you pick up a hobby you once had as a child, such as playing the piano or creating pottery, you can bring back the pleasant feelings you once had. When you're stressed, your hobby is a breath of fresh air.

Here are some great suggestions.

COLLECT SOMETHING. I love collecting. Each year, my husband buys me the new Santa teapot from the Fitz and Floyd holiday collection. I display these teapots in a china cabinet, which I pass several times a day. When I do, I smile and reflect on sweet memories. Each year, we purchase an annual holiday ornament from the Lenox collection with the year on it. Every time I go on a business trip where I'm speaking at a convention, I purchase a collectors' spoon from the airport gift shop with that city's name on it for Meagan. She has a spoon rack in her room where she displays her prized collection. Knowing she will receive a new silver spoon when I return helps her not miss me so much. For myself, I purchase a magnet from that city and enjoy adding it to the collection of places I've been.

START A COLLECTION FOR SOMEONE ELSE. I started buying teapots for my mentor as a thank you gift after each of our monthly phone calls. Each of the teapots represents something about one of the countries where her communications training programs is distributed or presented. My daughter is a horse fanatic, so I collect Breyer horses for her and even have programmed an eBay search to help me find good deals.

These are small, seemingly meaningless collections. They don't take much time or money. But they help me remember the past and provide an anchor for my children. I suggest you pick something that you want to collect, whether it's thimbles, mugs, or bells. It's fun to search for additions to your collection everywhere you go. Don't get too carried away and have hundreds of things all over the house—that would qualify as clutter! Limit the occasions when you would add to your collection, be selective, rotate your displays with the seasons, or purge it if it gets out of control.

TAKE UP SOMETHING NEW. When my daughter Meagan went horse crazy, she wanted to redecorate her room with a wild horse theme. Flowers were no longer cool enough for a big ten-year-old girl. We picked out new border, paint, wall hangings, and decorations; even the knobs on her dresser were horse heads. The only difficulty we had was finding a bedspread she liked. We found lots of rocking horses and carousels and domestic horses, but we couldn't find wild horses. Elaine Dumler, one of my girlfriends and fellow speakers, is a fabulous quilter, so I called her with the idea of making a horse quilt. Was I nuts? I'd never made a quilt in my life! But I did know how to embroider and cross-stitch from projects as a little girl. Elaine convinced me I could do it and took me shopping. Meagan and I picked out iron transfer patterns, fabric, and floss colors, and we're right in the middle of hand-making a quilt! So don't be afraid to try something new.

ORGANIZE A HOBBY AREA. First, find somewhere in your home where it's quiet and you can work without too many interruptions. My friend Lisa Hill, who is really into Creative Memories scrapbooking, dedicates most of her basement to this activity. She has a huge table, lots of storage space for paper, photographs, stickers, and decorative-edge scissors. Be sure to store your materials in an organized fashion until you're ready to use them. Stores like Office Max, Target, and Wal-Mart have aisles with great storage solutions, such as portable filing boxes, see-through stackable plastic containers with lids, rolling bins and drawers, and photo boxes. When you're finished using your hobby supplies, put them back in their designated homes. If you leave your things strewn about, they're bound to get lost or damaged. I guarantee that your creativity will diminish if your area looks chaotic.

USE YOUR HOBBY AS A REWARD. I use my embroidery time as an incentive to get my evening's work accomplished. Having hobby time as an artificial deadline helps you move in an efficient fashion throughout the evening. Once homework is checked, kids are bathed and in bed, the dishwasher is running, and everything is tidy, you can get started on something for yourself. If you give yourself a goal of chores to complete and challenge yourself to finish them in an efficient manner, you'll have more time left over at the end of the evening to relax and unwind with your favorite activity. A task expands to fit the time available, so setting a goal every evening will help you finish it more quickly than if you didn't set one.

PLAY quiz item 79

> 79. _____ Force myself to slow down and stop rushing around.

If I Got Dressed Quickly, Did I Do a Better Job?

My seminar attendees often lament, "There's just not enough time!" To the contrary. I always state, "You've got all the time there is." Time management doesn't mean packing your day like a moving van, ensuring every single square inch (or minute) of space is full. If you actually had more time, you'd just stuff it with more of the same: more appointments, more projects, and more paperwork.

What's really at issue is not the quantity of time, but its texture and its tone. Not the texture of minutes and hours—each to be filled and measured—but the seamless texture of life itself. When I'm working too hard, I crave a different kind of time: slow . . . loose . . . alone . . . and suddenly a different side of me emerges.

People have become spoiled by speed. Before the facsimile machine came out, all we had was the mail. Then came the fax, then voice mail, then the cell phone and pager, and then e-mail. Because of these technologies, people expect you to react faster than ever before. What happened to all those studies in the 1960s that said one of the biggest challenges of the future would be what to do with all our time? Amazing inventions were predicted to free up long stretches of time in our days.

Do you remember when hotel rooms didn't have coffeemakers? I recall vividly the first time I walked into a hotel room and discovered a coffeemaker. I didn't even drink coffee back then, but I made it, simply because having the coffeepot was so cool. Then people got used to it. Customers got spoiled. They wanted more. If you go to a hotel today and your room does *not* have a coffeemaker, it's a cause for dissatisfaction. Now we expect hotels to provide robes, irons and ironing boards, hair driers, refrigerators, and microwaves. Where does it stop?

The bad news is that it *doesn't* stop. People will always get used to things the way they are, become more demanding, and want more. So it is with technology and speed. Everyone wants to know when things will "return to normal" and "slow down." They won't! The speed at which you're operating is now what's expected. Welcome to the new normal!

The trouble is, raising kids, making friends, and creating artistic work all run counter to the demand for speed. Fast speeds aren't a natural fact of the universe. So when do you want speed?

You may have heard the distinction between Type A and Type B personalities. Type A personalities have six times more heart attacks than do Type B personalities. Type A people are:

- Competitive
- Preoccupied with work
- Highly driven (often to the point of obsession)
- Always in a hurry
- Unable to relax
- Fast moving and impatient

Psychologists describe some people who become addicted to adrenaline. Addicts create situations in which they can get a "fix" through chaos, crisis, and conflict. Some seminar participants have admitted they often create stressful situations to meet their need for excitement.

Most of us don't even think about varying the pace of our lives, because our culture at large considers moving fast to be productive. However, think about how fruitless it is to rush around during certain activities. Hurrying on the laundry, for example, doesn't make sense. When you look at the pile of laundry your family generates each week, you might get the sense it will never be done. That's the point. You will *never* get the laundry done. It is an insurmountable mountain. Hurrying with the laundry isn't going to cause you to get your clothing dirty less quickly.

A recent *Time* magazine/CNN poll found that 65 percent of people spend their *leisure* time doing things they'd *rather not* do. Things like . . . answering polls. Seriously, 65 percent? How depressing! What's the point of leading a full life if you don't have the time and energy to do what you enjoy doing?

Stop rushing around being busy with things that don't really matter to you. Move on. Make time for activities that are meaningful. When your values are clear, time will appear. Make time to do absolutely nothing. One of my girlfriends told me, "I have no down time. I'd love to have more free nights during the week with no commitments. But it's hard for me to just *sit* here. I feel like I should be doing something."

How do you begin to apply the brakes in your life when the world around you is pushing on the gas pedal? Here are some ideas.

DECIDE TO MOVE SLOWLY. Decide, on purpose, to *not* be speedy during certain times, when speed doesn't alter the outcome or might even make it worse. Does it increase the quality of your work? If you rush while driving, does it improve your safety? If you gulp your food, does it taste better or digest more easily? Recognize the times when speed seems ridiculous. Notice yourself rushing and decide to take a slower pace. Or eliminate an activity or task if you're rushing just to get to the next one.

CUT BACK ON COMMITMENTS. Most people have such busy, complicated lives, they don't have time to stop and look at what's happening—much less figure out how to create time for the things they enjoy. Look at your life and decide to cut back in the areas where, ultimately, it just doesn't matter. Do you have to be a member of that organization? Do you have to chair that committee? Do you really want the job or volunteer position you're working so hard to achieve? Are you content with the personal relationships in your life? Make your goal to spend time on the activities that are meaningful instead of rushing around being busy with things you don't really care about.

CLEAR A SPOT ON YOUR CALENDAR. For me, it's a purple spot. Literally. Every month, I find a good day to stick a round, purple sticker on my calendar. This indicates which day I will totally devote time to doing nothing. I may call a friend to have lunch. I may go to the recreation center and sit in the Jacuzzi. I may drive to Cold Stone Creamery and get my favorite full-fat, full-sugar vanilla custard, mixed with Heath Bar *and* Butterfinger bits. I may sleep in. I never really know until I get there. I schedule purple days during the week, so I can truly take a mini-vacation *by* myself *for* myself.

SEIZE THE MOMENT. In my field of study, productivity, I've heard of too many people who have put off something that brings them joy because they haven't thought about it, don't have it on their schedule, didn't know it was coming, or were too rigid to depart from their regular structure. What about all those people on the *Titanic* who passed up dessert at dinner that fateful night? (That's why I eat ice cream on my purple day.) I can't count the number of times I've invited one of my brothers to attend a family event, such as his niece's or nephews' birthday parties, a holiday get-together, a dinner, and he says (check one):

- I'm too busy.
- I wish I'd known yesterday.
- I have plans with my *friends*.
- I don't want to be around noisy children.
- (He doesn't call back at all.)

We'll die someday, and we'll never have spent time together. Sadly, he doesn't even know what his niece and nephews look like except through annual photos I dutifully send. I suspect he schedules his headaches. He and I live on a sparse diet of promises that he makes when all the conditions are perfect. Guess what? The conditions have never been perfect, and I have stopped asking from fear of rejection.

Seizing the moment can mean being open to a spontaneous adventure, dropping into an interesting-looking store just because you're driving by, or taking the long way back home because you wanted to drive around a beautiful lake. At the end of it all, make sure you don't keep reciting a litany of "I'm going to . . ." and "I plan on . . ." and "when things settle down a bit."

PLAY quiz item 80

> 80. _____ Take care of myself on a regular basis.

Can You Give Me a Minute?

Did you know that having an active social life as an adult may help prevent Alzheimer's disease and other types of dementia as you get older? We've always known that mental activity is good for the brain, but a new study from the University of Florida School of Aging Studies shows that the brain loves leisure. In fact, researchers found a 38 percent less risk of dementia in adults having the highest level of leisure activity. In the study, researchers analyzed data from the Swedish Twins Registry, which tracked same-gender identical twins who were born between 1886 and 1925 and followed them through the 1990s. Specifically, researchers compared 107 twin pairs in which one twin was diagnosed with some type of mental impairment and the other was not. Even when factors such as education level were taken into account, greater involvement in leisure activity—social visits, reading, and vacations—was shown to reduce the risk of dementia. All work and no play will make Jack's brain a dull thing indeed.

It's not enough to sit on the sidelines and watch others play. *You* have to be personally involved in activities. Take a class, meet a friend, or take a tour. Get involved in church activities, intramural sports, service clubs, and charitable organizations. Remember, you're working to live, not living to work.

Here are a few ways you can engage yourself.

REVISIT YOUR CHILDHOOD. For years, I took for granted living at the Air Force Academy in the gorgeous Rocky Mountains of Colorado Springs. I had no idea that I was living what many would consider an idyllic, sheltered life. On many occasions, I would open the curtains in my bedroom to stare into the big brown eyes of a deer. We would spend hours in the woods behind our house, playing Indians, building forts, and just lying in the sun. To this day, when I need to refresh and reconnect with myself, I take a long walk so I can reconnect with nature and the rustling wild grasses.

RECONNECT WITH YOUR CHILDHOOD. What did you used to love to do? Work with clay? Paint? Draw? I used to spend hours playing the piano and learning new music. Today, finding a few spare minutes to plink out a few tunes is a delicious treat. I also used to spend hour upon hour reading the *Little House on the Prairie* books as well as countless *Nancy Drew* and *Black Beauty* novels. Especially around the holidays, sitting down to relax with a good book brings back warm memories of childhood: sometimes I can almost see a twinkling Christmas tree and smell spicy wassail in the air. Do the things you loved to do as a child and cherish yourself as an adult.

SCHEDULE A DAY OF PAMPERING. You need time to yourself to relax, refresh, and rejuvenate. I don't feel the least bit guilty about taking my monthly personal day. I work hard, and so do you. You deserve some personal attention! Do what you love, whether it's a manicure or a massage or a bike ride or a round of golf. The money invested is well worth the decreased stress level you will experience.

DON'T WASTE ALONE TIME. If for some odd reason, I find myself alone in our house, besides shouting "Whoo-hoo!" in my head, I resist the urge to do something productive. Funny as it seems coming from me, this is *not* the time to throw in a load of laundry or tidy up the house. Instead, I do something I can't do when the kids or my husband are home. I ask, "Can I do this activity when James is around?" If the answer is yes, I find something else creative to do. For example, I like getting out the photographs I've been stacking for the last few months and putting them into their file boxes. Praying and exercising are good options for me. I also like calling a friend, so I can have a decent conversation for once without a child's interrupting chatter.

GET RID OF THE GUILT. I find that women, especially, have been programmed to sacrifice everything in the name of what's good and right for everyone else. If there's anything left over, they get the scraps. I find that men are much better at saying, "I need to relax!" A man might say, "I'm playing a round of golf with Joe this afternoon," whereas my girlfriend would say, "I'd really like to go get a pedicure tomorrow, but I should take Jimmy shopping for school clothes."

One thing I know for sure is that *you can't give what you don't have*. If you don't take care of yourself, your ability to take care of others becomes severely compromised. Being skilled at taking care of yourself improves your capacity to care for others; if you weren't fulfilled, you'd only be able to see other people through the filter of your unmet needs. Not taking care of yourself is actually unhealthy for those who depend on you. And as my husband likes to say, "If Mommy's not happy, then no one is happy."

If you're running on an empty tank and fumes of habit, everyone loses. So rid yourself of the guilt you feel when you relax, refuse a request, or take time for yourself. You need it and deserve it, if you want to be at your productive best!

Remember, play is not frivolous behavior. The word "recreation" contains the two words "re" and "create." Play is the way to re-create yourself, every day, and remind yourself *you are not your work*. Your work is part of your life—an important part, yes—because it allows you to live, but it's not the most important part. You must find time to play. Because, after all, that's what the rest of this book was about. Now take the time you've gained and do something for yourself!

CONCLUSION

CONGRATULATIONS on finishing this book! As you've discovered, becoming more productive is hard work. But spending time to strengthen your pillars will save you more time in the future and hopefully improve the quality of your life—which is, after all, the ultimate goal.

So don't stop here! Keep working to improve, grow, and strengthen your pillars. When you feel deeply connected to how you live your life, you can get past any obstacle that keeps you from getting things done. When you're clear about your priorities, it's easier to put the distractions of daily living out of your mind so you stay focused.

When something is *really* important, you will find time for it, no matter what.

I'd love to hear your thoughts and comments about how you are productive at home. Please contact me at Laura@TheProductivityPro.com or visit my Web site at www.TheProductivityPro.com. Here's to finding more time together!

ABOUT THE AUTHOR

Laura Stack, MBA, CSP, is a professional speaker and personal productivity expert. She is the president of The Productivity Pro®, Inc., an international consulting firm in Denver, Colorado, specializing in productivity improvement in high-stress industries.

© Ray Ng

Laura presents seminars and keynotes on improving output, lowering stress, and saving time in today's workplaces and homes. She is one of a handful of professional speakers whose business focuses solely on time management and productivity topics. Since 1992, Laura has taught her original principles on information overload, stress reduction, performance improvement, time management, and life balance to Fortune 500 companies, associations, and government agencies.

Laura holds an MBA in Organizational Management from the University of Colorado. She is on the board of directors for the National Speakers Association (NSA) and is the recipient of the Certified Speaking Professional (CSP) designation, an earned award held by fewer than 10 percent of professional speakers worldwide. She was awarded a Board Approval in Productivity

Improvement from the Society for the Advancement of Consulting (SAC). Her popular monthly electronic newsletter has subscribers in thirty-eight countries.

Laura Stack is the author of the bestselling book *Leave the Office Earlier* (Broadway Books, 2004), which was hailed as "the best of the bunch" by the *New York Times* and listed on the June 2004 Book Sense Business and Economics Bestseller list. *Leave the Office Earlier* has been published in seven countries and in five foreign languages: Japanese, Korean, Chinese, Taiwanese, and Italian. Laura is featured in three audio success series with other well-known speakers such as Zig Ziglar, Denis Waitley, and Brian Tracy.

Widely regarded as one of the leading experts in the field of employee productivity and workplace issues, she has been featured nationally on CNN, NPR, Bloomberg, CBS radio, NBC TV, WB News, and in the *New York Times*, the WashingtonPost.com, the *Chicago Tribune*, *Working Mother* magazine, *Ladies' Home Journal*, *Entrepreneur*, *Redbook*, *Reader's Digest*, *Cosmopolitan*, *Woman's Day*, and *Parents* magazine.

Laura draws from her background as a corporate manager, a University of Colorado instructor, CareerTrack speaker, radio talk show host, newspaper columnist, and small business owner. Her client list reads like a Who's Who of Fortune 500 companies, including Microsoft, IBM, Qwest, Coors Brewing Company, Lockheed Martin, Lucent Technologies, the Denver Broncos, StorageTek, Wells Fargo Bank, Mobil Chemical Company, Coastal Companies, Time Warner, and VISA, plus a multitude of associations and governmental agencies.